PREFACE

The present work has been prepared mainly with the view of meeting the wants of University students.

Two works of similar character were available, *The Outlines of Moral Philosophy,* by Dugald Stewart, whose name shed lustre over this University, published in its final form in 1808; and *A Manual of Moral Philosophy* by Professor Fleming of Glasgow, published in 1860. Both of these are text-books of high value. As, however, a want has been felt, and pressed upon my attention, for a book dealing with the subject in view of more recent discussions, I have here attempted to meet the demand.

My aims have been to present the chief problems of Ethical Science; to give an outline of discussion under each, allowing fundamental questions greatest prominence; and to afford a guide for private study by references to the Literature of the Science.

In order to secure space for discussion of the more important problems, details have been omitted such as may be found in the histories of philosophy more commonly in the possession of students.

In some parts, the work wears a controversial character. In the present state of Ethical inquiry, this was unavoidable. The Development Theory (Sensational and Utilitarian) is well represented, both critically and constructively, in the works of Mr. John Stuart Mill, and of Professor Bain. The present Handbook offers an exposition and defence of the Intuitional Theory of Morals, with the criticism of Utilitarianism. The uniform object, however, has been to give a careful representation of the conflicting theories, supplying the reader with materials for independent judgment.

While the interests of University students have been constantly considered, I have endeavoured to provide a book suited for those who wish, apart from academic arrangements, to prosecute the study of Ethical questions.

H. C.
University of Edinburgh,
30th October 1872.

INTRODUCTION
SPHERE AND METHOD OF ENQUIRY

1. Moral Philosophy is the rational explanation of our moral actions, moral nature, and moral relations. It is a science of the knowledge of moral distinctions, of the practice of morality, and of the existing moral system, or order in the universe. It is a theory of knowing and of being, but only of such *knowing* as is concerned with moral distinctions, and only of *being* which is capable of possessing and applying such knowledge.

The designations 'Moral Philosophy' and 'Ethics' are commonly and properly used as synonymous. Etymologically, the Greek designation, Ethics ('H$\theta\iota\kappa\alpha$ from $\eta\theta o\zeta$, custom, habit, disposition), refers to a more limited department of enquiry than that belonging to Moral Philosophy. Strictly taken, it applies only to individual conduct or manners. The same limitation, however, exists in the Latin designation, Moral, since *mores* concerns primarily manners or customs. The Greek term, as having more distinct reference to the source of action within the mind, has even the advantage over the Latin term. According to the best usage, however, the names Moral Philosophy and Ethics are equivalent; Moralis Philosophia, '$H\theta\iota\kappa\alpha$; German, Ethik or Sittenlehre.

2. In its beginning, Moral Philosophy takes rank as a Science of Observation. In its higher development, when dealing with relations which transcend the facts of experience, such as our relations to the Absolute Being, it wears the form of a Speculative Science. The denial of a speculative branch of the science must rest on the denial either of the need for a philosophy of the fact of man's existence, or of the possibility of such a philosophy. Moral Philosophy is further described as a Practical Science, because it embraces knowledge requisite for the guidance of human conduct. As a philosophy or science, it is a system of truth, scientifically discovered and arranged.

The term 'observation' has by some been unwarrantably applied to the recognition of external facts only. 'Observation' refers to the mental *exercise,* not to its *objects.* The mental sciences, as truly as the physical, are sciences of observation, though in their higher departments the mental sciences are speculative.

3. As a Science of Observation, Moral Philosophy is *subject,— first,* to the laws of evidence, which require that facts be carefully ascertained, distinguished, and classified; and *second,* to the rules of logic, which require that generalization be reached by legitimate induction from ascertained facts. As a Speculative Science, it is dependent for its start, and also for the final test of all its results, upon the accuracy and completeness of the underlying Science of Observation.

The inductive method determines the foundations of the science; the deductive method finds application in the speculative department. In the inductive method, the critical method of Kant is included, by which he distinguishes between the *a posteriori* and the *a priori* in knowledge; but the dialectic method is excluded, such as that of Spinoza *(Ethics),* which elaborates a theory from a series of definitions, or such as that of Hegel *(Wissenchaft der Logik),* which starts from the highest abstraction, viz., Pure Being; (v. *Secret of Hegel,* by J. H. Stirling, LL.D., London, 1865.)

4. The Order of Investigation must, as in all sciences, be from the simple to the complex. Moral Philosophy must, therefore, begin with individual experience, and must pass thence to social life, and thereafter to the wider testimony of History. From these fields of observation it rises to grapple with problems which transcend observation, while they rise out of it.

Comte pleads for commencing our study in society, because the laws of human conduct are best inferred from the actions of men in the mass, *Cours de Philosophie Positive,* 1. 31; 2d ed. The following passage from Mr. Mill maybe taken in reply: — 'Human beings in society have no properties but those which are derived from, and maybe resolved into, the laws of nature of individual man;' *System of Logic,* ad ed., II. 543. But, for the reason indicated by Hume, *(Intro. to Treat, on Hum. Nat.),* observation of the actions of men is essential for completing our investigations.

5. Consciousness (Conscientia, Bewusstseyn) is the uniform condition of individual experience. To consciousness, therefore, must be our primary and ultimate appeal concerning the facts of personal experience. As here understood, 'individual

experience,' and 'the facts of consciousness,' are identical. Physical impressions are facts of experience only as they are recognised in consciousness. A distinction must, however, be kept between facts of experience and conditions of life. The play of vital organs, such as the heart or brain, is largely beyond the range of consciousness, though the action of both may be closely connected with our mental activity, and may thus have an important bearing on the interpretation of what is experienced.

Consciousness, though associated with physical energy, is not so closely connected with it as to make the latter the measure of the former. Accordingly, physical prostration, popularly named 'unconsciousness,' is not to be reckoned equivalent to a cessation of personal experience. On the contrary, it often happens that those said to be unconscious are aware of what is transpiring around them.

For a full investigation of the nature, evidence, and authority of Consciousness, Hamilton's *Metaphysics,* Lects. xi.-xvi., and Note H. in Reid's *Works.* Hamilton says, 'It is the recognition by the thinking subject of its own acts or affections;' *Metaph.* 1. 201. Rather, it is the recognition by the thinking subject of *itself* and its own acts and affections. 'What consciousness directly reveals, together with what can be legitimately inferred from its revelations, composes, by universal admission, all that we know of the mind;' Mr. J. S. Mill's *Exam. of Sir W. Hamilton's Philos.,* p. 132, 3d ed. For the grounds on which Mr. Mill holds that 'we cannot study the original elements of mind in the facts of our present consciousness;' *Ib.* p. 173.

6. The Introspective or Reflective Mode of Enquiry is an essential requisite for the construction of a science of mind. This mode of enquiry is named Introspective, because the individual must look *within himself* in order to discover the facts of his experience; Reflective, because he must *turn back* upon the facts as having had a place in experience. The necessity for the introspective line of enquiry arises from the application of an obvious law of evidence. A man roust attend to the facts of experience in order to interpret them. And it is only as the facts of our inner experience are subjected to observation and analysis that it is possible to attempt the construction of a philosophy of them.

Comte has declared Introspection impossible. His argument is this, 'In order to observe, your intellect must pause from activity; yet it is this very activity which you want to observe. If you cannot effect the pause, you cannot observe; if you do effect it, there is nothing to observe.'— (Miss Martineau's Translation, I. p. II.) The argument involves neglect of the following facts: that intellectual activity implies consciousness; that attention to its own states is a possibility of mind; that repetition in consciousness of the same act leads to increased familiarity with it; that memory admits of the recall of what has previously passed through consciousness. There is, therefore, no necessity for a pause in order to attain knowledge of personal activity. Dr. Maudsley not only accepts the argument of Comte, but supplements it thus: '(a) There are but few individuals who are capable of attending to the succession of phenomena in their own minds; (b) there is no agreement between those who have acquired the power of introspection. (c) As long as you cannot effect the pause necessary for self-contemplation there can be no observation of the current of activity; if the pause is effected, then there is nothing to observe.'— *The Physiology and Pathology of Mind,* p. 10, 2d ed. These statements may be summarised thus: — (1.) Few can use the introspective method; (2.) those who can are not agreed as to the results thereby secured; (3.) nobody can use it at all. Comte himself did not maintain his consistency. Take the following example: — 'Philosophers tell us of the fundamental difficulty of knowing ourselves, but this is a remark which could not have been made till human reason had achieved a considerable advance. The mind must have attained to a refined state of meditation before it could be astonished at its own acts,— *reflecting upon itself a speculative activity,* which must be at first incited by the external world.'— *Cours de Philos. Positive,* vi. 6, Miss Martineau's translation, II. p. 159. If it be possible by any process of refinement to attain reflection on our own mental activity, the objection to introspection is admitted to be untenable. On this subject see Sir H. Holland's chapter on Mental Consciousness, *Mental Physiology.* By Mr. Mill a 'Psychological mode of ascertaining the original elements of mind' is placed over against the Introspective. *Exam. of Hamilton's Philos.,* p. 170, and p. 173; with which compare 'the Natural History' mode in Prof. Bain's *Senses and Intellect,* with Append. A., and chapter on 'Consciousness;' *Emotions and Will,* p. 555; also Spencer's *Principles of Psychology,* 'On Consciousness in general,' p. 322, c. 25. Mr. Mill, 'for want of a better word,' calls his mode 'Psychological;' but the Introspective is Psychological, and his Psychological is Introspective. For an admirable statement on Introspection, see Mill's *Exam. of Hamilton's Philos.,* p. 169.

7. The testimony of Consciousness cannot be denied without self-contradiction. He who doubts it relies on Consciousness for the affirmation of his doubt.

This is the key of the Cartesian position, and the basis of modern philosophy; Des Cartes's *Method,* I. II. III. *Method* and *Meditations,* translated by Professor Veitch. Leibnitz, *Nouveaux Essais,* II. 27. Maudsley points to the madman's delusion as throwing discredit on consciousness, *Physiol. and Pathol. of Mind,* p. II. So far from such an objection having any force, the pathology of brain depends for its scientific validity on the reliableness of the madman's consciousness. If a man says that he constantly sees spectres which have no existence, or that a person resides in his stomach, it is because, knowing his statements to be erroneous, you nevertheless trust his consciousness, and do not regard him as a wilful deceiver, that you pronounce him insane. Consciousness thus discovers with certainty those forms of experience which give evidence of a morbid organism.

8. The Interpretation of Consciousness is the business of philosophy. This implies the discrimination and classification of facts, the determination of their origin or source, and the discovery of the legitimate inferences from these facts. In this way we may construct a rational explanation of our experience. The distinction between the testimony of consciousness to internal facts, and its testimony 'to something beyond itself,' is well put by Mr. Mill; *Exam.,* p. 166.

9. Every state of consciousness involves three elements. The shortest expression of such a state is, I — am conscious — of a perception. An act of perception thus standing as the illustration, there are in the single state, the conscious knower, the consciousness, and the present experience, viz., a perception. Consciousness is the uniform characteristic of our experience; in

consciousness, the recognition of self is invariable; the special exercise recognised is variable. While, therefore, Consciousness is knowledge of a present state, it is always knowledge of Seh as Intelligence,— Self-consciousness, Selbstbewusstseyn.

This is the meaning of Des Cartes's — Cogito, ergo sum,— I think, therefore I am. This celebrated utterance is not an argument, but a simple statement of the fact, that each thinker is as certain of his own existence as of his own thought. Hamilton, though giving the threefold analysis of a state of consciousness, reduces the component elements to two, by identifying consciousness itself with the fact recognised, thereby making the present fact a modification of consciousness. He says, 'Consciousness is not to be viewed as any thing different from these modifications themselves;' *Metaph.* I. 193, and Reid's *Works,* 932. On the lower physiological theory, Mind is known only by physical manifestation, and thought is a function of brain; *Rapport du Physique et du Moral de l'Homme,* P. J. G. Cabanis. At the other extreme of transcendental metaphysic, developed by Kant, Mind is a transcendental conception, separated from the smallest trace of experience. For the history of philosophic thought on this subject, Pt. I. Div. ii. c. i.

10. Among states of consciousness, there are some which discover that we are not pure intelligences, but that we are also *sentient* beings. We are conscious of sensation, through an organism so truly a part of our being, that its affections are our own. Touch, taste, smell, hearing, and vision, afford distinct illustrations. The physical organism, through which sensations are received, provides for a wider area of knowledge. The organism itself is not known in consciousness, but only. the experience resulting from its affections. For example, the organs of vision and hearing are not known in consciousness, but the sensations and perceptions obtained by means of them are thus known. If then Consciousness be always Self-knowledge, and physical organism is not recognised by consciousness, that organism is more properly described as belonging to Self, than as essential to its very nature.

11. The organism which is not known in consciousness must have its functions determined by scientific enquiry distinct from that prosecuted by the analysis and interpretation of consciousness. While the knowledge of the internal Self is by

internal observation, the knowledge of the organism must be by external observation. There are thus two departments of science concerned with our existence, the Psychological (ψυχη *psyche* the soul, and *logos,* science), and the Physiological (φυσις, *physis,* nature, and *logos).* These are quite distinct from each other, yet closely related, and capable of rendering mutual aid.

For a most important contribution from the Physiological side, see *Preliminary Observations,* and the first part of Chap. III. in *The Principles of Medical Psychology,* by Baron Ernst von Feuchtersleben, M. D., published by the Sydenham Society (1845). Feuchtersleben's little book, *The Dietetics of the Soul,* London (Churchill) 1852, is well deserving study. The German work is in its thirty-third edition. The union of mind and body involves what Professor Laycock has happily designated 'the correlations of consciousness and organization;' *Mind and Brain,* see specially the Preliminary Dissertation on Method, chap. v. See also *Psychological Inquiries,* 1st and 2d series, by Sir Benj. Brodie; *Chapters on Mental Physiology,* by Sir H. Holland; Maudsley's *Physiology and Pathology of Mind;* and Paine's *Physiology of the Soul and Instinct:* New York, 1872.

12. To speak of the Introspective line of enquiry and of the Physiological, as if they were two distinct, and even conflicting, *methods* of philosophizing, is an abuse of language. They deal with two distinct *departments* of investigation, in which the same method, namely, observation, is employed on two sets of facts altogether different. While the method of philosophizing is in both cases the same, the spheres are so distinct that Introspective enquiry cannot reach organism, and External observation cannot reach consciousness. No examination of the organ of vision leads to the discovery of perception; and no contemplation of a perception discovers the organ of vision. Prof. Bain (*Senses and Intellect,* p. 91) speaks of 'the influence spread over the *conscious centres* when muscular contraction takes place.' But there is no physiological or anatomical evidence warranting us to fix upon certain spots in the brain as 'conscious centres.' Jouffroy has well said, 'The senses cannot penetrate into the sphere of consciousness, nor the consciousness into the sphere of the senses;' *Introd. to Edition of Stewart's Outlines* — Jouffroy's *Philosophical Essays* (Clark, Edinburgh), p. 9. J. G. Fichte has said, 'We are conscious of the seeing, hearing, or feeling; but can

12

by no means, on the other hand, see, feel, or hear our
consciousness;' *Anweisung zum seligen Leben,* 1806, *The Way of
the blessed Life,* translated by Dr. William Smith, Edinburgh, p.
43.

The fields of enquiry belonging to Physiology and
Psychology are, however, so related, that neither science can
adequately interpret its own facts without reference to the other.
Those phenomena of consciousness known as sensation and
perception expressly require Physiological aid for their
explanation. And the Physiology of nerve and brain needs no
less the testimony of consciousness in order to interpret
ascertained facts. In one respect the Pathology of nerve and brain
comes even more closely into contact with Psychology, as all
diseased or disordered action of physical organism throws in
upon consciousness forms of experience otherwise unknown.
This holds true in the widest and most important sense of the
Brain, which is distinctively the organ of Mind or Self. All the
facts connected with a disordered brain are thus fitted to cast
important light on the action of mind as related to the action of
brain. Hence the peculiar value to mental philosophy of all
scientific investigation as to the experience of the insane.

Nerve and Brain are the physical conditions of sensation
and external perception on the one hand, and of locomotion on
the other. To what extent they afford conditions for other forms
of mental exercise is not yet made out. The nerves of sensation
in minute ramifications come from the surface of the body, join
in ganglia, and stretch up to the great nerve centre, in the brain.
From the brain, on the other hand, go the whole sets of motor
nerves, or nerves of movement, by which control is maintained
over the muscles. The brain itself is in the form of two lobes or
hemispheres, adapted for communication with the two sides of
the body, and specially with double organs of sense. The matter
of the brain is of two kinds,— the outer or grey matter, which is
vesicular, having as its function, to supply nerve energy, and the
inner or white matter, which is fibrous in nature, embracing the
termini of the nerve ramifications. Such is the organism which
affords the physical media of sensation and external perception,
and of control of the bodily movements. This organism every
human being employs, while ignorant of the laws and appliances
which determine its use. For the nature and functions of Brain

and Nerve, *v.* Quain's *Anatomy,* 7th ed. vol. II. 501; with Carpenter's Principles of Human Physiology, 7th ed. chap. xiii. p. 503. There is a valuable statement on the relation between Physiology and Psychology in Jouffroy's *Introd. to Stewart's Outlines,— Philosophical Essays,* Edin. 1839, p. 37, onwards.

Sensitive organism is the physical condition, and Consciousness the psychological condition, of sensations. On the other hand, excepting only a limited circle of spontaneous movements, conscious volition is the psychological condition, and nerve energy the physical condition, of motion. In sensation the impression is made on the organism, and is transmitted from the extremity of the nerves to the nerve centre; and though the transmission is not matter of experience, the resultant sensation is known in consciousness. In movement of the limbs, the volition to move the foot or fingers is known in consciousness, and thereupon there is a transmission of nerve energy from the brain along the appropriated nerve lines providing for movement, but of this transmission there is no record in personal experience.

13. Consciousness discovers Self-determination in our activity. With thinking, there is conscious self-determination of the order of thought; with observation, self-determination of the objects to be observed, with use of an organ, such as the hand, there is self-direction of its use, even though consciousness gives no information as to how this is accomplished.

14. Consciousness of Self-determination is consciousness of power exercised by me over my mental activity, and over physical organs which belong to me. Self is thus known, not merely as Intelligence, but also as Power. I am a self-conscious, intelligent, self-determining Power. I am a Person, not a mere living Organism, and not a mere Thing. Personality thus involves self-conscious being, self-regulated intelligence, and self-determined activity. But there is no warrant to say, with the elder Fichte, that the Ego (I) posits itself, or with Hegel, that the Ego comes to itself,— or, with both, that the Ego is Universal Reason manifesting itself. Neither by direct evidence, nor by inference, can these positions be sustained.

Personality is here taken as involved in the consciousness of mature life. Whether this knowledge of Personality is capable of development from Sensation, as the lowest form of experience, is a question held in reserve. For answer, see Part I. Div. ii. c. i.

15. Besides the characteristics of experience already indicated, there are conditions of existence known as *external* to Self. These are conditions of our physical existence, as part of the material world; and conditions of intelligence, in so far as it is concerned with the facts of an outer world.

16. Moral Philosophy concentrates attention on what applies to Self as the determiner of personal activity. It is because Self-knowledge implies knowledge of myself as directing my own actions, in accordance with knowledge, that a Moral Philosophy is possible.

The characteristics of our physical nature, and those of the purely intellectual nature, belong to two distinct departments of science, the one physical, the other mental; but, Moral Philosophy, as distinct from both, makes reference to the results of the Physiological and Intellectual sciences, only in so far as its territory borders upon theirs.

17. In view of the sphere of action open to me as a Personality, I recognise my relation to other living beings, some of which, by speech and action, discover themselves to be possessed of the same personality as that which belongs to me. Of these living beings, there are others which do not discover their possession of personality. Within the sphere of personal activity, there is thus established the general distinction between Persons and Things, or more specifically, the threefold distinction between Persons, Living Organisms, and Things.

18. The Philosophy of Morals must be as applicable to the persons by whom I am surrounded as to myself, and must be capable of verification by them. But it need not be applicable to other living beings around me, or capable of verification in their experience.

19. Personality is the first requisite for philosophising. Where there is not self-consciousness, or knowledge of Self, as possessing power for self-direction, under conditions of intelligence, there cannot be a philosophy either of our own nature, or of any other form of being.

20. Personality is the basis of Morality. Where there is not knowledge of Self, as the intelligent source of action, there is no discrimination of motive, act, and end; and where such

discrimination does not exist, there is no morality. The knowledge of moral distinctions, and the practice of morality, are in such a case equally impossible, Shaftesbury, *Inquiry concerning Virtue,* I. II., § 3. 'The idea of person involves determination to individual morality;' Trendelenburg, *Naturrecht,* § 86, p. 158, Leipzig, 1860. 'Personality, as the universal characteristic of man, advances to the phenomenal in the form of individuality;' Martensen, *Die Christliche Ethik,* Gotha, 1871.

21. Actions as contemplated in Moral Philosophy are the outcome of intelligence and will, and are properly named Personal Actions. Other forms of activity, popularly denominated 'Actions,' do not come within the sphere of Moral Philosophy.

THE PSYCHOLOGY OF ETHICS PHILOSOPHY OF MAN'S MORAL NATURE

PRELIMINARY

1. In seeking the rational explanation of our Moral Nature, it is better, in point of order, to begin with our knowledge of moral distinctions, and only after that to extend observation to the springs of activity, namely, desires, affections, judgments, and volitions.

This order has been very frequently reversed in works on Moral Philosophy.

The Scotch Philosophy, swayed by the old classification of the powers of the Mind into the Understanding and the Will, has commonly begun the treatment of Moral Philosophy with an enquiry as to the Impulses of our nature, denominated Active Powers. Hutcheson's *Passions and Moral Sense;* Reid's *Active Powers;* Beattie's *Moral Science;* Stewart's *Philosophy of the Active and Moral Powers.* The German Philosophy has commonly taken the other course, seeking first to ascertain what is the Ethical idea or conception.

2. In the Intellectual department of Mental Science, Psychology deals with the facts of our experience belonging to morals, as with all the facts of consciousness, but simply to determine their nature as mental facts. In the Ethical department of Mental Science, Psychology ascertains the nature of Mental facts only as a preliminary step for determining their Moral significance.

3. The Psychology of Ethics is completed only by constructing a philosophy of all that belongs to our personality as Moral beings. Each characteristic must be looked at, not only apart, but also in relation to other features of our Moral Nature. 'The value of every ethical system must ultimately be tested on psychological grounds;' Mansel's *Prolegomena,* Pref. (Oxford, 1860).

4. In a system of Philosophy, every affirmation is liable to have its truth determined by a variety of tests. In no case are we shut up to a single avenue of enquiry. In Moral Philosophy there is uniformly a double test,— the true in theory must be the consistent in practice.

PART I
MAN'S MORAL NATURE AS COGNITIVE
DIVISION I
INTUITIONAL THEORY
CHAPTER I
KNOWLEDGE OF MORAL DISTINCTIONS

1. There is in consciousness a knowledge of Moral distinctions among personal actions. This is apparent in the discrimination of actions into right and wrong; *Honestum (rectum), malum;* καλον, κακον; *Recht, Unrecht.*

The same distinction is otherwise expressed by the phrases 'morally good,' and 'morally bad.' In these phrases, the term 'morally' is used to indicate the specific nature of goodness or badness alleged to exist, namely, such goodness or badness as can belong to personal actions, and to the agents, in contrast with other forms of goodness or badness, such as may belong to things. 'The right' thus comes under a wider generalization, namely, 'the good.' Happiness is a good within a man; property, on the other hand, is an external good; but the morally good is distinct from both, as good connected with what a man is and does, in contrast with what a man experiences and has. The greatness of contrast between actions and things makes it exceedingly undesirable to lay the foundations of Moral Science on such a generality as the Good.

The whole Ethical Philosophy of ancient times was seriously encumbered by discussing the question of Morals under the general conception of *The Good,* as a character of *things,* rather than under the conception of *The Right,* as a quality of *actions.* It commonly led to an estimate of moral good by its utility, as in the part taken by Socrates in the *Protagoras;* or to the use of good and evil in a double sense, as when Socrates makes the doing of injustice a greater evil, and the enduring of it a less.— Plato's *Gorgias,* 509. As a compensation we receive from the Ancient Philosophy most valuable discussions in support of the unapproachable superiority of Moral good, among all forms of good attainable by man.

Ultimately, as with Plato, The Good comes to be identified with God himself.— *Repub.* vii. 517; Jowett, ii. p. 351. The disposition to make The Good the basis of Morality has recently reappeared in some adherents of the *à priori* school, as well as among Utilitarians. For example, Schleiermacher, *Die Sittenlehre,* Werke, Philos. vol. v.; the younger Fichte, *System der Ethik,* ii. I, p. 27; Rothe, *Die Theologische Ethik,* vol. iii.; and in one of the most recent works, translated from the Danish into German, Bishop Martensen's *Die Christliche Ethik.*

In modern times the universally acknowledged distinction between actions right and wrong, has commonly been accepted as the primary fact, giving occasion for a Moral Philosophy. 'Those who have denied the reality of Moral distinctions may be ranked among the disingenuous disputants; nor is it conceivable that any human creature could ever seriously believe that all characters and actions were alike entitled to the affection and regard of every one.'— Hume's 'Inquiry concerning the Principles of Morals,' *Essays,* vol. ii. p. 223.

It is of essential moment to distinguish between the *foundation* of moral distinctions and the *knowledge* of them. Hume has confounded these at the outset. He treats of the problem 'concerning the general foundation of Morals; whether they be derived from reason or from sentiment, whether we attain the knowledge of them by a chain of argument and induction, or by an immediate feeling and finer internal sense.'— *Ib.* These are two perfectly distinct questions. Mackintosh's *Dissertation,* sect. i. As to the foundation of moral distinctions, I wish to insist that that is independent of human personality; while as to the knowledge of moral distinctions, that is derived from Reason, not from feeling.

2. Of the duality of moral distinctions, these may be taken as examples: — persevering use of personal powers, courageous endurance of privation, truthfulness in utterance, kindness of disposition, and efforts to mitigate the sufferings of others, are right actions; while vanity on account of possessions, envy of others in prosperity, secret satisfaction at their trials, dishonest dealings, and wilful infliction of injury, are wrong actions.

3. The actions possessed of moral quality are the actions of intelligent agents. If the term 'action' be employed in a wider sense, such application goes beyond the moral sphere, as when

we speak of the 'action' of water on the rock; organic action, as the action of the heart; and the action of an animal in walking or eating. When deliberate reflection on the nature of the act is impossible, moral quality does not belong to the action. The terms 'right' and 'wrong' are misapplied, when used in relation to any actions other than personal actions.

4. All moral actions, being the actions of persons, presuppose intelligent observation, and are carried out by personal determination for a definite end. Every moral action, therefore, is capable of being regarded in three relations, according to its origin, progress, and result. With all these, intelligent self-determination is concerned. A moral action, therefore, includes motive, act, and end. As these may be distinguished from each other, they may differ in moral quality. The motive may be right, though the act is wrong. And still further, the rightness of the end does not determine the character either of the motive or of the means.

5. All personal actions are not known as moral actions. The varieties of activity possible to man are according to the powers which belong to his nature. That nature may be contemplated as physical, intellectual, and moral. Action which is merely physical, or purely intellectual, does not necessarily come within the moral sphere. For example, walking, leaping, and lifting; efforts of attention, reasoning, and memory, are not in themselves moral actions.

6. Actions not in themselves recognised as moral actions may acquire moral character by being involved with the action of our moral nature. The complex nature, physical, intellectual, and moral, may in all its parts be concerned with a definite line of action, in which case the whole extent of activity wears a moral character. Every power belonging to us as moral beings is thus capable of being turned to a moral or an immoral use. Physical exercise is a merely physical good; but physical strength can be employed for the attainment of moral good or the doing of moral evil. Intellectual exercise is an intellectual good, but it also can be employed in moral relations, for good or evil.

7. Actions which are not in themselves Moral actions, cannot with philosophical warrant be denominated actions 'morally indifferent.' The reason for this statement is contained in the previous paragraph, from which it appears that the

distribution of our actions into 'good, bad, and indifferent,' is inadmissible.

The designation 'indifferent' comes to us from the Stoic Philosophy, αδιάφορα, things neither good nor bad.— See Zeiler's *Stoics*, etc., p. 218. The distinction was accepted by Cicero, who translated ἀδιάφορον by *indifferens:* 'Quod illi ἀδιάφορον dicunt, id mihi ita occurrit, ut *indifferens* dicerem.'— *De finibus*, iii. 16. Cicero also described things indifferent by the designation *res mediae*, things lying in the middle, between right and wrong. This phrase is as unsuitable as the other, for things morally right are not separated in things morally wrong by an intermediate territory. Moral distinctions belong to a single sphere, which is the inner and more sacred sphere of human life. All beyond that sphere, moral characteristics cease to apply. The contrast is interesting between this classification of things (possessions rather than actions), without moral quality as *res mediae*, and Aristotle's *mean, μίσοτης*, as determining the nature of virtue. The Stoics aimed at a classification of different kinds of good, and placed such external good as health of body, honours, and wealth, as *res mediae*. Aristotle, looking at activity, makes the mean to be the test of virtuous action in all cases.

In the Scotch Philosophy, Reid accepted the classification of actions into 'good, bad, and indifferent.'— *Active Powers*, Essay v. c. iv. (Hamilton's Ed. p. 646.)

8. Whether moral distinctions are recognised by men generally, may be ascertained by reference to the testimony coming (1) from individual conduct, and (2) from social life. What has been reached introspectively may thus be tested by external observation. *First*, Testimony from personal conduct. Every man is seen to experience self-approbation and self-condemnation on account of his actions. Shame because of wrong-doing may be taken as an illustration, with the admission that there is a distinction between the shame felt on account of awkwardness, and that on account of wickedness. *Second*, Testimony from social life. Men are agreed in approving certain actions as right, and all nations inflict punishment on evil-doing.

The sufficiency of the evidence from these sources is not affected by the question whether that evidence is applicable to all forms of moral distinctions. For the present purpose, it is of no moment whether the actions punished by society do or do not embrace the whole range of actions morally wrong. The fact of the punishment of some actions is sufficient. Even on Professor Bain's theory, which makes punishment and moral distinction co-extensive *(Emotions and Will,* p. 257), there arises no difference at the present point.

9. While all men agree in accounting certain actions right and others wrong, they may not agree as to the actions so regarded. The explanation of such disagreement is connected with the later enquiry regarding the ground or criterion of moral distinctions, but such disagreement does not affect the evidence for the fact, that men do recognise moral differences among actions.

10. Problems.— (1.) Indicate the grounds on which The Good is not to be taken as affording a commencement for Ethical Enquiry. (2.) Does the identification of pleasure with the good, in the *Protagoras,* rest on sufficient grounds? (3.) Animals may be trained to obedience; a dog will rush into the water to save a drowning child; animals undomesticated and untamed will die for the protection of their young: do such facts as these indicate a knowledge of moral distinctions? Darwin's *Descent of Man,* I. c. iii. 'The Moral Sense.' On the opposite side, Wallace's *Contributions to the Theory of Natural Selection.*

CHAPTER II
MORAL JUDGMENTS
(INTUITIONAL THEORY)

1. A Philosophy of personal experience, to be adequate, must account for the origin and nature of each fact in experience.

2. As the knowledge here to be explained is my knowledge, it involves the relation between me and mine, and its explanation must in part at least be in myself. Personality contains the primary explanation of personal experience.

3. As the knowledge here to be explained is the knowledge of moral quality in the actions of myself and others, it involves a further relation between me and others, and its explanation may be in part beyond myself, in so far as it may be concerned with what is neither me nor mine. The explanation of some personal experience may in part be found in what is beyond my personality. In so far as my experience implies the recognition of

moral distinctions by others, it may find part of its explanation in other personalities.

4. As the fact now to be explained is KNOWLEDGE, not Feeling, it can be accounted for only by the existence of a cognitive power belonging to our personality. Whether this power be an original power of mind, or the result of development from simpler elements, is a question belonging to a later stage of enquiry. However attained, this knowing power belongs to our personality, and its exercise from time to time depends upon our personality.

5. The only philosophic warrant for acknowledging distinct powers in mind, is the discovery in consciousness of facts essentially different in nature. Facts which differ must have different explanations. If different facts have a common source, it is because diverse powers exist in the same source of activity. By distinct powers of mind, therefore, is meant nothing more than the mind's power to produce facts essentially different.

6. Knowledge of the moral qualities of actions is knowledge of matters of fact. Of such knowledge there are three distinct forms. These are: — *Sensation,* knowledge of impressions made on our physical nature; *Perception,* knowledge of objects by self-directed observation; *Judgment,* a more advanced knowledge of objects, either by simple comparison, or by inference.

These generally admitted distinctions are here simply accepted as the product of Psychology in the purely intellectual department of mental science.

As Affections and Sentiments presuppose knowledge, and as the Laws of Association merely provide for the combination of the facts of knowledge, these cannot afford any theory of the origin of our knowledge of moral distinctions. Sentimental and Associational theories are thus excluded on exactly the same ground.

Jonathan Edwards (1703 — 1758) made Benevolence the standard of rectitude. 'Virtue is the beauty of those qualities and acts of the mind, that are of a *moral* nature, *i.e.* such as are attended with desert or worthiness of *praise* or *blame.'* 'Virtue is the beauty of the qualities and exercises of the heart, or those actions which proceed from them.' 'True virtue most essentially consists in benevolence to being in general.' 'The first object of a virtuous benevolence is *being*, simply considered: and if being, *simply* considered, be its object, then being *in general* is its object; and what it has an ultimate propensity to, is the *highest good* of being in general.'— *A Dissertation concerning the Nature of true Virtue*. Chap. i.

David Hume (1711 — 1776) referred to 'the original fabric and formation of the human mind' for the explanation of moral distinctions. He held 'that Reason and Sentiment concur in almost all moral determinations and conclusions,' but 'the final sentence, it is probable, depends on some internal sense or feeling, which nature has made universal in the whole species.'— *Essays*. II. 222 — *Principles of Morals*, sect. I. The nature of this sense or feeling is thus indicated: 'Every quality, which is useful or agreeable to ourselves or others, is, in common life, allowed to be a part of personal merit:'— the censure of the disagreeable and the approval of the agreeable are thus 'the universal sentiments of censure or approbation which arise from humanity.'

The theory of Adam Smith (1723 — 1790) is founded on Sympathy. *Moral Sentiments*, Part iii. (1759); 'We either approve or disapprove of our own conduct, according as we feel that, when we place ourselves in the situation of another man, and view it, as it were, with his eyes, and from his station, we either can or cannot entirely enter into and sympathize with the sentiments and motives which influence it.'— Part iii. c. I. For his argument that 'general rules of morality' are formed 'by finding from experience that all actions of a certain kind are approved or disapproved of,' *v*. Part iii. c. 4.

Dr. Thomas Brown (1778 — 1820) agrees with Adam Smith in so far as he grants that emotions are the basis of moral distinctions, *Philos. of the Human Mind*, Lect. 59. He says: 'The action excites in us a certain feeling of vivid approval. It is this irresistible approvableness . . . which constitutes to us who consider the action, the virtue of the action itself,'— Lect. 73. 'On the undue place often given to the Emotions," Chalmers's *Sketches of Ment. and Mor. Philos.* chap. vi. Of Associational Theories see detailed examination in Div. II.

7. Knowledge of moral quality in an action is not of the nature of Sensation. Sensation is neither an act, nor the knowledge of an act, but an involuntary experience consequent

on personal relation to a sensitive organism, and to objects capable of making impressions on that organism. Take, for example, the sensations of heat, cold, weariness, and pain.

Those who originally described the moral faculty as a 'Moral Sense,' meant by that either a power of perception, or of judgment, with attendant emotions, not a mere capacity of feeling or of sensation. Thus Shaftesbury (1671 — 1713), 'In a creature capable of forming general notions of things, not only the outward beings which offer themselves to the sense, are the objects of the affection, but the very *actions* themselves, and the *affections* of pity, kindness, gratitude, and their contraries, being brought into the mind by reflection, become objects. So that by means of this reflected sense, there arises another kind of affection towards those very affections themselves which have been already felt, and are now become the subject of a new liking or dislike.' Behaviour and actions are said to be 'presented to our understanding,' and the faculty is said to be 'a sentiment of judgment.'— *Inquiry concerning Virtue.* 1. 2, sect. 3; *Characteristics,* vol. ii. 29. So Hutcheson, *Syst. Of Mor. Phil.;* and *Passions and Moral Sense.*

8. Knowledge of moral quality in an action is not of the nature of Perception. Perception being a simple recognition of fact, can include only such facts as are capable of being known by simple observation, that is, without comparison and inference. For example, Perception gives knowledge of an extended surface, but not of its measure; knowledge of a signal, but not of its meaning; knowledge of an action, but not of its moral character. Knowledge of an extended surface,— of the presence of a signal,— and of the performance of an action, is possible by simple Perception. But knowledge of the measure of the surface, of the meaning of the signal, and of the character of the action, are three examples of knowledge requiring the application of a standard, that is, the cognition of one thing by means of another, and this is knowledge of a higher and more complex order than simple Perception.

A theory of the knowledge of moral distinctions by means of a moral sense, as an organ or power of perception, is thus shown to be impossible.

9. Knowledge of moral quality is of the nature of Judgment. The knowledge of an action as fact is one thing, the

knowledge of that action as right or wrong is another thing. The former involves simple perception, the latter is attained only by comparison. For example, the infliction of pain by one upon another, as a simple act, may be seen in a variety of circumstances. In one case we may regard it as morally right, in another as morally wrong. In any case we must first know the relation of the persons concerned, the motive of the agent, and the contemplated end. If the relations of persons be that of parent and child; if the motive of the parent be desire of the child's improvement; and the warrant, a parent's right to restrain disobedience in a child, we pronounce one verdict. On the other hand, if the persons concerned are related as neighbours, and if the suffering is inflicted in malice, we give an opposite verdict. In either case we form a judgment. Again, restricting attention to our own consciousness, take for example the experience of an envious disposition. The knowledge of the presence of envy in the mind, is simple perception; the knowledge of its character as morally wrong is knowledge of a higher order, implying a prior knowledge, however obtained, as to rightness and wrongness, and the application of that prior knowledge to the particular fact perceived. It thus appears that the knowledge of moral quality is not obtained without comparison.

10. Moral Judgment does not result from the comparison of individual objects, but from the comparison of a particular act with a general truth. The comparison of an envious disposition present in consciousness, with a former experience of the same kind, only warrants the affirmation that these are two examples of the same disposition. Their similarity of nature being recognised, and the accuracy of a judgment of condemnation upon the earlier experience being assumed, there is a legitimate inference to the wrongness of the present disposition; but it is thereby proved that the judgment is not attained by simple comparison of particular cases. The first judgment,— and by consequence, every dependent judgment,— must be accounted for by reference to a general truth applicable to all examples of the same form of experience. Moral Judgments, therefore, take rank as judgments which apply a definite standard in particular cases.

11. Moral Judgments are not distinguished by moral quality, as right or wrong, but by intellectual quality, as true or

false, correct or incorrect; and they are as liable to error as other judgments.— Hutcheson's *Syst. of Mor. Philos.* 1. 4, 9.

12. Every accurate moral judgment affirms a particular application of a general moral truth. It contains a principle valid as a law of activity, not only in the particular case, but in all similar cases; not only at this time, but at all times (Id quod semper aequum et bonum est); a principle whose validity is in its own nature. There are other judgments which apply a standard altogether adventitious, the result of agreement, or of common association. Judgments of morality differ in this respect from judgments of measurement. The judgment that an honest or benevolent act is right, contains an element of self-evident truth. The judgment that an extended body is seven yards long, contains an element of truth dependent on common consent. In morality, the standard of judgment is invariable, because independent of personal or national choice. In measurement, the standard of judgment is variable, because dependent upon national sanction. There may be various standards of measurement, but only one standard of morality. Truthfulness, and nothing else, must be the standard of morality in utterance. Honesty, and nothing more nor less, must be the standard of morality affecting property. It is therefore an essential feature of a valid moral judgment that it carry in it a general truth.

13. Problems.— (1.) Distinguish between the rightness of an action, and the approbation of the action. (2.) In discussing the manner in which moral qualities are recognised, is the question as to 'that which renders morality an active principle' (Hume, followed by Mackintosh) legitimately introduced? (3.) Distinguish between the rightness of an action, and the merit of an agent. (4.) How is the moral quality of an action distinguished from obligation to do or not to do it?

CHAPTER III
FIRST PRINCIPLES OF MORALS
(INTUITIONAL THEORY)

1. As Moral Judgments involve the application of a general truth to a particular action, they pre-suppose knowledge of First Principles as a requisite for the discovery of moral distinctions among actions. For example, approval of a man who

speaks the truth, is implicitly approval of truthfulness itself The ultimate intellectual basis of the approval may be very dimly perceptible to the person pronouncing the judgment; but when such a judgment is scientifically tested, its philosophical warrant is found in the general principle that Truthfulness itself is right, that is, that Truthfulness is of the very nature of rectitude. Mr. Martineau denies that Morality is a system of truths.— *Essays,* second series, p. 6.

The term Principle *(principium, αρχή)* signifies literally a beginning, and may refer to any commencement. Within the mind, it applies either to first principles of knowledge or to sources of activity, such as the passions. It is here employed in the former sense exclusively. See Reid, *Intell. Powers,* Essay vi. c. 4, and Hamilton's Notes, p. 761; very particularly Kant's *Critique of Pure Reason,* Transcend. Dialectic, Intro. II., Meiklejohn's transl. p. 212. In the latter sense it is employed by Hume, Adam Smith, and others who assign superiority to sentiment.

2. The general truths involved in moral judgments are such in their nature that a reasoned contradiction of them cannot be maintained. Their opposites are incapable of vindication by any test, either from the forms of knowledge, or from the facts of experience. That Falsehood is right, that Malevolence is right, that Cowardice is right, are positions which cannot be reasoned out as applicable to human conduct.— Hume's *Essays (Prin. of Morals,* sect. i.); Reid's *Intell. Powers,* vi. 6 (Hamilton's Ed., p. 454).

3. The general truths involved in moral judgments are not generalized truths dependent for their validity on an induction of particulars; but self-evident truths, known independently of induction. They are as clearly recognised when a single testing case is presented for adjudication, as when a thousand such cases have been decided. In this relation, the Inductive Method guides merely to the fact that such truths are discovered in consciousness. But Induction as little explains the intellectual and ethical authority of these truths, as it settles the nature of the facts pertaining to physical science. The rightness of Honesty is not proved by an induction of particulars. But the conclusion that 'Honesty is the best policy,' is essentially a generalization from experience.

For elucidation of the former statement, it is needful to distinguish between the Action,— the Judgment, as to its moral character,— the Warrant for that judgment,— and the Abstraction which represents the particular form of moral quality present, namely, Honesty. Exchange of property by mutual consent may stand for the example. The judgment is that the acquisition of property in such a manner is morally right. What then is the warrant for this judgment? The purchaser pays his money and receives the property. Purchase depends on possession of the purchase-money. Honesty consists in paying the price. In pronouncing upon an exchange of property, therefore, we lean on a principle which determines what is right in acquiring property. How did the purchaser obtain his money? In reply, we are led back to personal effort, where we come upon the natural law of production — the ultimate law on which Political Economy rests — man possesses wealth by producing it. The source of property is in the man himself. His first possessions are the natural powers which belong to him. The moralist is thus led into the inner circle of human life. He deals with the activity which has its source within and only its ultimate results in the outer world. Moral quality does not belong to property, but only to personal activity; consequently, moral considerations are not concerned with variety in the kinds of property, but only with the lines of action taken for securing it. Rightness or wrongness applies to personal action in *acquiring* property. And the question of morality in acquisition, must depend upon what is right in *producing* property. This result is reached by simple analysis of the facts, discovering their relation to each other. By the use of his understanding in the direction of his energies, man becomes a producer. This is, in point of fact, the origin of property.

This analysis brings us to Personality as the centre and source of the activity to which alone moral distinctions are applicable. The question as to property thus becomes ultimately a question as to the use or non-use of our powers. By the use of our powers property is produced; without such activity, production is impossible. The enquiry is thus concerned with what is right in the use of our powers. Here there are two preliminary facts essential to the case. These are, the existence of powers to be used, and ability for self-direction in their use. The latter is obviously itself a power, which might be included in the first statement, but it is here distinguished as different from the producing powers, and concerned in their control. There are then powers, physical and mental, by the use of which man becomes a producer, and he has power of self-direction, by means of which he can determine, with due regard to external circumstances, what he shall produce. These being the facts, the principle which decides rightness of acquisition is, *that it is right in a man to use his powers for their natural ends.* This principle comes from the depth of our nature; it is the outcome of Personality; and the knowledge of it is a necessary condition of an intelligent, self-directed life. This is Intuition. It is the immediate recognition of the moral law, which appoints man to be a producer. By a power inherent in our Reason, the principle is recognised as self-evident. Thus, in the recognition of moral principle, the mind is the source of simple ideas, as Price maintained. By our Will, the principle may either be voluntarily accepted as the guide of conduct, or voluntarily rejected. But, to prove that the natural use of our powers is right, and the neglect of their use wrong, is as needless, as the attempt would be vain. That it is *right* to use our natural powers, is a proposition quite distinct from these two;— that it is *agreeable* to exercise our powers, and that it is *useful* to employ them. The *first* expresses a principle, or rule of conduct; the *second and third* merely affirm distinct facts. The *first* is a preliminary rule of action, presupposed as a requisite for the guidance of personal conduct; the *second* applies simply to an accompaniment of action, and is discovered only in acting; while the *third* applies to the external results of effort, which can be ascertained only by experience. Self-direction presupposes the knowledge of the distinction between right and wrong in conduct, originating in self-knowledge; the agreeable and the useful both presuppose action itself as the condition of their discovery.

Now, in distinguishing between right and wrong, the rightness of using our natural powers for their natural ends may be accounted the earliest and most general form in which the distinction is recognised. It may even be regarded as the foundation principle of morality. If unity is attainable in morals, it is here. (For discussion of the question whether virtue is one, *v.* Plato's *Protagoras.*) Viewing this principle as affording guidance

32

in the acquisition of property, every step may be taken by means of its application, until we reach the lightness of exchange. When we say, Industry is right, we only give an interpretation of the principle. By use of our powers, we originate property, and the rightness of such acquisition is implied in the principle. The use of our powers for their natural ends, clearly covers the attainment of these ends. And once more, the rightness of acquiring other property through means of that which has been self-originated, is only a more extended application of the same principle.

In this principle, that which is *wrong* becomes equally apparent. The right implies the wrong. Self-direction means, doing the right, and avoiding the wrong. If the natural use of our powers is right, the non-use of our powers is wrong, and so also is their unnatural use. An inactive life is wrong. Put abstractly,— Idleness is wrong. Viewed in relation to property, an unproductive life is wrong; and so of necessity, the waste of property is wrong.

This principle, springing from the very nature of Personality, must apply equally to all persons. Rightness in the use of natural powers, and consequently rightness in acquiring property, must hold in the case of all men. The cheat, the thief, and the robber are doubly condemned: *first* in respect of the violation of the law of their own personality, by the unnatural use of their powers; and *secondly,* in respect of the violation of the personality of another, by obstructing the use of his powers for natural ends. The idler, being distinguished only by the non-use of his powers, and not coming into view by direct action as a deliberate injurer of others, may less rouse our indignation, but he no less comes under the double condemnation. He violates the law of his own personality, and at the same time interposes to check the legitimate application of the law of personality in the case of others, by drawing upon their powers of production for the supply of his own wants. By another course, he occasions the same results to others, as are occasioned by the cheat.

Having thus seen how the rightness of personal activity, in harmony with our nature, involves the rightness of acquiring property, we have reached the point where the transition is made from right action, to personal Rights connected with property. From the origin of property, the Rights of property arise, namely, the right to hold and the right to use. These rights do not constitute Morality, they are its consequents. Rightness comes with the person. Rights come with the property. Personal Rights there are besides, no doubt, but they also are consequent upon what belongs to the person, and presuppose a law of conduct superior to social arrangements. These Rights cannot be constituted by Law; they afford to Law an original basis, so that the law is unjust which disregards them. Rights of Property come to be affirmed only in connexion with Risks of Property, and so point to social relations in which possession may be disputed or endangered, and not to the fundamental question of rightness in acquiring property. That there is an advantage to the community from guarding the rights of private property, is a consideration still further removed from the fundamental question of morality, and is to be settled by induction of particulars. When thus settled, as it very easily can be, and uniformly has been settled in every civilized nation, the advantage reaped from the protection of property becomes a sanction of morality, which, however, presupposes morality itself.

Recognising, as we are thus led to do, a manifold application of the moral law regulating acquisition of property, we are on the way for generalizing as to the form of moral excellence which appears in all these cases. We trace the common feature equally in the small and in the great. Thus we form a generalization as to the use of our powers, and designate it by the name of INDUSTRY; and another generalization as to the acquisition and exchange of property, and designate it by the name of Honesty, Fairness, or Equity — The Just, *justitia;* The Equal, το ἴσον. These abstractions belong to the intellectual furnishing of every man. As generalizations they are more or less clear and full, according to the reflection of the individual. But the law of morality bearing on acquisition of property is prior in knowledge and fundamentally requisite for the formation of the abstract conceptions of Industry and Honesty.

When we speak of an Intuitional Theory of Moral Distinctions, we mean that the Law which decides what is right is so connected with the nature of the Person, that the recognition of it is involved in intelligent self-direction. The knowledge is immediate, and its *source* is found within the mind itself. When we say of moral truth that it is self-evidencing, we mean that the Law carries in itself the evidence of its own truth. Taking Mr.

Herbert Spencer's form, we may say, it is 'indisputable.' Indisputability, however, may apply in two directions — to facts and to principles. The Moral Law affords an example of the latter. As to the *Validity* of the principle, the evidence of that lies in its own nature as a proposition or formulated truth. When we say that moral truth is its own warrant, we mean that it is by its nature an authoritative principle of conduct. Its credentials belong to its nature. Such laws of human conduct are 'the unwritten laws,' which Socrates says cannot be violated without punishment.— *Mem.* iv. 4, 13.

After the same manner as that adopted above, we must vindicate the essential rightness of each form of moral excellence falling within the range of human action, such as truthfulness, purity, temperance, kindness, etc., and the essential authority of the law which requires these of man. Such truths as those now described as self-evident principles of action, are also designated 'necessary truths.' This expression is very suitable in many ways, but the risk of ambiguity is considerable. Professor Bain explains the distinction thus: — 'The *necessary,* or what must be true, is opposed to the *contingent,* which may or may not be true.'— *Mental and Moral Science,* B. ii. c. 6. This cannot be accepted. 'Necessary' and 'contingent' are adjectives which qualify truth. The contrast is between 'necessary truth' and 'contingent truth,'— not between what must be true and what may be false. The distinction is between the true in principle and the true in fact. The one is truth recognised by the Reason, which is superior to all occurrences. The other is the truth of facts, things done, occurrences, and is recognised by Observation.

Besides this, there has been another source of ambiguity. 'Necessary truth' has sometimes been made to mean truth which we are necessitated to think. Consequent upon this use of the phrase, with which usage the Scotch Philosophy unfortunately is peculiarly chargeable, and the German Philosophy has its own share of blame, it has been made to appear as if these truths, instead of being by their own nature irreversible, drew their authority only from the necessities of our Intellect, a doctrine which I do not think has any evidence in its support. That our intellectual constitution is such as to fit us for the recognition of the principles of action seems plain in point of fact, whatever difficulty there may be in explaining the process of recognition.

But truths recognised as self-evident, have their authority in their own nature, so as to be essentially irreversible. Their contraries cannot be made to wear even the semblance of truth. Such principles as these, that truthfulness, justice, and benevolence are right in themselves, are authoritative as rules of conduct, and capable of enduring the test of application to the minutest details of life. So difficult is it to keep to an opposite view, that we could not wish the position better taken than has been done by Hobbes: 'The Laws of nature are immutable and eternal; for injustice, ingratitude, arrogance, pride, iniquity, acceptance of persons, and the rest, can never be made lawful. For it can never be that war shall preserve life, and peace destroy it.'— *Leviathan*, Pt. 1. 15, Molesworth's ed., vol. iii. p. 145. This feature of essential validity is what Kant has expressed by saying that moral principles have 'unlimited, universal validity,'— unbeschränkte allgemeine Gültigkeit. That these truths are seen by us to be self-evident, is a fact which adds nothing 'to their authority, but involves only the recognition of an authority which is inherent. As self-evident, the truth in the proposition is instantly recognised,— a fact well expressed by Cicero's word *promptu*, and also by our derivative *prompt*. As to the Psychological question concerning the mode or manner in which instantaneous recognition is secured, that seems inexplicable. These self-evident truths are brought from within in some manner not discovered in consciousness, and are instantaneously accepted. Quae ita sunt in promptu, ut res disputatione non egeat.— *De Officiis*, 1. 2.

Here the dividing point in the history of philosophic thought is reached. For an outline of the course taken by the two distinct currents of thought, see close of present chapter.

4. The general principle which gives validity to an accurate moral judgment, is present in that judgment only by implication, not by formal expression. Its formal recognition is not matter of common observation, but is dependent upon a philosophic process. The ordinary moral judgment deals with the concrete, not with the general or the abstract. Men do not enunciate general truths, when they decide on the rightness or wrongness of an action. Philosophy is not needed for any such decision.— Kant's *Metaph. of Ethics*, p. 164 (3d ed.); Cousin, *Philos. of Kant*, Henderson's transl. p. 167. But Moral

Philosophy must determine how a prompt decision in morals may be given without formal recognition of a principle, which by implication is nevertheless accepted.

5. Viewed simply as an exercise of mind, simultaneous with rational exercise, the recognition of general truths or principles is perception or intuition of a higher order, as the recognition of simple fact is perception or intuition of a lower order. Knowledge of the former kind implies direct insight into necessary truth. The possibility of such insight is the highest characteristic of our intelligent nature.

6. The power to recognise such self-evident truth has been named Reason, in contrast with Reasoning or Understanding. (Νοῦς in contrast with Διανοια;— Vernunft in contrast with Verstand). Kant formally enunciated this distinction.— *Kritik der Reinen Vernunft*, Die Transc. Dialectik II. A., Werke, ed. Rosencranz, II. 242; Meiklejohn's transl. *Critique of Pure Reason*, p. 212; Coleridge's *Aids to Reflection*, 8th ed. p. 167; Hamilton's *Reid*, Note A, sect. 5; M'Cosh's *Intuitions*, Pt. III. B. I. ch. ii. sect.

6. Knowledge of fact is knowledge by onlook; knowledge inferred is knowledge of one thing through means of another; knowledge of first principles is knowledge by insight into truth higher than fact.

7. Viewed simply as a form of knowledge, knowledge of first principles is distinguished by intellectual quality, not by ethical. It is knowledge of truth, but it is not in any proper sense right action. Insight into absolute moral truth, arising from the unfolding of intelligence itself, is a necessary function of mind, and therefore not capable of being reckoned among moral actions, which must be self-determined, as matters of choice.

8. The first principles of morals, being concerned with personal activity, are essentially laws of conduct, while they are principles of truth. That principle which determines what is right, determines what is law for me. As by our constitution we are appointed to a life of activity, so from the same source comes the discovery of the law for the guidance of our conduct. As the first principles of morals are of the nature of absolute truth, so are they absolute law, involving a *'categorical imperative,'* to use the renowned expression of Kant.— *Metaph. of Ethics*, p. 27, 3d ed.;

Price, *Principal Questions of Morals,* c. vi.; Hutcheson, *System of Mor. Phil.* II. ii. 3, Glasg. 1755.

It cannot be held with Kant in his Intellectual Theory, that the *a priori* elements of our knowledge are merely *regulative,* not *assertive.*— See Cousin, *Philos. of Kant,* p. 174. The position, which seems to me untenable even in reference to Pure Reason (the purely Intellectual), is manifestly so in reference to Practical Reason (the Moral). For whereas in the former case, the *a priori* elements of knowledge may be said to be merely regulative of *thought,* in the latter they are regulative of *conduct,* thereby making our actions, with dependent experience, a continual test of their validity. A moral principle is first a truth discovered as an element of knowledge; and next a law, recognised as a determinator of action. It is first a revelation (Offenbarung) of truth, in order that it may next be a law of life for an intelligent being.

9. While the principles of morality belong in their nature to the sphere of the absolute, they belong in their application to the sphere of the phenomenal or transitory: this is involved in parag. 4. Kant holds that 'Right cannot appear as a phenomenon.'— *Critique of Pure Reason,* Doct. of Elements, Pt. i. sect. 9. In ordinary experience, when a moral principle is recognised by us, it appears in its application to some line of conduct. To formulate and interpret the principle implies a philosophic process, but it also requires a definite example from which to begin. Only on the acknowledgment that absolute truth can be manifested in transitory forms, can there be a common rule of conduct for humanity. Only by the harmony of fleeting actions with absolute truth, which is at the same time absolute law, can there be consistency of human life. Without these, uniformity of law and consistency of action are lost in the specialities of Individualism. In such a case, each man is a law to himself, not by personal submission to recognised common law, but by express denial of it, and assertion of self-will.

It is impossible with philosophic warrant to maintain, as Kant has done, that man as intelligence exists in a cogitable world entirely separated from the phenomenal world.— *Metaph. of Ethics* (3d ed.), pp. 52, 63, 71, 147. Rather, it is clear that the spheres of *a priori* truth, and of experience, are so essentially related, that they cannot be separated, or contemplated as contradictory.

10. First principles of morals do not contradict each other, either in their nature as truths, or in their application as laws.

It has been a common objection against the Intuitional theory, that in attaining a variety of sovereign moral laws, it fails to provide for adjudication between them. The objection is thus stated by Mr. Mill: — 'In other systems, the moral laws all claiming independent authority, there is no common umpire entitled to interfere between them.'— *Utilitarianism*, p. 37. This objection is connected with the application of the principles, not with their nature. But, in order to conflict in practice, they must contradict each other in nature, which does not happen. The principle of truthfulness does not conflict with that of justice, nor the latter with that of benevolence. Each principle of morals applies to a line of activity all its own, and always its own. 'The same general principles are common to all men, nor does one such principle contradict another.'— Epictetus, i. 23. Further it is to be observed, that moral principles, as applying to perfectly distinct lines of activity, do not, on the ground of inherent authority, make a claim for extending that authority over spheres of activity which other principles regulate. In practical application, therefore, they do not contradict each other. Further, if perplexity arise as to the time when a principle of morality should have application, while other principles are left in abeyance, this perplexity affects neither the validity, nor the authority, of the principles; but is a question of present duty, which is quite distinct, and will afterwards have attention under the head of Moral Obligation.

11. There are first principles of intellectual truth, as there are of moral truth. The former are laws of intelligence, as the latter are laws of conduct. Of the former, the laws of non-contradiction and of causality are examples. Regarded as facts in consciousness, both are distinguished by the same character of self-evidence. In so far as they may be referred to a distinct power of mind, the power is one. The name commonly given to this Power — Reason, as distinguished from the Understanding or Reasoning power — is merely a name for Intelligence as competent to the function of recognising self-evident truths. This

is its highest function, the power for which is a fundamental condition of intelligent activity.

12. As of self-evident truths, some are applicable in purely intellectual relations, others in exclusively moral relations, this difference of application gives such warrant as high scientific convenience can afford, for distinguishing Intellectual or Speculative Reason from Moral or Practical Reason. Other warrant there is none. There is no such difference in the nature of the power exercised in the two cases, as to provide a philosophic basis for the distinction in classification and terminology.

As however the two spheres of application are concerned with two separate departments of science, the distinction is inevitable, for the sake of scientific accuracy. The more effectually to secure such accuracy, it is of consequence to make the popular term, CONSCIENCE, apply to Reason in its moral applications; as contrasted with Reason in its speculative bearings. Kant's distinction between Pure Reason and Practical Reason, however suitable in some respects, is not a distinction philosophically valid. If the recognition of *a priori* truth be the function of Pure Reason, then the Practical Reason is also Pure Reason.— *Metaph. of Ethics* (3d ed.) p. 64. Speculative Reason and Practical Reason might mark the difference.

13. Problems.— (1.) If a *priori* principles are confessedly conditions necessary for the attainment of human experience, are these principles more than conditions, and entitled to rank as Truths? The problem is, To find the philosophic interpretation of 'condition' in this case. (2.) If *a priori* truths are not always present to all minds (and the hypothesis which Locke controverted, is confessedly ridiculous), how is the recognition of them possible? The problem is, To attain the Psychological law under which *a priori* truth may at any time be presented in consciousness.— For Kant's Spontaneity of Reason, *Met. of Eth.* 71 — 75. (3.) Granting that there are *a priori* truths of Intelligence and of Practice, and that both are laws of mind, in what respect do they, as Laws, differ from each other? The problem is — To interpret legality in the two cases. (4.) If Moral Principles are at once Truths, and Laws, can we draw rigidly the distinction between these two aspects of the same Principle? (5.) If the mind is itself the source of primary truth, how far is mind dependent upon experience for the use of what it possesses? (6.)

Can Truth be at once absolute and phenomenal? Can these two characteristics be found in combination? (7.) Can Truthfulness as a law of Personal Conduct, come into conflict with Justice as a law regulating the relations of Persons? (8.) Can *a priori* moral truth be represented as expressing nothing 'except general legality,' or 'the form of law in general'? — Kant's *Met. of Ethics,* p. 13, 3d ed.

SKETCH OF THE HISTORY OF PHILOSOPHIC THOUGHT AS TO THE SOURCE OF OUR KNOWLEDGE OF MORAL TRUTH

The standard of moral decisions is the test of every system of Ethics. With this is closely connected the source from which the knowledge of the standard is drawn. The briefest outline of the history of thought on this subject is all that can be attempted.

In contemplating the Ancient Philosophy, it is needful to keep in view that the questions as to the ultimate standard of morals, and the source of our knowledge of that standard, were not so definitely raised as in modern times. The utmost care is required in order to guard against judging the terminology of ancient times by modern distinctions.

Socrates, born about 470 B. C., made it his chief business to reach a proper understanding of such general conceptions as piety, justice, bravery, temperance, and virtue. In this, as Aristotle affirms, *Metaph.* xii. 4, he simply carried out a process of generalization, in order to form a general or abstract conception, which might be afterwards applied to any variety of examples. These general conceptions he constantly subjected to the test of experience. He insisted that knowledge is essential to virtue, or, even more broadly, that knowledge is virtue. This last declaration, which is commonly represented as the central position of the Socratic philosophy, involves a theory of practice, rather than of knowledge, resting on the allegation that no man is knowingly vicious. While concerning himself with the significance of ethical conceptions, he did not raise the question as to the ground on which general conceptions are held to afford a standard of moral distinctions. If, however, we may regard the Platonic Socrates in the *Theœtetus* as the historic Socrates, he argued strenuously against the doctrine of Protagoras, which reduces everything to the phenomenal. Our best authorities as to the theory of Socrates are Xenophon's *Memorabilia*, and Plato's *Apologia*. After these in importance come the Platonic *Dialogues*, and references in Aristotle's *Metaph.* and *Ethics*. See Stanley's *Lives of the Philos.;* Ritter's *Anc. Philos.* vol. ii.; Schwegler's *Hist. of Philos.*, Dr. Hutchison Stirling; Zeiler's *Socrates and Socratic Schools*, Reichel; Ueberweg's *Hist. of Philos.*, G. S. Morris, Michigan,— *Theol. and Philos. Lib.;* Lewes's *Hist. of Philos.;* Sir A. Grant's *Aristotle*, Essay ii.

Plato, born about 427 B. C., rises into a higher region of enquiry. He gives to the general conceptions of Socrates the character of Ideas, which constitute the fundamental ideas of Reason,— the perfect essences of things — the eternal laws of being,— and belong to a super-sensible state, 'a world or sphere of ideas.' Intelligence is confused with the shadows of the sensible state, and is ever striving to rise into this 'upper world' of higher knowledge. Here the Good, which he ultimately identifies with God, is supreme. See specially the *Republic*, B. vii., Jowett's transl. ii. 348; Aristotle's *Metaph.* i. 6. The power to know these primary ideas 'is already in the soul,' *Rep.* vii.; and their presence may be explained by a theory of *reminiscence*, possible on account of our having descended from a higher sphere: *Meno*, Jowett's Transl. i. For the student of Moral Philosophy, the most important of the Platonic Dialogues are Protagoras, Meno, Gorgias, Phsedo, Philebus, and Republic, i.-iv., and specially B. vii. On Plato's Philos., see Ritter's *History*, and the admirable representation of it in Archer Butler's *Ancient Philos.* vol. ii. From an opposite point of view, Grote's *Plato*.

Aristotle, born 384 B. C., formally separates Ethics from other sciences. He commences the Nicom. Ethics with a discussion of the chief good,— *summum bonum*, ἀριστον,— or the perfect good, το τελειον αγαθον,— which he declares to be Happiness. He is thus led into the doctrine of the Mean, μεσοτης, or avoidance of extremes, previously touched upon by Socrates, *Mem.* ii. I. II. The leading part of the Ethics assumes the utilitarian or the Eudæmonistic form. A different phase of theory appears in Books v., vi., vii., on account of which it has been disputed whether these books were written by Aristotle himself, or by Eudemus as an amplification of the sayings of his master. In Book vi. the rule of practical life is, to act according to right reason,— κατα τον ορθον λογον. Reason is distinguished into Scientific, επιστημονικον, which contemplates necessary matter, and the Reasoning or Discursive Faculty, λογιστικον, which deals with contingent matter. Even here, however, it is left uncertain what is the standard by which to determine the mean, and there are admissions which seem to imply that there is no certain invariable standard. If the genuineness of Books v., vi. and vii., be allowed,— and the internal criticism against them is not conclusive,— it is difficult to harmonize them with the forms of life enumerated in B. i. c. 5. In any case, the theory is burdened with the admission, i. 4, that while happiness is the *summum bonum*, men are not agreed as to happiness, or what is most desirable. Grote maintains that 'by referring the principles to Intellect (Νουζ), Aristotle does not intend to indicate their generating source, but their evidential value and dignity.' 'To say that they originate from Sense through Induction, and nevertheless to refer them to Intellect (Νουζ) as their subjective correlate,— are not positions inconsistent with each other, in the view of Aristotle.'— Grote's *Aristotle,* vol. ii. App. ii. p. 293. That both positions were taken by Aristotle seems plain; that he raised the question of their consistency is not clear. That they did not seem to Aristotle inconsistent, can be maintained on no better ground than that he accepted both. But this is rather lofty as a canon of internal criticism,— That an author is never inconsistent. On Aristotle's Ethical system, see Ritter, Schwegler, Ueberweg, Sir A. Grant's *Aristotle's Ethics,* Essays and Notes; Whewell's *Systematic Morality,* p. 140. From the Utilitarian standpoint, Lewes's *Aristotle,* and Grote's *Aristotle.*

Here it should be remarked that the prominent defects of ancient systems are such as to render them, on the practical side, incompatible with a theory of necessary or universal moral law. They are systems constructed for the State, not for Humanity; for friends, but not for foes. Human in their origin and development, they became more or less sectarian in their application. The inconsistency is glaring even in the midst of the grandeur of Plato's Ideal system. Zeller dwells on some of these defects in the 1st chap. of *Stoics,* etc.

The two conflicting elements of Aristotle's theory part company, and form two distinct and conflicting philosophies in the later movements. The two antagonistic theories are represented by the Stoics and the Epicureans, and thenceforth these two divisions continue down the line of history. The separation of the conflicting elements was attended on each side by a disparagement of that which was rejected, and a consequent undue exaltation of that preferred. The Stoics selected the Rational nature as the true guide to an ethical system, but they gave to it supremacy so rigid as to threaten the extinction of the subject affections. The Epicureans, laying hold of the doctrine that happiness is the chief good, gave such ascendency to the desirable as to threaten the mob-rule against which Plato had protested.

The Stoic Philosophy was essentially a moral philosophy in which right action was rational action, and in this light the Stoic maxim is to be interpreted, to live according to nature, ομολογουμένως τη φυσει ζην. For while this implies harmony with the universe, it is by Reason that such harmony is recognised; and this is made so vital, as practically to lean on the Socratic doctrine, that knowledge is virtue. But with the Stoics, as with Socrates, there is indecision as to the standard, though it is commonly said that the knowledge of right is given by nature. For the Stoic Philosophy, see *Diog. Läertius,* B. vii., specially lives of Zeno (about 350 B. C.), Cleanthes, Chrysippus. See also Plutarch; Cicero, *De Finibus* and *De Officiis;* with Seneca, Epictetus, and Marcus Aurelius. *Histories,* as above, very particularly Zeller's *Stoics,* etc., Reichel.

The system of Epicurus, B.C. 342, made Happiness the chief good, and declared the end of Philosophy to be the guidance of man in the attainment of it. The pleasure of the soul is placed above that of the body; but there is no standard higher or more authoritative than the agreeable. Diogenes Läertius, B. x.; Plutarch, Cicero, and references as above.

Cicero, 106 B. C., gave moral philosophy the precedence. In all his thought, he was swayed by the Greek Philosophy, and though vacillating and undecided in many points, was avowedly (*De Off.* i. 2) an adherent of the Stoics. Though far from being consistent as to the criterion of truth, he held to 'innate notions,' *notiones innatœ,* and the common consent of the nations, *consensus gentium.* He maintains, that a man cannot say that he is ignorant of duty, *Acad. Pr.* 34; and that the conviction of the wisest men has been, that Law was neither invented by the genius of men, nor an institution of the popular will, but something eternal, *De Leg.* ii. 4.

It is necessary here to pass, as transcending needful limits, the Neo-Platonic Philosophy of Plotinus, A. D. 204 — 269, Aurelius, and Porphyry; the Patristic period, when Christianity did so much to quicken and expand philosophic thought; and the age of the Schoolmen, with the controversy between the Nominalists and Realists. For the history of thought during these periods, see specially Ueberweg's *History of Philos.,* Cudworth's *Immutable Morality,* and Sir W. Hamilton's *Dissertation* A., supplementary to Reid's *Works.*

Des Cartes (1596 — 1650), the father of modern philosophy, made innate ideas a distinctive feature of his system. He held that these ideas are given by the light of nature, *lumen naturæ.* He divides ideas into innate, adventitious, and factitious, *Medit.* iii., where see his definition of *Nature.* His theory is more fully unfolded in the *Principles of Philosophy.* In a letter to the French Translator of the *Principles,* he gives an important explanation of his views as to these innate ideas or principles of Knowledge. 'They must be so clear and evident that the human mind, when it attentively considers them, cannot doubt of their truth; in the second place, the knowledge of other things must be so dependent on them as that though the principles themselves may indeed be known apart from what depends on them, the latter cannot be known apart from the former.' Prof. Veitch's Translation, p. 94, and note, 207. Des Cartes did not enter formally on Ethical Philosophy.

Spinoza (1632 — 1677), a disciple and expounder of Des Cartes, developed a system very different from the Cartesian. His thinking was directed chiefly to the grandeur of the Divine nature, and our dependence upon God. His theory, developed in *The Ethics,* is dialectic in form, depending almost wholly on definitions of terms, not upon observed facts, and is Pantheistic in substance. It holds the conception of the Deity to involve such all-pervading existence, and all-efficient agency, as to make *The Ethics* really an exposition of the impossibility of Ethics, Still, Spinoza is to be interpreted not from the standpoint of Scepticism, but from that of Faith. His definition of Substance is the basis of his whole system. 'By substance I understand that which is self-existent, and is conceived only through itself'; that is to say, Substance is that the conception of which requires the conception of nothing else from which it must be derived.'— *The Ethics,* Pt, I. Def. 3. This is the beginning and end of all that Spinoza maintains. From this it follows that 'no substance can exist, or be conceived to exist, except God.' All existence is a manifestation of Deity, and can be in no sense distinct from the Deity. 'All things are determined by the necessity of the Divine nature.' 'Things could not have been produced by God in any other way than they have been.' From these positions in Part I., there necessarily follows, in Part II., a view of the human mind directly contrary to Personality or self-originated activity. The human mind is 'constituted by certain modes of the Divine attributes.' The False is 'merely want of knowledge.' 'Men deceive themselves when they fancy themselves to be free.' 'Belief in freedom is possible only because we are 'ignorant of the causes which determine our actions.' On this Psychology rests the Ethical system of Part in. 'Affections or Emotions' are states of body and their ideas, Def. 3. Things awaken in us pleasure or pain, Prop. xv., they are accordingly liked or disliked, loved or hated, Prop. xvi.; we strive to do whatever men regard with pleasure, and to avoid the contrary, Prop. xxix.; as different men are differently affected, they love and hate different things. Morality is thus the play of love and hate, based on likes and dislikes. The mind is grieved by contemplating its own inability to act; grief occasioned by our own weakness is humility,— joy occasioned by our own power is self-satisfaction,— humility is intensified when we imagine ourselves to be blamed by others, Prop. LV. Spinoza's Definitions of the Affections of the mind are found at the close of Part III. The system is a theory of human conceptions, in which the highest transcendental conception rules, and logical deduction carries the theory of human practice down to the lowest type of sensationalism. In the Ethics of Spinoza the extremes meet.— Benedicti de Spinoza *Opera Philosophica Omnia,* vol. i. ed. Bruder, Leipzig, 1843 — 1846; *Benedict de Spinoza: his Life, Correspondence, and Ethics,* translated by Willis, London, 1870.

Malebranche (1638 — 1715) held the Cartesian doctrine, affirming that there are necessary truths, which are truths of the Universal Reason.— *Recherche de la Vérité,* I. 4; *Search after*

Truth, translated by Taylor. On this basis he founds morality.— *Traité de Morale.*

Leibnitz (1646 — 1716) accepted the same account of the source of our knowledge of fundamental truth.— *Nouveaux Essais,* B. I., ed. Erdmann, p. 204.

Hobbes (1588 — 1679) devoted himself to Moral Philosophy. Contemporary with Des Cartes, he founded his theory on an opposite view. 'Concerning the thoughts of a man, . . . the original of them all, is that which we call Sense, for there is no conception in a man's mind which hath not at first, totally or by parts, been begotten upon the organs of sense.'— *Leviathan,* I. I. At the same time, he held 'Eternal laws of Nature,' I. 15,— a chapter of great interest, though difficult to harmonize with the preceding theory. For the statement of the fundamental feature of his ethical system, see below, Div. ii. ch. 2.

Cudworth (1617 — 88) maintained, in reply to Hobbes, that there is 'a natural, immutable, and eternal justice' *(Immutable Morality,* I. I); and that 'there are some ideas . . . which must needs arise from the innate vigour and activity of the mind itself.'— *Ib.* iv. 2. An able discussion, but depending too much on argumentation as to the essences of things.

Locke (1632 — 1704) made it a primary aim to oppose the theory of 'innate ideas.' He insisted that there are neither speculative nor practical principles belonging to the mind by its original constitution. 'Children and idiots have not the least apprehension or thought of them.'— *Essay* I. ii. sec. 5. Recognition of them by children seems to him the only conceivable view of 'innate truths,' although it is altogether different from Des Cartes's theory, or any other that had been maintained. According to Locke, all our knowledge is obtained through Sensation and Reflection. In support of moral law, the Christian refers to 'Happiness and misery in another life;' the Hobbist, to the power of the state; the old heathen philosophers to the dignity of man and the highest perfection of human nature. 'Hence naturally flews the great variety of opinions concerning the moral rules, according to the different sorts of happiness they have a prospect of, or purpose to themselves.'— I. iii. 5, 6.

Wollaston (1629 — 1724) denied 'innate maxims,' and also rejected the happiness theory. He held that the reasoning power, or rational faculty, is the judge of actions and the governing principle of life. He thus made 'right' identical with 'truth.'— *Religion of Nature Delineated.*

Samuel Clarke (1675 — 1724) insisted that there are 'eternal and necessary differences of things,' and a consequent 'fitness or unfitness of the application of different things or different relations one to another.' This fitness determines rightness.— 'Unchangeable Obligations of Natural Religion,' published in same volume with *The Attributes.*

Joseph Butler (1692 — 1752) held that 'there is a principle of reflection in men, by which they distinguish between, approve, and disapprove their own actions. We are plainly constituted such sort of creatures as to reflect upon our own nature.'— *Sermon* I. 'There is a superior principle of reflection or conscience in every man which distinguishes between the internal principles of his heart, as well as his external actions; which passes judgment upon himself, and thus . . . magisterially exerts itself . . . and goes on to anticipate a higher and more effectual sentence.' It is, 'considered as a faculty, in kind and in nature, supreme over all others, and which bears its own authority of being so.'— *Sermon* II. 'You cannot form a notion of this faculty, conscience, without taking in judgment, direction, superintendency.'— *Ib.* 'Had it strength, as it has right; had it power, as it has manifest authority, it would absolutely govern the world.'— *Ib.* Beyond this Butler does not push the inquiry.

Price (1723 — 1791) held that the understanding is the source of simple ideas, that 'our ideas of right and wrong are simple ideas, and must therefore be ascribed to some power of immediate perception.'— *Principal Questions of Morals.*

Hume (1711 — 1766) propounded a Sceptical Philosophy which reduced existences to a series of appearances, and mind to a bundle of perceptions.— *Treatise on Human Nature,* I. i. I.; and I. iv. 6. He advocates the Utilitarian theory of morals, but not with complete consistency. He says, 'Those who have denied the reality of moral distinctions may be ranked among the disingenuous disputants.'— *Essays,* II. 223, *Principles of Morals.* In the Appendix on Moral Sentiment, he adds, p. 348, 'Virtue is an end, and is desirable on its own account, without fee or reward, merely for the immediate satisfaction which it conveys.' The inconsistency of such a sentence is a curiosity of the Sceptical philosophy. To Hume's Scepticism, Intuitionalism has been peculiarly indebted for a powerful impulse experienced in Scotland, Germany, and France. On the relation of the Scotch and German Philosophies, see Cousin on Kant, Henderson's Translation, p. II.

Reid (1710 — 1796), in reply to Hume, maintained that the mind has a knowledge of truth superior to that gathered by experience. 'There are propositions which are no sooner understood than they are believed . . . there is no searching for evidence, no weighing of arguments; the proposition is not deduced or inferred from another; it has the light of truth in itself, and has no occasion to borrow it from another.' These truths are called 'first principles, principles of common sense, common notions, self-evident truths.' Of these, some are 'first principles in morals.'— *Intell. Powers* (1785), Essay vi. chaps. 4 and 6. 'I call these first principles, because they appear to me to have in themselves an intuitive evidence which I cannot resist.'— *Active Powers* (1788), v. I. The closing words here are objectionable, because they make it appear as if it were by some constraint that we acknowledged the truth of the propositions.

Dugald Stewart (1753 — 1828) was the resolute upholder of the same theory.— *Elements of the Philos. of the Hum. Mind* (1813), vol. II. I; Works, III. 23. First Truths, Stewart designates 'the fundamental laws of human belief, or the primary elements of human reason.'

Kant (1724 — 1804) is the leading champion of an *a priori* philosophy, whose singular ability, with adaptation of the national mind, has given Germany the first place in prosecuting the investigations of mental philosophy. It was by Hume's Sceptical philosophy that Kant was roused 'from his dogmatic slumber,'— Introd. to the *Prolegomena*, Werke, Rosencranz, in. 9,— a rousing of more than common significance to the philosophic world. For Kant's view of Hume, see *Kritik der Rein, Vern, Critique of Pure Reason*, Meiklejohn's Transl. pp. 453 and 464, and Introd. to *Prolegomena*. Cf. Cousin's *Philos. of Kant*, Henderson's Transl., p. 145.

Kant set to work critically, to ascertain how much in consciousness is to be assigned to experience, and how much is *a priori*, or original to mind. The result led him to maintain an *a priori* element in the exercise of the Senses, *Sinne*, of the

Understanding, *Verstand,* and of the Reason, *Vernunft.* Exercise of the senses is possible, only under the *a priori* forms of space and time; of the understanding, under the primitive pure notions, denominated Categories. The exercise of the Reason gives Ideas, out of which principles originate. The three grand Ideas of Reason are the Soul, God, and the Universe. Still, we know only phenomena, or passing appearances. Of things-in-themselves,— noumena,— we can know nothing. Even the ideas of Reason themselves, involve us in hopeless confusion. At this point, Kant does not part company with Hume. Yet they completely differ in this respect, that Kant maintains the reality of things-in-themselves. With him, the Mind is a noumenon, existing in a supersensible or cogitable world, superior to the laws of causality. With certain marked differences, the theory of Kant here becomes analogous to that of Plato. With the ancient philosopher, the supersensible world is one from which we have descended, and to which we may climb again by philosophy; with the modern, we are now both in the supersensible world, and out of it, being within it as pure mind, but without, in so far as we are concerned with the sensible and phenomenal. According to Kant, the *a priori* forms, notions, and ideas, which are not criteria of truth, are conditions of our intelligence which we impose on phenomenal experience. This is akin to that formula of Reid which represents first principles of intelligence and morality, as convictions which we cannot resist; but quite inferior to Reid, who maintains that *a priori* principles have 'the light of truth in themselves.' With Kant, the ideas of pure reason, though involving us speculatively in contradictions, are nevertheless regulative of intellectual life. Kant's intellectual theory, with all its speculative insight, and grandeur of conception, is negative and sceptical in its conclusion, from which its cognitive or supersensible world cannot be accredited as a philosophic deliverance.— *Kritik der Reinen Vernunft,* Werke, Rosencranz, II.; *Critique of Pure Reason,* Meiklejohn's Translation; Mahaffy's *Kant for English Readers;* Schwegler's *History,* translated by Dr. J. Hutchison Stirling; Ueberweg's *History,* translated by G. S. Morris; Cousin's *La Philosophie de Kant,* translated with admirable Introduction by A. G. Henderson, London, 1854; *Inquisitio Philosophica,* by M. P. W. Bolton, London, 1866; *Time and Space,* by Dr. Shadworth

Hodgson, London, 1865; *Kant,* article in *Encyclo. Britann.,* 8th
ed., by Rev. Professor John Cairns, D. D. For the terminology of
Kant, see *Critique of Pure Reason,* Meiklejohn's Transl. p. 224;
Encyclo. Worterbuch der Kritischen Philosophic, by G. Mellin,
eleven vols. Leipzig, 1797; Krug's *Handwörterbuch,* Leipzig,
1832, 2d ed.

Kant's Ethical Theory, in accordance with the Intellectual,
is *a priori* in its structure. It is in the region of practice that we
transcend the phenomenal, and attain the real. 'The Practical
Reason' discovers truth; the 'Autonomy of the Will' carries us
beyond the phenomenal into the cogitable or supersensible
world. Here the Categorical Imperative or Moral Law, our own
Personality, Freedom of Will, and the Being of God, are all
certainly discovered. In accordance with the nature of the
categorical imperative, the formula of all morality is,— Act from
a maxim at all times fit for law universal.— *Grundlegung zur
Metaph. der Sitten,* 1785; and *Kritik der Praktischen Vernunft,*
1788, both in vol. vii. of Werke, Rosencranz; *The Metaphysic of
Ethics,* translated by Semple, which I have edited, with
Introduction, 3d ed., Edinburgh.

Johann Gottlieb Fichte (1762 — 1814), adopting pure
Idealism, discarded the Speculative Reason of Kant, and
regarded Reason as practical. In Ethics, he first developed the
Science of Rights.— *Grundlage des Naturrechts,* 1796, Werke
by J. H. Fichte, Ill., translated by Kroeger,— *Science of Rights,*
Philadelphia, 1869; and afterwards the *Science of Morals, System
der Sittenlehre,* 1798, Werke, Th. iv. With Fichte, Self-
consciousness is the test of rationality, and the Rational Being
necessarily posits itself as a free-will agent. To such a rational
agent, Morality is action according to the ideas of Reason, in
order to attain perfect or absolute freedom.

Georg W. F. Hegel (1770 — 1831) made the Idea the
source of all reality. His system is developed as a Dialectic,
proceeding from Pure Being as its starting-point. It is more a
Philosophy of Logical Possibilities than a Philosophy of Mind or
known existence, though of necessity it is wrought out with the
materials which experience affords.— *Wissenschaft der Logik,*
1833 — 34, Werke, iii.-v. His Ethical Theory is in accordance
with his general scheme. It is divided into three parts, Abstract
Right,— Morality in the individual life,— and Moral Principles

applied to social life.— *Grundlinien der Philosophie des Rechts,* Berlin, 1821, Werke, viii. Hegel's line of progress is as follows,— starting from a conception such as Being, to pass over to its opposite, Not-Being, and then by the combination of both to reach a higher unity, or stage in advance, Becoming. The notion is thus the first moment,— reaching the antithesis, is the second moment,— and the combination, is the third moment. This tripartite movement, Hegel regards as involved in every stage of philosophic progress. In accordance with its character, universality and Necessity are the prominent features of the scheme. 'The philosophical science of morals possesses the Idea of Right,— the Conception of Right,— and its realization in objects,' sec. i, p. 3. In harmony with Fichte, he says, 'The ground of the Right is the mental, and its primary position and starting-point, the Will, so that freedom constitutes its substance and distinction, and the system of Right is the realm of realized freedom, the world of mind brought out from itself, as a second nature,' sec. 4, p. 14. Then comes the development, according to the Hegelian system, of the pure or indeterminate Ego (I), into the determinate, by a metaphysical process. After this, the immediate or natural Will, encountering Impulses, Desires, and Inclinations, realizes itself in action, by an ethical process. In this, Personality is reached, sec. 31, p. 41. The Mind has objects and aims, and so is a Person. 'Personality involves capability of Right.' 'The Law of Right is therefore,— Be a Person and respect others as Persons,' sec. 36, p. 42. In application of this the Right of the moral Will involves three sides,— (1.)the abstract or formal right of the action, (2.) the speciality of the action, as having a determinate aim, in harmony with abstract right,— this is the Well (Wohl), and (3.) the realization of this in act,— which is the Good, and its antithesis, the Bad, where appears the application of Conscience, sec. 114, p. III.

In judging of Hegel, it is needful to distinguish between his method and the substance of his system, keeping at the same time in view, that this philosopher of abstractions held that 'everything true is concrete' (alles Wahre ist concret), sec. 7, p. 19. The substance of the theory has for the most part been previously and otherwise obtained. Without Kant there could have been no Hegel. The critical method preceded this dialectic, supplied the materials, gave the key — and the later philosophy has come after, with a splendid dialectic exercise, working up these materials into a new form, affording ample proof of the validity and consistency of the fundamental conceptions of Reason. But as a separate and independent system of philosophy, I cannot think it capable of enduring. The basis of all real philosophy lies where Kant uncovered the distinction between the *a posteriori* and *a priori*,— knowledge by experience, and knowledge original to mind; and the beginning of all philosophizing is where Des Cartes began,— I think, therefore I am. If both philosophers seriously failed in rearing the superstructure, this is only in keeping with the analogy of discovery; but certainly both achieved, as Hegel also has done, a very grand part in the work which belongs to ages.

Friedrich E. D. Schleiermacher(1768 — 1834) discussed the whole system of Ethics from the point of view afforded by the highest good. He maintained that 'the activity of Reason upon the nature, expresses the beginning and ending of the science of morals.'— *Sittenlehre* (1835), sec. 91; Werke Philos. v. p. 52. 'As Moral Philosophy is completely unfolded as a doctrine of Good, or of the Highest Good, so is it the full expression of the whole unity of Reason and Nature.' But the highest good is not to be taken as a single good, but as a totality,— 'the organic connexion of all good,'— a doctrine which comes closely upon the Utilitarian Theory, though it is not so regarded by Schleiermacher himself.

The French philosophers belonging to the latter half of the eighteenth century, carried out the sensationalism of Condillac, by developing a utilitarian system of morals. Thus Helvetius (1715 — 1771) argues from sensation as the origin of all knowledge, to the pleasurable as the ground of moral distinctions.— *De l'Esprit,* Paris, 1758; *De l'Homme,* London, 1772; and *Les Progrés de la Raison dans la Recherche du Vrai,* London, 1775. D'Holbach (1723 — 1789), making actions the necessary product of our organism, develops a moral system similar to that of Helvetius.— *Système de la Nature; ou Des Lois du Monde Physique et du Monde Moral,* 1770.

The French School of the nineteenth century, drawing its inspiration mainly from the Scotch School, partly from the German, finds the basis of morality in necessary principles of rectitude. Following Laromiguière, Maine de Biran, and Royer-

Collard, Victor Cousin (1792 — 1867) is a conspicuous example. The critic at once of Locke and of Kant, he was the vindicator of Reid, and the upholder of universal and necessary principles as the basis equally of speculative and of practical science.— *The True, the Beautiful, and the Good*, translated by O. W. Wright, Edinburgh, 1854. See specially Lects. I.-III. XI. and XIV.

Theodore Jouffroy (1796 — 1842) was the distinguished disciple and colleague of Cousin. Travelling along a course of independent investigation, he reached the same conclusions in morals. The main steps are these: — There are 'primitive tendencies' in our nature, and 'faculties' for attaining the ends sought by these tendencies, 'pleasure' results from the use of these faculties. Reason finds these tendencies and faculties developed, enters into the meaning of all things connected with our nature and circumstances, and acquires an idea of the true end of our being. Thus man attains to morality in self-guidance, for he is moral only by the attainment of universal absolute ideas. From a survey of the relations of distinct personalities, there comes the conception of Universal Order. The idea of Order awakens the reverence of Reason, and is accepted as 'the natural and eternal law.' 'All duty, right, obligation, and rules of morality spring from this one source, the idea of good in itself,— the idea of Order.'— *Cours de Droit naturel*, Paris, 1834; *Introduction to Ethics*, translated by W. H. Channing, Boston, 1840, 2 vols. Jouffroy's own theory is given in vol. I. I — 82.

Auguste Comte (1798 — 1857) has, more recently in the history of France, become leader of a reaction. In his desire to attain certainty, he seeks, under the name of Positivism, to restrict philosophy to the recognition of facts and laws, to the exclusion of causes. He proposes to abandon 'metaphysical idealities' for observed realities, as if external observation discovered the only realities, or as if metaphysical investigation involved rejection or disparagement of external facts.

For the student of Moral Philosophy, the most important parts of the *Cours de Philosophie Positive*, are the Introductory discussion on the nature of Philosophy, and Book vi., *Social Physics*, chaps, v. and vi.; the one entitled Social Statics, or theory of the spontaneous order of human society; the other entitled Social Dynamics, or theory of the natural progress of human society.

Comte is profuse in his charges of 'imbecility' all round, and of 'transcendental idiocy' in a special direction, while he assures his readers that the Positive Philosophy 'reorganizes everything that it touches,' and that 'Social Science has nowhere yet risen to the positive except in this book.' In spite of such blemishes, the parts of his work mentioned above well deserve careful study.

I have already indicated, Introd. sect. 4, that Comte rejects Psychology, on account of the alleged impossibility of following the introspective line of inquiry, instead of which he offers a Biology, or theory of life. I have also explained, Introd. sect. 6, that he further insists that the laws of human conduct must be studied in society, not in the nature and experience of the individual. The moral system which he proposes is thus a Sociology, with no law of personal life save that which may be deduced from the data recognised in social organization and progress. I will now give the main points of Comte's system, in so far as it is concerned with human conduct. In doing so, I shall quote from the translation given by Miss Harriet Martineau, *The Positive Philosophy of Auguste Comte,* 2 vols., London, 1853.

Comte denies that society originates in utilitarian considerations, and holds that there is 'a spontaneous sociability of human nature,' ii. 127. There is in our nature a 'preponderance of the affective over the intellectual faculties,' 128. There is 'a certain degree of spontaneous activity as the chief cerebral attribute of humanity,' 136. 'The intellectual faculties are naturally the least energetic, and their activity, if ever so little protracted beyond a certain degree, occasion in most men a fatigue which soon becomes utterly unsupportable. Nevertheless, it is on the persevering use of these high faculties that the modifications of human life, general and individual, depend.' To produce and sustain intellectual effort, some impulse is needed from 'lower but stronger propensities.' 'The individual nature of man becomes lofty in proportion as incitement proceeds from propensities which are of a higher order,' 129. 'Our affective faculties must preponderate,' in order to give 'a permanent aim and direction' to the activity of our reason. 'Our social organism is, then, what it ought to be, except as to degree; and we must observe and remember that it is in our power, within certain narrow limits, to rectify this degree of difference.' 'The lowest and most personal propensities have, in regard to social relations, an unquestionable preponderance over the nobler,' 'our social affections are inferior in strength and steadiness to the personal,' 'this condition is necessary,' in order to stimulate exertion, and 'it is only its degree we have to deplore.' 'All notions of public good must be based on those of private advantage, because the former can be nothing else than that which is common to all cases of the latter,' 130. By Comte our moral nature seems to have been regarded as consisting of our affective faculties — our social and personal propensities — though this is not expressly affirmed. 'Our moral nature would be destroyed and not improved, if it were possible to repress our personal instincts,' 131. 'The statical analysis of our social organism' shows that the development of the race rests on 'a certain system of fundamental opinions,' or common beliefs, 156; and what Positive Philosophy aims at is, to ascertain 'how those habits and views are to be rationalized, so as solidly to establish the universal obligations of civilized man,' and thus to generate 'universal moral convictions,' 475. 'When the morality of an advanced society bids us love our neighbours as ourselves, it embodies, in the best way, the deepest truth, with only such exaggeration as is required in the formation of a type, which is always fallen short of in practice,' 131. 'The sympathetic instinct, and the intellectual activity,'— 'those two chief moderators of human life,' 132 — 'are especially destined to compensate mutually for common social insufficiency,' 131; and 'the first function of universal morals, in regard to the individual, consists in increasing this double influence,' 132. 'So much for the first Statical division — the Individual.'

From this fundamental part of the theory concerning human nature, I pass to the Dynamical, or theory of human progress. ' If we regard the course of human development from the highest scientific point of view, we shall perceive that it consists in educing more and more the characteristic faculties of humanity, in comparison with those of animality.' 'While the radical dispositions of our nature are necessarily invariable, the highest of them are in a continuous state of relative development,' 149. The order of evolution is thus determined: — 'Though the elements of our social evolution are connected, and always acting on each other, one must be preponderant, in order to give an impulse to the rest, though they may in their turn so act upon it as to cause its further expansion.' 'We must find out this superior element, and . . . we cannot err in taking that which can be best conceived of apart from the rest, while the consideration of it would enter into the study of others. This double characteristic points out the *intellectual* evolution as the preponderating,' 156. One consequence is that 'we must choose for consideration in this intellectual history, the most general and abstract conceptions, which require the exercise of our highest faculties. Thus, it is the study of the fundamental system of human opinions with regard to the whole of phenomena . . . which must regulate our historical analysis.' 'The scientific principle of the theory' (of human progression) 'appears to me to consist in the great philosophical law of the succession of the three states: — the primitive theological state, the transient metaphysical, and the final positive state,— through which the human mind has to pass in every kind of speculation,' 157. The Theological period or state is explained thus,— 'The necessity of the intellectual evolution, I assert, lies in the primary tendency of man to transfer the sense of his own nature into the radical explanation of all phenomena whatever.' 'The only way in which he can explain any phenomena is by likening them, as much as possible, to his own acts,' 159. This theological period is necessarily the first stage, 'for the facts which must form the basis of a positive theory could not be collected to any purpose without some preliminary theory which should guide their collection. Our understanding cannot act without some doctrine, false or true, vague or precise, which may concentrate and stimulate its efforts, and . . . those who expect that the theory will be suggested by the facts, do not understand what is the course necessarily pursued by the human mind, which has achieved all real results by the only effectual method,— of anticipating scientific observations by some conception (hypothetical in the first instance) of the corresponding phenomena,' 161. 'The only alternative from total inactivity was, in those days, in the pursuit of the *inaccessible subjects* which are represented by the theological philosophy.'

'The metaphysical philosophy takes possession of the speculative field after the theological has relinquished it, and before the positive is ready for it.' 'The method of modification consists in substituting gradually the entity for a deity when religious conceptions become so generalized as to diminish perpetually the number of supernatural agents,' 171. 'The increasing subtlety of metaphysical speculation is for ever reducing their characteristic entities to mere abstract denominations of the corresponding phenomena, so as to render their own impotence ridiculous when they attempt explanations,' 172.

The metaphysical period is only a transitional stage to the Positive, for 'men are unable to emancipate themselves' from the theological system, 'except by abandoning altogether these inaccessible researches and restricting themselves to the study of the laws of phenomena, apart from their causes,' 160. 'Under this system of general education, morality will be immoveably based upon positive philosophy as a whole, and Human nature being one of the branches of positive knowledge, it will be understood how childhood is to be trained in good habits, by means of the best possessions, and how those habits and views are afterwards to be rationalized, so as solidly to establish the universal obligations of civilized man,— duties personal, domestic, and social, with the modifications that will be required by changes in civilisation,' 474. The positive spirit is the only one which can 'generate universal moral convictions,' and develop 'the social sentiment as a part of morals.' The metaphysical system 'bases morality on self-interest,' but 'positive morality, which teaches the habitual practice of goodness, without any other certain recompense than internal satisfaction, must be much more favourable to the growth of the benevolent affections than any doctrine which attaches devotedness itself to personal considerations,' 473. *V.* Huxley's *Lay Sermons,* viii. p. 162.

I proceed to consider briefly the value of this system, regarded as an Ethical Theory. Its first distinctive feature is, that it is a Sociology, or theory of society regarded as a unity, not a theory of personal conduct according to which each individual is a separate factor. A man is not regarded as a representative of the race, in whose nature the characteristics of the race may be fairly studied, but merely as an atom in a great totality apart from which the individual is deserving of no scientific consideration. It is said,— 'As every system must be composed of elements of the same nature with itself, the scientific spirit forbids us to regard society as composed of individuals. The true social unit is certainly the family,' II. 132. This is obviously correct as to society, in contrast with mere association of individuals, but in making this essential also to the theory, it is shown to be a Sociology, not a Moral Philosophy. That social phenomena are governed by laws as rigorous as those of the physical universe is admitted. But, as a matter of fact, actions originate with individuals, and therefore, as a matter of scientific demand, there must be a law of personal action determining right conduct for an individual, in absence of which Positivism has no claim to be regarded as a Moral Philosophy.

The next distinctive feature of Positivism is its rejection of Psychology, on the radical ground of a denial of the possibility of introspective observation. Mr. Mill has with great effect pointed out the incompleteness of Positivism as a philosophic system, on account of the exclusion of Psychology from the circle of the sciences.— *Auguste Comte and Positivism,* by J. S. Mill, 62 — 67. I am specially concerned with the bearing of this omission on an ethical theory. Comte has a biological theory of human nature, in contrast with a psychological,— a theory of life instead of a theory of mind. That any theory of human life must include mind, is admitted. But, can a theory of life include mind without introspective observation? Comte meets this with the statement that introspection is impossible. But, let the reader look back on the summary of Comte's Statical theory given above, and he will find a whole series of statements, most admirable in their nature, as to passions, higher affections, and intellectual faculties. All these are based on introspective observation,— they are parts of a psychology,— but they are nothing more than parts, because thoroughness of investigation in this department Comte did not attempt. The consequence is that, while there is a true morality running all through Comte's discussion, there is no moral philosophy. He has not even come in sight of the difficulties to be encountered in attempting to construct a doctrine of moral obligation. But the morality which he proclaims is clearly reached by a use of the psychological method, in contradiction of his own assertion of the impossibility of its use. The defenders of Comte have taken up defensible ground in alleging that the founder of the system did observe mental processes by the same method as that which Mr. Mill supports. But the correctness of the defence is admitted only at the cost of surrendering the absurd allegation that Psychology is impossible. Dr. Bridges pleads quite reasonably, and with strict accuracy, that 'if by Psychology be meant the study, by every means that are available, of the moral and intellectual functions of man, it is very certain that Comte was a psychologist, though he naturally avoided a word which connected him with a contemporary school of metaphysicians . . . . The study of the intellectual and moral functions was prosecuted by Comte throughout his life, and that on methods, not, I imagine, materially different from those which you would adopt.'— *The Unity of Comte s Life and Doctrine; a Reply to Strictures on Comte's later Writings, addressed to J. S. Mill, Esq., M. P.,* by J. H. Bridges, M. D., London; 1866. Mr. G. H. Lewes accepts this defence, quoting with approval the passage from which the above extracts are taken.— *Hist. of Philosophy,* II. 627. Undoubtedly Comte used introspection, while he declared it impossible; and thus he was a psychologist, in a hesitating imperfect way. That he *'naturally* avoided a word which connected him with a contemporary school of metaphysicians' may be admitted, when we remember how he charged metaphysicians with imbecility and idiocy,— how he condemned the metaphysical stage of evolution,— and proclaimed fiat Positivism is not only superior but perfect. Comte was a Psychologist,— a Metaphysician. How could he help if? In restricting philosophy to what we can *know,* was he not bound to inquire into our powers of knowledge, as well as into the facts known? If he were to treat of moral problems, how could he do otherwise than enquire into our mental constitution, so as to distinguish between passions and intellect? Mr. Lewes, speaking of Religion, has well said, that 'to regulate the Feelings, it must furnish an explanation of man, such as enables us to understand, and by understanding adapt ourselves to the Internal Order, which constitutes the moral life.'— *Hist. of Philos.* II. 639. And so, to give any theory of the Internal Order which constitutes moral life, Philosophy must be introspective and analytic.

The last distinctive feature of Positivism in this connexion is the Dynamical theory, based on the law of the three stages of social evolution. In this part, the system is not properly a Sociology, but a theory of the intellectual conditions under which men have attempted explanations of the phenomena of the external world. That these explanations have exercised a mighty influence on the intellectual development, and on the social, moral, and religious condition of the race, Comte has shown with great ability, and with a success which will command general admiration. But this is not Sociology, and, though often concerned with morals, it does not contribute anything towards the formation of a Moral Philosophy. He has given a history of speculations, not a philosophy of human nature, nor a theory of moral life. An ethical theory cannot take the form of speculation as to the most probable explanation of the occurrences in the physical world. Even if the law of the three stages were accepted as affording a key to intellectual progress, it cannot provide a theory of right practice. Even as a theory of intellectual development, it does not explain much. It merely says that the human race began its efforts with incipient philosophy, that it gradually attained a developed philosophy, and that it is now recommended to abandon philosophy, and content itself with the classification of facts. The two first declarations will be admitted; the closing advice is not likely to be taken. Was it the folly and not the glory of the first stirrings of thought, that they prompted men to attempt to scale the inaccessible? Is it the glory, and not the folly of philosophy to teach man to aim low? Are men to escape their troubles, and perform life's duties only by 'restricting themselves to the study of the laws of phenomena, apart from their causes'? If the 'habits and views' of men are to be 'rationalized, so as solidly to establish the universal obligations,'— and this is what all moralists admit must be done, if a science of morals is to be constructed,— Comte has not given us any help in explaining the rationalizing process. It may be true, as he suggests, that there is 'something astonishing in man's expectation of understanding matters which are inaccessible to reason.' But if man has a natural craving for knowledge of causes, it is needless to denounce that craving; while it is plain that what is accessible to reason can be determined only by examining reason itself.

Professing to be a philosophy of the universe, Positivism has not provided a philosophy of human nature. It may be true that men from early times have concerned themselves with explanations of the phenomena of the outer world; but the first necessity was to guide their own life. If they were intellectually interested in physical events, they were practically concerned in human actions. If they gave some thought to the rising and setting of the sun, the flowing of the waters, and the growth of trees,— they must have given more thought to the direction of their own energies. How did they recognise a rule of personal conduct? Positivism gives no answer. And while constructing a Sociology, with professed denial of the possibility of knowing causes, it fails to account for that most conspicuous fact in the procedure of Society, that it has always regarded men as the causes of their own actions, and has punished them for their evil deeds.

Returning again to Germany for a rapid glance at what has been done more recently, I refer first to Johann Fried. Herbart (1776 — 1841). He may be regarded as a philosopher who, about the time of the elder Fichte, Schelling, and Hegel, was lilting his voice in favour of Psychology, though he was still an adherent of the transcendental philosophy. His Ethical system was first published in 1808, under the title of *Allgemeine Practische Philosophic,* which, with his other ethical writings, is to be found in vol. viii. of the Collected Works.

He begins by asking 'what is the Good? Who is the Good? the Better? the Worse?' (vol. viii. p. 4) and insists that the approval and condemnation implied in these words, both in ordinary conversation and in the exercise of Conscience, makes it necessary to raise these questions,— 'Is such a judgment admissible'? And, if this may be affirmed, Which judgments are correct?' The verification or rectification of such a judgment, 'may be expected from practical philosophy as its sole vocation,— if it has a vocation, and if it is anything,' p. 4. He treats of morals under the three conceptions,— the Good, Virtue, and Duty, showing that all three are concerned with the Will,— 'Good stands as the boundary for man's Will; Virtue is the strength of his Will; and Duty is the rule of his Will,' p. 10. In view of the judgments pronounced as to the condition of the Will, he holds two main positions,— '(1.) The judgment pronounced upon a volition never marks it out as a single volition, but always as the member of a relation; (2.) The judgment has originally no logical quantity, but the sphere of its authority comes to it from the universality of the conceptions through which the members of the relation were thought,' p. II. He assigns the knowledge of moral distinctions to Taste, saying that it should be obtained from a universal Æsthetic. His system is seriously hampered by the need for explaining and vindicating this Æsthetical doctrine, which places Ethics along with Poetry, Sculpture, and Music, p. 12. At this stage, the theory has some analogy with that of Jonathan Edwards, who begins his theory by saying that Virtue is a species of beauty. This, however, is only an incidental resemblance. After defending the position that the recognition of moral quality is by a moral sense or taste, Herbart proceeds to enquire, 'How far a practical philosophy can attain to universality.' As morality is a matter of proportion or harmony, he says it is founded on the 'harmony between conceptions and real things,' p. 29. 'Universal conceptions, being abstracted from reality, lose a great deal of its determinateness.' On this account, they do not afford a measure of degree of moral excellence. That is found only when we contemplate the real, and compare it with the universal conception. 'Harmonious or inharmonious proportions' between volitions and conceptions, afford the ultimate test of moral actions, p. 30. On this basis, he builds up a theory of ideas, of which the following are the fundamental,— (1.) The idea of internal freedom, (2.) the idea of perfection; (3.) the idea of good volition; (4.) the idea of right.

Heinrich M. Chalybaus (1792 — 1862) published at Leipzig, in 1850, his *System der Speculativen Ethik,* in 2 vols.— a work of very great ability. The system is divided into three parts,— 1. The primary principle or fundamental doctrine of Ethic; II. Phenomenology of morals; III. System of Ethic — that is, applied Ethics. A brief statement will indicate the author's fundamental position. He begins by considering Ethic in its relation to knowledge in general. 'Science is in so far a formal conception, as there is included under it the manifold and particular contents of the whole empirical knowledges; but in a more restricted sense, Science is pure, highest, philosophical (ἐπιστήμη). As among the sciences, Ethic does not take the place of the most fundamental, pure, and original, but belongs to the mixed or applied sciences, so must we give to it that which is fundamental and pure . . . . It raises, therefore, in the foreground the demand (1.) to indicate this relation of Ethic to pure philosophy, (2.) particularly to show the basis of the Ethical principle in the absolute Idea, and its development from the same; and lastly (3.) to determine the special principle of Ethic itself as, to content and application,' p. 3. 'It behoves us to make a path' to 'Pure or Fundamental Philosophy.' 'If such a general ground-science were not yet attained, the moralist himself must strive to unfold it, that thereby he may be able to give his principle the necessary foundation,' p. 4. From these opening statements the author's standpoint is clearly seen,— his conclusion being that the Reason discovers necessary moral law, and that morality consists in the harmony of volition with reason.

Immanuel Hermann Fichte, son of Johann Gottlieb Fichte, born 1797, published his *System der Ethik,* in 3 vols., Leipzig, 1850 — 51 — 53,— a work of great merit. The volume in which his own system is developed is vol. ii. part i., Leipzig, 1851, sold separately. He says that 'Ethic is for us the science of the nature of the human Will.' It may also be treated as 'a system of practical ideas,' for the very conception of Will involves possession of such ideas, p. i. 'Ethical ideas are the ideal notions of perfection of Will.' 'The idea of the Good' is the proper object of Moral Philosophy. The science shows how 'the abstract idea becomes a distinct and manifoldly articulate conception in the system of Ethical ideas; and how thence there arises for Moral Philosophy the threefold point of view of a Science of Virtue, of Duty, and of Good,' p. 28. The conception of the Will, 'resting on the depth and background of human consciousness,' recognises the will of the individual as 'a law for itself,— as command or prohibition,' p. I. 'The source and internal basis of the Shall and Shall-Not is the simple internal nature of man, and specially of that which is fundamental to his Will,' p. 29.

One of the most notable of quite recent books is that of Bishop Martensen, published at Copenhagen, the German translation at Gotha, 1871, entitled *Die Christliche Ethik.* 'Only in the domain of freedom is morality possible,' p. 3. 'The Moral itself is an idea, which has not its source in conduct and experience, but rather itself exists as the unconditioned law of such experience,' p. 4. 'All research . . . points to the idea of an absolute aim and last end for the human will and voluntary action. This all-embracing end for the will of man is THE GOOD.

The Good is what secures its end or object.' 'The Idea becomes also the Ideal when it presents itself as the pattern which, in the exercise of freedom, shall be reduced to a specific form,' p. 5. Moral Philosophy may be treated from three different standpoints,— The OUGHT, Duty, a demand on man's will; VIRTUE, the ability to do good, the law admitted into the will; and the GOOD, the realization of the sum-total of all good, p. 9. 'The Ideal of self-government is essentially the good, or the idea of Ethics. And if we inquire as to the content of this ideal, it can only be described as man himself,— human personality, conceived in its purity and perfection.' 'The universal human,'— *Allgemeine Menschliche,*— thus becomes with Martensen the test of all natural Ethics.

Recent British and American developments may be more briefly traced, as the books themselves are more readily accessible. See Professor Masson's vigorous and vivid sketch — *Recent British Philos.,* 2d ed., London, 1867. Dr. Thomas Brown's theory I have already given, p. 25. The most important works in support of the Utilitarian basis of Morals will be found in the following Division, where the theory is examined. Dr. CHALMERS in his *Sketches of Mental and Moral Philosophy* did not enter upon a systematic development of the Science. The most valuable portions of the book are, chap. i.— On the distinction between mental and moral philosophy; and chap. vi.— On the undue place which is often given to the Emotions, and the delusive estimate of human virtue to which it leads.

Dr. William Whewell published the *Elements of Morality* in 1845, 2 vols.; and *Lectures on Systematic Morality* in 1846. In the earlier and larger work, after treating of Reason and the Springs of Action, he proceeds to maintain that 'moral rules exist necessarily,' I. 32. The gratification of natural desires 'must be a part of the order of Society. There must be Rules which direct the course and limits of such gratification. Such Rules are necessary for the peace of Society.' 'Reason directs us to Rules,' I. 33. 'As there is a universal human reason, common to all men, ... so there is a universal moral sympathy, common to all men, so far as it is unfolded; a conscience of mankind to which each man's conscience must conform,' 35. 'Moral rules must be necessary truths, flowing from the moral nature of man,' 50. 'An internal moral standard is one part of Conscience, and Self-knowledge or Consciousness is another part,' 235. But 'each man's conscience may err, and lead him to a false moral standard,' 238. 'Conscience is the Reason employed about questions of right and wrong, and accompanied with the sentiments of approbation. and condemnation, which, by the nature of man, cling inextricably to his apprehension of right and wrong.'— *Systemat. Mor.* p. 144.

Dr. M'Cosh, formerly of Queen's College, Belfast, now President of Princeton College, United States of America, published in 1850 his work on *The Method of the Divine Government, Physical and Moral,* which is now in its eighth edition. Book III. contains an able treatment of the main ethical questions. President M'Cosh strenuously supports the inductive method as ruling in Moral Philosophy; begins by considering the nature of the Will, maintaining its freedom; and distinguishes the following questions concerning morals,— the mental process by which the distinction between virtue and vice is observed; the common quality or qualities in all virtuous actions,— the rule by which to determine whether an action is virtuous; and the consequences which follow from virtue and vice. He supports the doctrine of first principles in morals, which are distinguished by 'self-evidence, necessity, universality.' He says Conscience may be viewed in three aspects: (1.) 'as proceeding upon and revealing a law with authoritative obligations;' (2.) 'as pronouncing an authoritative judgment upon actions presented to it;' (3.) 'as possessing a class of emotions, or as a sentiment.' Dr. M'Cosh has also a criticism of Utilitarianism in his *Exam. of Mr. Mill's Philos.,* chap. xx.

In America, Dr. Francis Wayland published as a textbook his *Elements of Moral Science.* Its ninth edition, from which I quote, was published in Boston in 1839. 'As soon as a human being comprehends the relation in which two human beings stand to each other, there arises in his mind a consciousness of moral obligation,' p. 44. This is a 'peculiar and instinctive impulse; arising at once by the principles of our constitution, as soon as the relations are perceived in which we stand to the beings, created and uncreated, with whom we are connected,' 46. Further than this he does not press the inquiry. According to him, Conscience is imperfect. 'There are many obligations under which man is created, both to his fellow-creatures and to God, which his unassisted conscience does not discover,' p. 113.

Francis Bowen, in his Lowell Lectures on *The Application of Metaphysical and Ethical Science to the Evidences of Religion,* Boston, 1849, has a Lecture on Conscience, in which he maintains 'the absolute certainty of its decisions,' p. 274, and declares that 'the sense of *obligation,* the recognition of an act as something which *ought* to be done, or to be left undone, is the capital fact in our moral being: it is the foundation and superstructure of our moral nature,' p. 277.

Dr. Laurens P. Hickok, well known for his ability as a mental philosopher, has a treatise entitled *System of Moral Science,* published in London, 1853. 'We do not apprehend pure truth, except we have some ground in which the truth is, inasmuch as truth always particularizes, and can give no criterion of itself in general. This is the same in moral truth, as in mathematical and philosophical. Hence the necessity of finding some ground on which the truth of the ultimate Rule of the right shall be made immediately manifest. This can be done only by a clear apprehension of the Highest Good, since that must be the ground on which the ultimate rule shall reveal itself,' p. 41. 'No sensible appearance nor mental conception can be scarcely ever given to the mind as a mere dry intellect.' All our feelings will range under two distinct classes: (1.) 'Feelings which cannot rest in mere contemplation' (Desires); (2.) 'Feelings which rest in the object itself . . . for its own sake' (Sentiments), 42, 3. Those of the second class 'are called forth only in the presence of some pure ideal excellency, which the mind holds up to its own view, or some copy which it may compare with the pure ideal,' 43. There are thus two kinds of Good, the one *utility,* the other *dignity.* Spiritual life is the dignity given to humanity. This is proved, (1.) by Taste, through which the pure forms of art are put upon every object which ministers to the gratification of the appetite;' (2.) by Science, since 'Philosophy is cherished for its own sake, and the universal truths are attained by which both man and nature are interpreted;' (3.) by 'the Imperative of the spirit's own excellence.' There is to each spirit, 'an inner world of conscious prerogative . . . from which comes forth perpetually the imperative that every action be restrained by that which is due to its own dignity,' 47. 'The Highest Good,— the Summum

Bonum,— is worthiness of spiritual approbation.' 'That this is ultimate, *intuitively* appears in many ways,' p. 49.— See also Hickok's *Empirical Psychology,* New York, 1859, Divisions second and third.

Another work deserving attention is that of Dr. Joseph Haven, *Mental Philosophy,* Boston, 1857. 'Among the conceptions which constitute the furniture of the mind, there is one which, in many respects, is unlike all others, . . . that is, the notion or idea of *right,'* p. 303. 'The ideas in question (the right and wrong) are *intuitive;* suggestions or perceptions of *reason.'* 'Regarded subjectively, as conceptions of the human mind, right and wrong . . . are simple ideas, incapable of analysis or definition; *intuitions of reason.* Regarded as objective, right and wrong are realities, qualities absolute and inherent in the nature of things, . . . not relative merely to the human mind, but independent, essential, universal, absolute . . . . Judgment decides that such and such actions do possess the one or the other of these qualities, . . . there follows the sense of obligation, . . . and the consciousness of merit and demerit, . . . and certain emotions which we are constituted to feel,' 312 — 13. But 'Conscience is not always a safe guide,' 324.

Of quite recent books, the following are worthy of attention: — grote's *Utilitarianism,*— a posthumous publication, and at times more diffuse than it might have been under the author's revision; but a candid, careful, and very powerful criticism. With this, take the able critique in Lecky's *Hist. of Europ. Morals,* chap. i. *The Theory of Practice,* 2 vols., Lond. 1870, by Dr. Shadworth Hodgson, an exceedingly able and elaborate work, in which the author seeks to reach moral law by a path in harmony with a theory of evolution, though distinct from that taken by the Utilitarian school. Professor Blackie has given us a valuable addition to Ethical literature in his *Four Phases of Morals,* full of important exposition and criticism. *The Conscience,* by the late Prof. F. D. MAURICE, a book more of popular than of scientific structure. It opens with an admirable chapter on the Ego or I, and then proceeds to treat of Conscience, saying that 'Conscience is that in me which says I ought or I ought not.' This word 'ought' is inseparable from Self. *Ethics of Theism,* by Dr. LEITCH, the second part of which contains a discussion of the leading ethical questions; and in dealing with the criterion of morals shows that neither the will of God, nor utility, nor sentiment can afford the criterion. *The Philosophy of Ethics,* by Mr. SIMON S. LAURIE, taken with *Notes, Expository and Critical, on certain British Theories of Morals,* by the same author, in which the leading points of each theory are brought out with marked felicity. The student is further referred to the exceedingly valuable article in the Encyclopaedia Britannica on *Moral Philosophy,* by the Rev. Dr. LINDSAY ALEXANDER, Edinburgh; Mackintosh's Dissertation; and Whewell's Lectures on the Hist. of Mor. Philosophy.

CHAPTER IV
CONSCIENCE
(INTUITIONAL THEORY)

1. Conscience (conscientia, συνειδησιζ, Gewissen) is that power of mind by which moral law is discovered to each individual for the guidance of his conduct. It is the Reason as that discovers to us absolute moral truth — having the authority of sovereign moral law. It is an essential requisite for the direction of an intelligent free-will agent, and affords the basis for moral obligation and responsibility in human life.

2. Conscience, in discovering to us truth, having the authority of moral law, is seen to be a cognitive or intellectual power. Either it does not discover truth; or, if it does, it is not a form of feeling, or combination of feelings, or affections, or emotions, or desires. Feeling may exist as fact, and thus have reality; but it is not in itself of the nature of regulative truth, and it cannot by its action produce such truth. Truth is that which we can see, and implies seeing power. Moral law is that which we can know, and implies knowing power. Hume, while allowing the action of intellect, assigns to feeling 'the final award.'— *Essays,* App. 1. Mackintosh makes conscience a combination of our moral sentiments or feelings, 'which have no other object but the mental dispositions leading to voluntary action.'— *Dissert. Encyc. Brit.,* Whewell's edit, pp. 152, 215, 323.

The popular name for the Moral Faculty applies to a cognitive power: Con-science (con-scientia, συν-ειδησιζ). *Conscience* and *Consciousness* are similarly compounded, and are in fact originally the same word — conscientia.

Consciousness is now employed as the more general term to include the knowledge of every mental state. By analogy, conscience is immediate knowledge of moral law, as clear and indubitable as a simple fact of consciousness. Conscience is, however, popularly applied to the whole moral nature of man. Thus Remorse is popularly an exercise of Conscience, while moral law is discovered by the same faculty. This free use of the name makes it often synonymous with consciousness, or the knowledge of the harmony of personal conduct with moral law. The prefix, *con, with,* has very frequently been held to mean knowledge of moral law along with the Moral Governor.— So Thomas Aquinas, *Summa Theo. 2.* 79, 13; Martensen, *Die Christliche Ethik,* sec. 117, p. 498, in course of translation for dark, Edinburgh; Trench's *Study of Words.*

3. Conscience, in discovering to us moral law for the guidance of our actions, has authority over all other springs of activity within us. We may with clear philosophic warrant attribute to the power discovering to us all moral law the authority which belongs to each of the laws thereby made known. 'The authority of Conscience' is an abbreviated form for expressing the authority which is common to all the laws of morality. In affirming that Conscience has authority over the other powers of mind, we merely indicate that moral law, being concerned with the guidance of our actions, is authoritative for the regulation of all the other motive forces, and restraining forces, which operate within human nature.

Every spring of activity within us operates according to a law of its own nature. Thus every affection and desire comes into play under a definite law determining its exercise. But neither affections nor desires are competent for their own guidance. All these forces of our nature are dependent upon intelligence for direction, while, for performance of its special function. Intelligence is dependent on its possession of Moral Law. All other powers are thus subordinated to moral law. The power which discovers such law is necessarily excluded from this subordination. And it thus appears that the recognition of moral law is not a moral action, but a condition essential for the performance of moral action. On the ground thus stated, we must regard as insufficient the theory that Conscience is either the acquiescence or the antagonism of the whole nature on occasion of the play of some appetite or desire. This theory, hinted at by Plato, when he described Injustice as 'a rising up of a part of the soul against the whole soul' (*Repub.* iv.), has been advocated by Trendelenburg in a passage of great eloquence and power.— *Naturrecht*, sec. 39, p. 56. The leading parts of the paragraph are translated by Professor Lorimer, *Institutes of Law*, p. 152. The fact of such antagonism or acquiescence of our nature in the exercise of our propensities, is admitted. That the resentment or consent is with varying degree in different persons, and in the same person at different times, is also granted. The ground is solid, but not sufficient. In two respects the insufficiency appears. 'The whole man' does not always resent the action of the 'self-seeking part;'— den selbsüchtigen Theil,— and what then? But, more especially, we want an explanation of antagonism or acquiescence. And if we may progress in our feeling of resentment or approval, we need knowledge in order to determine the line in which progress shall be esteemed true moral culture.

4. Conscience in discovering truth absolutely authoritative as moral law is vested with sovereign practical authority in mind. This appears from its nature, and is confirmed by comparison of the functions of the moral faculty, with those of all other powers and capacities in mind.

That which discovers moral law has the teaching authority which belongs to the law itself. This law, as absolute truth, admits of no contradiction. Every other power of mind inferior in teaching function is subordinate to this. Other truths, recognised as in their nature absolute, such as the first principles of understanding, called laws of thought, have their complete application in another sphere, and do not in nature or authority come into competition with the laws of morality. 'The supremacy of conscience' is an abbreviated expression for the sovereignty of moral laws over the forms of activity to which their authority applies. In its reference to motives, acts, and ends, moral law has unquestionable and unchangeable authority.

The high honour of establishing the supremacy of conscience belongs to Butler.— *Sermons* I. II. III. and *Dissert. on the Nature of Virtue.* Conscience is the 'moral approving and disapproving faculty,'— 'a principle of reflection or conscience.' That principle by which we survey, and either approve or disapprove our own heart, temper, and actions, is not only to be considered as what is in its turn to have some influence; which may be said of every passion, of the lowest appetites; but likewise as being superior; as from its very nature claiming superiority over all others; in so much that you cannot form a notion of this faculty, Conscience, without taking in judgment, direction, superintendency.'— *Ser.* II. Butler has not gone with much care into the question as to the nature of conscience, but he has placed the fact of 'superintendency' or supremacy on such a basis that it has been admitted with wonderful unanimity by upholders of most conflicting theories as to the nature of conscience.

5. The authority of conscience is not found in any predominating force belonging to it as a faculty, but altogether in the character of the truth which it discovers. The authority is not found in the nature of the faculty itself. The faculty is a power of sight, such as makes a perception of self-evident truth possible to man, and contributes nothing to the truth which is perceived. To the truth itself belongs inherent authority, by which is meant, absolute right of command, not force to constrain. Professor Bain mistakes in saying that a purely mental origin 'is held to confer a higher authority' on certain ideas, if he intends this as a representation of Intuitionalism.— *Mental and Moral Science,* II. 6, sec. 2.

6. Conscience is a faculty which, from its very nature, cannot be educated. Education, either in the sense of instruction or of training, is impossible. As well propose to teach the eye, how and what to see: and the ear, how and what to hear: as to teach Reason how to perceive the self-evident, and what truths are of this nature. All these have been provided for in the human constitution.

The opposite view has been commonly advocated, even by intuitionalists. For example, Reid's *Active Powers,* III. iii. 8, H. p. 595. Stewart is more guarded, *Outlines of Mor. Phil.,* sec. 174. Whewell puts it as broadly as possible,— 'We must labour to *enlighten* and *instruct* our Conscience,' and by consequence 'He who acts against his conscience is always wrong,' 'but to say that he who acts according to his conscience is always right' 'would lead to great inconsistencies in our Morality.'— *Elements of Morality,* I. p. 236, sec. 364 — 366. Very differently Kant,— 'An erring conscience is a chimera.'— *Metaph. of Ethics,* 3d ed., p. 217. So Rothe, *Theol. Ethik,* ii. 29. Whewell confounds opinion with conscience, as will appear from the following: — 'Whatever subordinate law we have in our minds is to be looked on only as a step to the Supreme Law,— the Law of complete Benevolence, Justice, Truth, Purity, and Order.'— *Ib.* sec. 366.

Moral training is something different from education of Conscience. Two things need here to be distinguished: *(a.)* Personal experience in the application of conscience. Since all knowledge begins in experience, though it does not all arise from experience *(v.* Introduction to Kant's *Critique of Pure Reason),* the application of moral law becomes known in personal experience, according as the forms of activity admit of it. But application of law presupposes the knowledge of it, and knowledge of moral law is not gathered from experience.— (Div. I. c. iii. sec. 3.) *(b.)* Personal attainment in the practical subordination of other powers to the authority of conscience. This is of the very essence of moral training, which is dependent upon the sovereign authority of Conscience.

7. Conscience, in subjecting our other powers to its authority, reveals the moral harmony of our natural powers, and provides what is essential for moral training of our whole being. All subject powers are powers naturally under regulation for their exercise, and all regulated powers are capable of training. In this way our dispositions, affections, and desires are placed under guidance, in accordance with the demands of moral law.

Dispositions, affections, and desires which are out of harmony with Conscience are out of harmony with our nature,— that is, are unnatural, and can have no place in healthy moral development.

8. Conscience, in revealing a law which absolutely condemns certain dispositions, desires, and passions known in human experience, authoritatively requires the suppression of moral evil within us, and thereby contributes still further to the necessities of moral training.

There are springs of action of which we are conscious, which moral law entirely condemns. Of these, pride, selfishness, jealousy, and envy may be taken as examples. What in teaching it condemns, conscience requires shall in practice be suppressed, since moral truth is by its nature moral law. Conscience thus contributes not only constructively, but destructively to the necessities of moral training.

9. Conscience, in discovering to us first principles for the guidance of conduct and formation of moral character, constitutes a leading distinction of human nature. The basis of personal life is thereby laid in self-evident, absolute truth. The application of that truth is left to us in the guidance of personal procedure; and this is an exercise unspeakably higher than guidance by detailed rules. The possibilities of such a life involve the possibility of likeness to the Deity Himself.

10. The name of Conscience has always been, and will always continue to be, popularly used in a much wider sense than that in which the designation can be employed under strict philosophic warrant. It is thus commonly made to embrace all that is connected with our moral decisions, within the sphere of personal consciousness. Thus our moral judgments are attributed directly to conscience itself, and that even when they are discredited as erroneous. So in like manner all experience of moral sentiment is referred directly to Conscience.

11. With this wide popular use of the term Conscience, a variety of phrases descriptive of the condition of the faculty has found currency in popular discourse. Of these, the following may be taken as examples: — An unenlightened Conscience, a scrupulous Conscience, a tender Conscience, a hardened Conscience, an upbraiding Conscience.

The philosophic interpretation of such phrases may be secured by discriminating between these three things — the Conscience properly so called, the moral judgments, and the moral sentiments, all of which are popularly referred to one power. In some of the phrases a mixed reference may be found; but they commonly apply either to the moral judgments or to the action of the moral sentiments.

12. The diversity of moral judgments among men is the main difficulty in vindicating an intuitional theory of Conscience, and is the great leading objection of its opponents.

In treating of this difficulty, the following points need attention: —

First, The extent to which diversity prevails. All nations admit a distinction between right and wrong in human conduct. There is very general agreement as to the forms of rectitude, such as truthfulness, justice, benevolence. There is no nation which is known so to transpose moral distinctions as to place these forms of moral excellence in the list of qualities morally wrong. Diversity of opinion on moral subjects is much more concerned with the determination of what is wrong, than with deciding what is right. Men excuse deceit, who do not condemn integrity; they. approve advantage taken of another, but they do not condemn honesty; they applaud cruel vengeance, but they still admire benevolence. There is thus a want of consistency in the case of many of the judgments pronounced. Compare the law of theft in ancient Sparta; in Caffre-land, famous for cattle-lifting; and in the nations of modern civilization.

Secondly, The philosophical explanation of diversity among the moral judgments of men. Men differ not as to the principles, but as to their application in given circumstances. Epictetus explains it thus,— 'The same general principles are common to all men . . . . Where, then, arises the dispute? In adapting these principles to particular cases,' I. 23. Contradictory moral judgments imply error somewhere; that error is capable of being detected and exposed; its detection and exposure imply possession of a common, unvarying standard of morals. An adequate explanation of diversity of moral judgments is therefore possible. The key to diversities in personal judgments, will afford the key to national diversities. The question is this — If the first principles of morals are self-evident truths, of which a reasoned contradiction cannot be given, how can the rational nature of man accept and act upon a tacit contradiction of them? The answer is twofold, partly Ethical, partly Psychological.

(1.) Ethical Explanations.— *(a.)* There are dispositions belonging to our nature, and impelling to action, which are out of harmony with conscience, and the exercise of which is a practical violation of the authority of conscience. Selfishness and Malice may be taken as the root forms of these. This fact affords, primarily, an explanation of wrong *acting,* but it is at the same time a step towards the explanation of erroneous *thinking.* Hence it happens that the diversity of opinion on Morals is much more concerned with what is wrong, by way of excusing it, than with what is right, by way of condemning it.

(b.) There is often great difficulty in deciding what is present duty, when there is none as to what is morally right.

Hence it happens that there is much more diversity of opinion as to the dutiful in special circumstances, than as to what is right in all circumstances. It is the relation of the agent to circumstances, which originates questions of casuistry, and not the decision as to what courses of conduct are right in themselves. All such diversity of opinion concerns the application of the standard, not the nature of the standard, and is therefore to be laid aside as irrelevant when the discussion is concerned with the standard of moral distinctions. Men may agree that Benevolence is morally right, and yet may altogether differ as to the duty of helping a beggar. Diversity of opinion on this latter point, though it is connected with morals, is not concerned with the standard of morality.

(2.) Psychological Explanation.— The following laws of mind come into view as bearing on the question: —

(a.) Dispositions swaying the conduct have power to bias the judgments. What a man inclines to do, that he is ready to think right. Liability to error being at any rate characteristic of the reasoning power, the risk of contentment with fallacious reasoning is greatly heightened, when cherished dispositions favour the accepted conclusions. In this way, the rational nature is often content to place false generalizations in the room of self-evident truths.

(b.) Prevailing opinions may be accepted without independent investigation. It is not merely in the ethical sphere, but in every department of thought, that illustration may be found of this tendency in the rational nature. In the development of mind, prevailing opinions are first accepted on authority, and then retained without personal investigation. Besides, if the practice sanctioned is in harmony with an evil disposition common to our nature, there is double inducement to adopt it. Authority and Inclination combine their forces. Where social custom establishes a practice, unreasoning acquiescence is easy.

(c.) The moral sentiments cluster around a false judgment, as readily as around a true. There is not, indeed, the same security in both cases for the continuance of these sentiments. But if a man, whether correctly or incorrectly, only approve an action, he will experience self-approbation in doing it. If, whether accurately or not, he only disapprove of an action, he will experience a sense of shame, or even of remorse, in doing it.

Of all the recognised laws of mind, this is the one to which most prominence is to be given, in accounting for the astonishing diversity of opinion, founded upon appeals to conscience. If a South Sea Islander approve of vengeance, he may have a sense of well-doing while he tortures an enemy. If an Indian believes that the Deity requires him to wash in the Ganges, he may have a sense of remorse in neglecting what he regards as duty. Moral sanctions may thus gather around even gross immorality. When this law of union between judgment and sentiment is recognised, it is clear that sentiments afford neither the basis of moral distinctions, nor any certain guidance as to such distinctions. Moral responsibility hangs upon the possession of rational nature.

Man, as a rational being, has intrusted to him the application of the principles of morality *(v.* sec. 9 of this chap.) In deciding questions of morals, he may either seek a clear view of moral law, or he may accept a current rule of conduct without inquiring as to its rational validity. In the former case, he accepts self-evident truth, capable of vindication by every test. In the latter, he proceeds upon a rule the rational insufficiency of which may be proved at every step. If individual and national history give evidence that men often prefer the latter course to the former, there is ample explanation, ethical, intellectual, and sentimental, and that explanation does not affect the reality of self-evident moral principles, or impinge upon their authority as moral laws.

13. Problems.— (1.) Can personal feeling possess the authority of moral law? (2.) Critically examine the following,— 'As each man's Reason may err, and thus lead him to false opinions, so each man's Conscience may err, and lead him to a false moral standard.'— Whewell's *Elements of Morality,* sec. 368, l. 238. Distinguish between what is here pointed to as fact, and what is presented by way of interpretation and explanation of the fact. (3.) If Conscience be represented as 'a power of reflection,' can its supremacy be competently maintained? (4.) Does the philosophical doctrine of an unerring Conscience imply infallibility of judgment in morals on the part of its possessor? 'The universal Conscience and Reason, of which Dr. Whewell speaks as infallible, must reside in some men endued with Conscience and Reason. We ask, who are these infallible men, or

this infallible Council?'— Prof. Bain, *Emotions and Will*, p. 267. (5.) When sovereignty is attributed to conscience, what is the nature and measure of power involved in this sovereignty? (6.) Are the functions usually assigned to conscience compatible with the hypothesis that this faculty finds exercise only in consequence of an action having been done?

CHAPTER V
DUTY OR OBLIGATION
(INTUITIONAL THEORY)

1. Besides the knowledge we have of rightness and wrongness as qualities of actions, we have the knowledge of duty, obligation, or oughtness, as a condition of personal activity. The general conception of obligation is subjection of personality to moral law. The measure of this obligation is therefore found in the full application of the whole law to the whole life.

Duty is *officium*, in contrast with *honestum:* καθῆκον in contrast with καλόν; *Die Pflicht,* in contrast with *Das Recht; devoir,* in contrast with *droit.* The *officium* of Cicero, like the καθῆκον of Zeno, is used in a wider sense than moral obligation, properly so called, applying to rational selection of desirable objects. 'Quod ratione actum sit, id officium appellamus.'— Cicero, *De Fin.* III. 17. According to Diogenes Laertius, Lib. vii., Zeno was the first to use καθῆκον in the strictly Ethical sense. See also Cicero, *De Officiis,* I. 3.

2. Personal obligation is recognised in consciousness by means of a judgment affirming present personal subjection to clearly recognised moral law. Such a judgment invariably affirms a definite measure and direction of obligation as resting upon me at the time.

3. The judgment of oughtness is so distinct from the judgment of Rightness, that the former applies to the agent, the latter to the action.

4. The judgment of oughtness is so related to the judgment of Rightness, that each implies the other, and both draw their warrant from the same moral law. The first principles of rectitude are the basis of all morality: in relation to intelligent beings, these principles wear the aspect of moral laws; each

78

moral being is thus by a necessity of his existence placed in subjection to moral law; subjection to law, or liability to obedience, is in each case commensurate with the application of moral law to the life of the moral being; and rightness is that quality in action which is recognised by its conformity with moral law.

5. The judgment of oughtness is such as to imply complete and uniform subjection to all the laws of morality. I am under constant and complete obligation to moral law, because it is known to me as moral law. Partial or incomplete obligation to moral law is impossible.

A distinction has been drawn in Morals and Jurisprudence between obligations 'perfect and imperfect,' otherwise named 'determinate and indeterminate.' The distinction has more commonly been maintained from the standpoint of Positive Law, by reference to what civil authority can enforce in view of human relations. From this standpoint, the distinction is concerned with the due limits of civil power in the enforcement of personal rights, and not with the real nature of moral obligation. The distinction has also been maintained from the standpoint of Philosophy by Hutcheson and Reid, and conspicuously by Kant and many of his followers.

6. A condensed account of the history of this distinction may be best presented by a classification of three examples of the use of the distinction between perfect and imperfect obligation.

First,— An Ethical use, That some duties are always binding, others only in certain circumstances. The former are perfect duties, the latter imperfect; κατόρθωμα, officium perfectum, and καθήκον μεσν, officium medium.

This is the view given by the Stoics, and accepted by Cicero as their avowed follower. It does not properly indicate two kinds of obligation. It is a classification of *duties*, not a philosophy of the fact of obligation. It points to the obvious truth that moral law not only imposes common obligation upon all, but has speciality of application according to the circumstances of each. The Stoics seem really to have used κατόρθωμα to signify an *action done* in acknowledgment of duty *(recte factum,* rather than *officium perfectum),* rather an action done in a perfect manner, than a perfect obligation requiring its performance.

Cicero has complicated technical phraseology by the use of *rectum* qualifying *officium* as equivalent to *perfectum.*— Diogenes Laertius, B. vii., Life of Zeno; Cicero, *De Officiis* I. 3; Ueberweg's *Hist. of Phihs.* I. 197; Zeiler's *Stoics,* etc., p. 269; Grant's *Aristotle* I. 262; Reid's *Active Powers,* Essay III. iii. 5, Hamilton's ed., p. 588, and two notes, p. 588, and p. 649.

Second,— A Juridical use, That in the dispensation of justice there are only some duties which can be enforced under sanction of positive law, whereas others must be left to individual choice for their performance. The former are perfect obligations, with equivalent perfect rights; the latter are imperfect obligations, with imperfect rights.

This is looking at the distinction from a point of view altogether different. Instead of considering what is common and what special in personal obligation, it is concerned with the question, how much of common obligation can be enforced by civil authority. It grants common obligation resting on Ethical warrant; acknowledges such obligation as the basis of natural law, but admits that social authority is not competent to enforce all obligations. This restriction is so far a thing of nature, as the limitation arises from the fact that there are obligations which belong to the internal sphere which social authority cannot enforce. But it is also in considerable measure a matter of general agreement, according to times and circumstances.

This view of perfect and imperfect obligation has been supported very generally by Jurists, and amongst moralists by Hutcheson, *System of Mor. Phil.* II. iii. 3; and Reid, *Active Powers,* Ess. III. pt. iii. c. 5.

Third,— A Transcendental use, That inasmuch as Moral law discovers only a maxim of conduct, and does not prescribe definite actions, all moral obligation is indeterminate, and only obligations enforced by positive law could be described as examples of determinate obligation.

This shifts the whole ground. It is not maintained that only some of our obligations are determinate, but that none are. It is the product of the transcendental philosophy of Kant which makes the essence of the law consist in its form, and so separates it from positive enactment. It is no doubt true that moral laws are general principles of action, which an intelligent being must apply for himself in the guidance of conduct, but the obligation

80

which encircles the whole life, and has sway over all its activity, is certainly obligation determinate and perfect. The opposite view led Kant to regard the subjective principles only as 'not unfit to be elevated to the rank of law in a system of universal moral legislation.' But this gave them 'only a negative character.' His translator, Mr. Semple, goes a step further, and ventures the assertion that 'Duty is a negative conception only.'— Kant's *Metaphysic of Ethics,* 3d ed., p. 204.

There is a very valuable discussion of this subject in Professor Lorimer's *Institutes of Law,* c. xi., Edin. 1872.

6. The subjection to moral law, which is recognised in a judgment of obligation, may be described as 'moral necessity.' It is *moral* necessity as determining the lines of activity which alone are in harmony with the laws of moral being.

For man, there are three forms of necessity, differing essentially in their nature. These are physical, intellectual, and moral. Physical necessity is concerned with our physical nature, and is not dependent on our will, as that we breathe, eat, and sleep, in order to support bodily life. Intellectual necessity concerns the exercise of our rational powers, determining the conditions on which they may be used for the discovery of truth, as in application of the laws of identity, non-contradiction, and causality. This form of necessity the will cannot alter, but may often disregard without loss of rational power. Moral necessity is that which imposes as a law of life implicit obedience to moral law. The will cannot alter this law, but may transgress it, yet only on penalty of destroying the harmony of the whole nature, and leading a life antagonistic to the moral government of the universe.

7. Common obligation is fixed for all by the necessities of moral law, but the recognition of it by each one for himself is dependent upon personal application of moral law to personal activity in the relations in which he is placed. Personal obligation in present time is determined between moral law and present personal situation.

8. Every judgment as to personal obligation has a threefold reference, viz., to moral law, as affording the rule of action; to personal power, as regulating the possibilities of action; and to present opportunity, as indicating the line of action open at the time. The decision may involve either obligation to act, or

obligation to refrain from acting. Beyond this sphere of judgment, because apart from the application of moral law, there is liberty of action according to personal preferences.

9. From personal obligation, there follows by necessary consequence, moral responsibility, or answerableness to God for the degree in which obligation has been fulfilled. The rational explanation of the universe is found in the existence of the sell-sufficient One (v. *Metaphysic of Ethics):* to Him as sovereign belongs the moral government of the universe: and to Him who imposes duty must answer be made as to its performance.

10. The relations of moral law, life, and action, may be thus represented: Rightness is absolute moral excellence discovered in all moral law; Oughtness is subjection of personal life to the authority of moral law; Goodness is rightness manifested in disposition and conduct under submission to moral law. The first is above all personality; the second is an essential accompaniment of personality; and the third is voluntarily wrought out in personal history.

11. Problems.— (1.) In what sense is obligation common to all moral creatures, and in what sense is it different to each? (2.) Distinguish between the knowledge of the fact of obligation, and the scientific explanation of the knowledge. (3.) From what sources may uncertainty arise as to present duty? (4.) How far is a performance of duty compatible with uncertainty as to which of two lines of action is the preferable? The problem is, to find moral certainty along with some degree of uncertainty as to the manner of its performance.

CHAPTER VI
MORAL RIGHTS
(INTUITIONAL THEORY)

1. As moral obligation signifies an imposed necessity of acting in accordance with moral law, it implies the right of the moral being, without restraint from others, to engage in the forms of activity thus required. This is the natural and inalienable right of personality,— To act according to Conscience. God has in the constitution of our nature provided for it; and our fellow-men can have no warrant to restrict it.

Right here is *jus* in contrast with *honestum* or *rectum*. Hence jurisprudence, the Science of Law, is properly the Science of human Rights, for, as Hutcheson says,— *'Jus* ensues upon *rectum.'* Jurisprudence is therefore based upon Ethics. For the distinction between rightness,— The Right,— as a quality of action, and a right, as a claim or title of a moral agent, *v.* Hutcheson, *Syst. of Mor. Phil.* II. iii. I, vol. i. p. 252; Reid, *Active Powers,* v. iii. H. p. 643; Whewell's *Elements of Mor.* I. iv. vol. i. p. 36.

2. As moral obligation requires from me right actions towards others, it implies rights on their part equivalent to those belonging to myself. Here also the measure of obligation is the measure of rights. The latter cannot be more restricted than the former. The right to fair judgment, the right to generous feeling, and the right to payment of money due, have all exactly the same ethical validity. The fact that the real acknowledgment of the right is more easily tested in the last-named example than in the other two cases, constitutes no difference in respect of the moral warrant for the claim.

3. Common obligations which determine the forms of right action towards others, mark out the common rights of those who are associated in the same sphere of action.

4. Special obligations resting upon some on account of speciality of relation to others, give to these others special rights in that relation. This discovers the ethical basis of the rights of parents and children, husband and wife, master and servant, for these rights are the exact equivalent of the relative duties. The child has a right to be educated, as the parent is under obligation to provide education for his child.

5. Moral rights are not self-exacted, nor can they be voluntarily surrendered. They are the necessary accompaniment of obligation under reign of moral law. They are as unchangeable as the nature of moral law itself, and the obligation which it imposes.

6. Duties and Rights are moral equivalents resting equally upon the unchangeable warrant of moral law as the universal rule of human action. The ground on which any man can claim a right entitled to acknowledgment by others is exactly the ground on which by necessity he must own moral obligation.

7. All moral rights are perfect rights, irrespective of their being claimed by the person or enforced by society. A moral right rests wholly upon moral law, and must be uniform as that law.— (See above, c. v. 5.) Positive law may not attempt to enforce all rights alike, because all rights do not admit of being enforced; but this does not affect the ethical validity of any of the rights of a moral being.

Hutcheson, while holding that 'the observing and fulfilling every proper right of others is matter of conscience, necessary to obtain the approbation of God and our own hearts,' nevertheless assents to the classification of rights into perfect and imperfect. He says,— 'Rights according as they are more or less necessary to be obtained and observed in society, are divided into perfect and imperfect.'— *Syst. of Mor. Phil.* II. iii. 3. In the former sentence he speaks as a moralist; in the latter as a jurist.

Dr. Thomas Brown was more accurate, when he said,— 'There is as little an imperfect right, in a moral sense, as there is in logic an imperfect truth or falsehood.'— *Philos. of Mind,* Lect. 91.

8. Besides natural moral rights, there are Acquired Moral Rights. These spring up as the direct result of natural rights. Of Acquired Rights, the distinctive rights of each person according to the nature of his property, and the rights acquired by contract, afford examples. The Rights of Property follow directly from the natural right to the use of personal power, and to the fruit of its exercise. The Rights of Contract arise from the natural right to dispose of personal power and property, according to personal choice, restricted only by the moral obligations which are the necessary attendants upon acquired as well as natural rights.

9. Acquired Moral Rights, depending upon natural moral rights, rest ultimately for their authority upon absolute moral law. The measure of any man's rights may depend upon the forms of contract into which he has entered; but the right of contract itself is determined by moral law, and is not dependent on voluntary agreement.

10. Problems.— (1.) Critically examine the statement,— 'Where no covenant hath proceeded, every man has a right to every thing.'— Hobbes, *Leviath.* I. 14, also in ch. 13. Molesworth, iii. p. 130, and p. 117. (2.) Does a state of war destroy the natural rights of the combatants'? Hobbes says,

'Force and fraud are in war the two cardinal virtues.'— *Leviath.* 1. 13; Molesworth, III. 115. (3.) How far is it in harmony with moral law to surrender a measure of personal right, in organizing society? (4.) Is there any natural limit to the surrender of personal rights under the requirements of civil government? The problem is,— To find the Ethical grounds for such limitation.

DIVISION II
DEVELOPMENT THEORY
CHAPTER I
ORIGIN OF KNOWLEDGE

1. 'Nothing is to be held innate that can be shown to arise from experience and education.'— Prof. Bain, *Ment. and Moral Science,* B. II. c. 6. This is common ground. A development theory of Moral Philosophy is sufficient if it can prove its competence to explain our recognition of moral distinctions, personal obligation, and personal rights.

2. The fundamental position of the development theory is, that all our most complex states of consciousness are merely developments, under natural law, from our simplest state. The mind, as known in present consciousness, is the general resultant of all previous experience. 'We have it not in our power to ascertain by any direct process, what consciousness told us at the time when its revelations were in their pristine purity. It only offers itself to our inspection as it exists now, when those original revelations are overlaid and buried under a mountainous heap of acquired notions and perceptions.'— Mill's *Exam.* p. 171. The development theory is, therefore, first a theory of mind, in order to become a theory of morals. Its ethical theory depends on the proved accuracy and sufficiency of its theory of mind. The preliminary stages of the theory are of consequence here only as bearing on a theory of morals. The history of the theory may be traced through the following works: — Locke's *Essay* (1690), giving the germ, in making sensation the origin of all knowledge, while attributing to mind a power of reflection. Condillac, *Essai sur l'origine des Connaissances Humaines* (1746), following Locke; but later, *Traité des Sensations* (1754), he derives reflection from sensation. Hartley's *Observations on*

Man (1749), tracing development by association. Priestley, *Disquisitions relating to Matter and Spirit* (1777). Erasmus Darwin, *Zoonomia, or Laws of Organic Life* (1793 — 96); criticised by Dr. Thomas Brown, *Observations on Darwin's Zoonomia* (1798). Mr. James Mill, *Analysis of the Phenomena of the Human Mind* (1829), and a *fragment on Mackintosh* (anonymously) 1835. Of the former, a new edition, edited by his son, Mr. John S. Mill, with notes by Prof. Bain, Mr. Findlater, and Mr. Grote, London, 1869,— a valuable compendium. Mr. JOHN S. MILL, *Examination of Hamilton's Philosophy,* 3d ed. 1867, Chaps., IX. XI. XII. Prof. Bain's Works,— *Senses and Intellect,— Emotions and Will,— Mental and Moral Science.* Herbert Spencer, *Principles of Psychology,* 2nd ed. Alfred Barratt, *Physical Ethics,* London, 1869,— a very able work, unfolding a theory hopelessly entangled 'between the irritability and contractility of animal tissue.' CHARLES DARWIN, *Descent of Man,* opening chapters, in contrast with which, see Alfred Russell Wallace, *Theory of Natural Selection,* Chaps. on Mind and Morals.

3. The development theory objects to the affirmation of original faculties of mind as explaining the states of consciousness. The old ground of original faculties is accounted a reproach to Philosophy. That a child is born with limbs, and organs of sense, is matter of observation; but that the child is born with power of observation, reasoning power, memory, and will, is pure assumption. Indeed, that there is in human nature such a thing as mind, or spiritual existence, in addition to physical organism, is not self-evident, but needs proof. It may, indeed, be questioned whether Mind is anything more than 'the sum of Subject-experiences,' so that 'operations and experiences *constitute* mind,' or even whether mind is not merely 'a function of brain.'

4. Since it is impossible to go back to the dawn of experience, the theory begins with Sensation, as the simplest fact in consciousness. Hence the development theory is called the Sensational theory.

5. The first test of the theory turns upon the account it gives of Sensation, as a fact admitted by all. What is Sensation? How does it arise? Where does it exist? How is it known? An answer to these four questions is essential to a philosophy of

Sensation. Take smell as the example — one of the Sensations furthest removed from intellectual power, or, as Prof. Bain puts it, one of 'the least intellectual Sensations.' Mr. James Mill says, 'In the smell three things are commonly distinguished. There is the organ, there is the Sensation, and there is the antecedent of the Sensation, the external object.'— *Analysis,* I. 4; 2d ed. I. 8. Sensation, then, is so connected with bodily organism that it implies an impression made upon some part of the nervous system by an external object. The Sensation is the fact requiring attention.

(1.) What is this Sensation? Mr. James Mill replies, it is 'a particular feeling, a particular consciousness,' 'a point of consciousness, a thing which we can describe no otherwise than by calling it a feeling.'— *Analysis,* I. 7; ad ed. I. 12.

(2.) How does the Sensation arise? Odorous particles which proceed from the object' reach the organ of smell, and, in some way to us unknown, make an impression on the nerve, of which impression, the sensation in some way unknown is the consequent. Or, as Hume says *(Treat. on Hum. Nat.* I. I, 2), 'Sensations arise in the soul originally from unknown causes.' That the impression is transmitted to the nerve-centre in the brain is acknowledged. Beyond this, Physiology makes no averment. Every one is able to tell from his own consciousness, when he has a sensation of smell. And, as Mr. Mill says, 'we can distinguish this feeling, this consciousness, the sensation of smell, from every other sensation.'— *Ib.* I. 7, or I.12.

(3.) Where does the sensation exist? Mr. Mill does not hold with Hume, 'that an object may exist, and yet be nowhere' *(Hum. Nat.* I. iv. 5), but replies, 'What is *in me* is the sensation, the feeling, the point of consciousness.'— *Ib.* p. 9, or 13. The sensation is in Me; not in my nose any more than in the violet. That Mr. Mill means to distinguish between the organ of smell, where the impression is, and the Me, where the sensation is, admits of no doubt. For he says the sensation is 'a part of that series, that succession, that flow of something, on account of which we call ourselves living or sensitive creatures.' He could not have meant that the nostrils belong to the 'flow.' In confirmation we have the following: — 'We can conceive *ourselves* as endowed with smelling, and not enjoying any other faculty. In that case, *we should have* no idea of objects, as seeable, as bearable, as touchable, or tasteable. We should have a train of smells . . . . Our life would be a train of smells, and nothing more.'— *Ib.* p. 8, or 13. To which account of life this must be added, our sensitive organism would be Nose and Brain, and nothing more.

(4.) How is the Sensation known? Much of the information now possessed as to Sensation is the result of Physiological Inquiry, and is not known by experience. But Sensation itself is always a form of experience. Our acquaintance with the facts, that odorous particles come from an object,— that there are within the nostrils olfactory nerves, sensitive to the influence of such particles,— and that these olfactory nerves are connected with the nerve-centre in the brain, is not obtained by us in experiencing the Sensation of smell. Such knowledge is obtained by external observation. But Sensation is known to me as a fact in my own experience. Sensation does not know itself, but is known by me. This knowledge is consciousness, which is characteristic of all internal experience. Sensation, then, is known to us 'as a part of that . . . on account of which we call ourselves living or sensitive creatures.' The simplest expression of the fact is this — I am conscious of a sensation of smell. This is our primary fact, out of which by development a Philosophy of Mind and of Morals is to be constructed. Here we start with absolute certainty, for, as Mr. J. S. Mill says, 'Consciousness of the mind's own feelings and operations cannot be disbelieved.'— *Exam.* p. 166. Here also we start with the greatest attainable simplicity in human experience. However great be the 'mountainous heap of acquired notions and perceptions,' this consciousness of a sensation of smell is the simplest fact in experience. Here, on the testimony of all the authorities of a sensational philosophy, we are underneath the mountain, and have come upon the primordial element of the whole formation.

As to this simple experience of sensation, four questions have been raised. In gathering the answers, facts have accumulated. We have objects — sensitive organism — impressions made upon it by the objects — and sensations known in consciousness. All these belong to the interpretation of the simplest element in human experience. Of these, three,— the object, the sensitive organism, and the impressions made upon it,— are acknowledged as realities affording an external explanation of the rise of the Sensation.

But the Sensation itself, as a fact of internal experience, is that which we need to have explained. I am conscious of the sensation as a fact 'in me.' This Consciousness is not identical with the Sensation. The latter is a sensation of smell, the former is consciousness of the sensation as mine. Sensation is 'a particular feeling;' consciousness is a general characteristic of all experience. With the capacity for sensation, I receive the particular feeling into myself; but with the consciousness as a characteristic of myself, the rise of the sensation is known as a present reality within. Consciousness of a sensation is therefore consciousness of Personality or Self, and of a particular experience as mine. Sensation of smell is feeling, to be classed among 'the feelings of Receptivity or Passivity, which arise in connexion with the Sentient or Incarrying nerves' (Prof. Bain). Consciousness is knowledge,— a double knowledge,— knowledge of self and knowledge of the present experience.

In opposition to this view, James Mill maintains the identity of Sensation and Consciousness, making the terms synonymous, and identifying both with feeling. Mr. John S. Mill and Professor Bain take the same position, but more guardedly. The views of all three are brought together in the new edition of James Mill's *Analysis,* chap. v., with Notes, 74, 75; vol. I. p. 226.

James Mill's identification of sensation and consciousness is inconsistent both in respect of expression and of the facts stated. As to expression, the following may be taken: — 'Though I have these various modes of naming my sensation, by saying, I feel the prick of a pin, I feel the pain of a prick, I have the sensation of a prick, I have the feeling of a prick, I am conscious of the feeling; the thing named in all these various ways is the same.'— *Analy.* I. 71, or I. 224. In this sentence there are plainly two distinct facts — the one expressing simple fact, the other possession or property in that fact: the one saying, I feel, the other, I have the feeling. The same thing is named in all the forms, but a second thing is named with it in the third and fourth. The fifth form is certainly different, but according to Mill it is tautological, therefore to be discarded as 'an impropriety of speech.' If it be an accurate statement, as is here maintained, it indicates a complex state, composed of three elements. (See above, Intro. sec. 8.)

As to the facts themselves, Mr. Mill admits such diversity as implies a distinction between Sensation and Consciousness. Sensations are 'feelings which *we have* through the external senses.' 'What is *in me* is the sensation.' It is not alleged that the object, making an impression on the organ, produces Me. On the contrary, I receive the sensation; its existence is accounted for by a power of Receptivity which belongs to Me. But, in receiving the sensation, I know the thing received, and I know myself as the receiver. I have the sensation, and I have the knowledge of it. Both belong to me as possessions at the same moment in the same state. Sensation is not Self-sensation, but Smell-sensation, or some other 'particular feeling.' Consciousness is the expression of Self-activity; Sensation is the expression of Receptivity in Self. Whether in lower forms of life there may be feelings or sensibility apart from consciousness, and by mere irritability and contractility of animal tissue, I do not undertake to say. But this is not what is involved in sensation as the simplest element in human experience, and Mr. Mill has not alleged that it is. The simplest fact in our experience involves knowledge of Self, Personality, or Mind, before you begin a theory of development. We are still on the old ground, and have gone back as far as Des Cartes. 'I feel,' is an affirmation which I myself make; and, in making which, I affirm my own existence, and my knowledge of a present state as mine. The existence of feeling is thus personal experience of feeling.

Mr. John Stuart Mill also holds the identity of Sensation and Consciousness, but he makes the avowal in a much more cautious manner, admitting that 'a slight correction seems requisite to the doctrine.'— *Analy.* 2d ed. I. 230. He says, Many philosophers think 'we cannot have a feeling without having the knowledge awakened in us at the same moment, of a Self who feels it. But of this as a primordial fact of our nature, it is impossible to have direct evidence; and a supposition may be made which renders its truth at least questionable. Suppose a being, gifted with sensation, but devoid of memory, whose sensations follow one after another, but leave no trace of their existence when they cease. Could this being have any knowledge or notion of a Self? Would he ever say to himself, *I* feel; this sensation is *mine?* I think not. The notion of a Self is, I apprehend, a consequence of memory. There is no meaning in the word Ego or I, unless the I of to-day is also the I of yesterday.'— *Analy.* 2d ed. 1. 229. It is matter of much interest that Mr. Mill, after his mature study of the question, should take his position so cautiously as to say, that it is 'at least questionable,' whether sensation involves a knowledge of self, and still more that he should ground this statement on a supposition. The supposition is a fair one, but it seems to me to fail in its purpose. Suppose a being capable of sensation but incapable of recollection. Suppose this being experiencing a sensation. 'Would he say to himself, this sensation is *mine?'* If he should say anything to *Himself,* he would say this; he could not possibly say anything else. Either he must experience a sensation without knowing it, or he must know it as his sensation. The argument to the contrary is based on the necessity of memory for the attainment of 'any knowledge or notion of a "Self." ' But a knowledge and a notion are two distinct things. A knowledge may be obtained in a single state; a notion is a general conception obtained by gathering up into one representation the various qualities recognised through successive forms of experience. Without Memory, a conception is impossible. But, on the supposition made, we deal with a being who has only a single sensation and no memory. A conception of a Self is to him impossible.— Hamilton's *Reid,* p. 360, and Note B, p. 804; Mansel's *Prolegomena Logica,* p. 9. But a knowledge of Self is not thereby excluded. On the contrary, if a conception of self can be obtained by the aid of Memory, a knowledge of self must be involved in each state, without the play of memory. Present Knowledge is the condition of memory. To say that memory recalls what was never present, is a contradiction in terms. A conception which contains what has not been gathered by direct knowledge, is a fabrication, and nothing more. A philosophic doctrine of Personality resting on such a basis, exposes its own insufficiency. The saying, that 'there is no meaning in the word Ego or I, unless the I of to-day is also the I of yesterday,' appears to carry the refutation of the theory. There must have been an I of yesterday, in order to say that the I of to-day is the same; and the I of yesterday must have had a meaning, if the I of to-day has any. A doctrine of Personality is, therefore, a prerequisite for a doctrine of Personal Identity. To identify these is to invent confusion. The conjunction has been attempted from the extreme of a transcendental philosophy, as well as from the other extreme of a sensational philosophy.

On the grounds thus indicated, it seems evident that the slight correction which Mr. Mill proposes, must be still further extended. The correction suggested is this: — 'There is a mental *process*, over and above the mere having a feeling, to which the word consciousness is sometimes, and it can hardly be said improperly, applied, viz., the *reference* of the feeling to our self. But this process, though separable in thought from the actual feeling, and in all probability not accompanying it in the beginning, is, from a very early period, inseparably attendant on it.' This is a large admission; too large to rest in. A *'reference'* to Self, however, implies a *'process,'* just as in the transcendental philosophy of Germany, the Ego or Self is said to *affirm* itself, so as to be an object to itself. There is thus the inconsistency of saying that Self refers its own state to itself, or that Self affirms itself to itself. For such statements there is no philosophic warrant. To know an experience as mine, I must obtain the knowledge in the act of experience itself. Later than this, is too late. If I do not know the sensation as mine, I cannot refer it to Self, if I do know it as mine, I have a knowledge which is superior to that obtained by any process or reference.

Professor Bain takes practically the same position. The modifications he proposes on the doctrine of Mr. James Mill are no less striking than those just considered. He says, 'We may be in a state of pleasure with *little or nothing* of thought accompanying; we are still properly said to be conscious, or under consciousness. But we may add to the mere fact of pleasure, the *cognition of the state,* as a state of pleasure, and a state belonging to us at the time. This is not the same thing as before; it is something new superposed upon the previous consciousness. When we take note of the fact that we are pleased, we proceed beyond the bare experience of the present pleasure, to an intellectual act of comparison, assimilation, or classification with past pleasures; we probably introduce the machinery of language to express ourselves as pleased: all this is so much *extra* consciousness. These operations are not involved in mere feeling; we may feel without them.'— *Analysis,* Note

74, I. 227. There is much in this paragraph which will be readily accepted hearing on the possibility of attention, or reflection, as a more complex exercise, than simple consciousness. It is agreed that we can make any mental state matter of attention, and can proceed to comparison of it with other states, and to appropriate classification of it. It is certainly accurate to say that 'These knowing operations are not involved in mere feeling; we may feel without them.' The real point in dispute, however, appears, when Professor Bain says, 'We may be in a state of pleasure with little or nothing of thought accompanying.' If 'thought' here mean 'consciousness,' whether are we to hold to 'little' or to 'nothing'? Leaving the 'little or nothing' indeterminate, Dr. Bain says, 'But *we may add* to the mere fact of pleasure the *cognition of the state* as a state of pleasure, and as a state belonging to us at the time.' Where is the evidence in support of this 'addition,' or the psychological provision for it? Does 'the mere fact of pleasure,' as a matter of experience, not imply that it is I who have the pleasure, or that the fact is one of personal experience? If not, I must, in order to 'add' the cognition of it as mine, have first a cognition of myself purely as a person, and then attribute the fact to myself as its subject; a process which, according to all the accredited results of Psychology, involves two impossibilities,— knowledge of pure self, and attributing to pure self of that which is not known as simple fact.

Hume says, 'I never can catch *myself* at any time without a perception.'— *Hum. Nat.* l. iv. 6. It is enough at any time to catch yourself with one. Kant, in opening up his grand scheme of transcendental philosophy, sought to reach what Hume here points to as requisite,— Mind as a Thing-in-itself. By that single effort, with its later developments down to Hegel, philosophic literature has been enriched to a wonderful degree. But we are still without the Thing-in-itself. We know Mind as Personality in every present state, the recognition of Personal Identity is another thing; and the conception of the Mind as possessed of a variety of powers is still another.

The extreme caution, almost hesitation, of the language which Professor Bain next employs, seems to indicate a sense of the greatness of the difficulty. He says,— 'It is thus correct to draw a line between feeling, and knowing that we feel; although there is a great delicacy in the operation. It may be said, in one sense, that we cannot feel without knowing that we feel; but the assertion is verging on error, for feeling may be accompanied with a minimum of cognitive energy, or as good as none at all.'— *Ib*. It must be kept in view, that 'to draw a line between feeling, and knowing that we feel,' involves an analytic or philosophic process, and the possibility of such a process depends upon the co-existence of the feeling and the knowing in a single mental state. If there be even 'a minimum of cognitive energy' accompanying each experience of feeling, the first and last hope of a development theory of mind dies out, and the true beginning of a mental philosophy is where Des Cartes began. For history of opinion on this subject, see end of this Chapter.

6. The next test of the development theory is found in the explanation it offers of the 'series, succession, or flow' of our experiences. That there is a series, involving unity in continuity, is admitted. A sufficient explanation must account for two things: (1.) The fact of a connected series of experiences,— 'a bundle or collection of different perceptions' (Hume); — 'a thread of consciousness' (J. S. Mill): and (2.) The diversity of nature belonging to successive parts of the series, bundle, or thread. Sensation being the primary fact, how is a connected series of sensations possible? and how does the series come to embrace more than sensations?

The *first* problem is this,— Given a sensation, how are we to account for the development of a series, conscious of its own unity? So far as the external conditions of sensation are concerned, it is clear that that which awakens one sensation may again awaken another. If there be Organism, with 'sentient or incarrying nerves,' and Objects fitted to make impressions on that organism, the external conditions are fulfilled. Permanence of externality, partly Mine, and partly Not-Me, make provision outwardly for sensation. Whether such externality is adequately explained by a sensational theory, the nature of the present problem does not lead me to inquire.

The essential question is this: Granting the possibility of sensations, how can a series of such sensations recognise itself as a series, or attain to a conception of Personal Identity? The theory most rigidly adhering to the conditions of Sensationalism is that presented by Mr. J. S. Mill, from whom we have ample acknowledgment of the perplexity. 'If we speak of the Mind as a series of feelings, we are obliged to complete the statement by calling it a series of feelings which is aware of itself as past and future; and we are reduced to the alternative of believing that the Mind or Ego is something different from any series of feelings, or possibilities of them, or of accepting the paradox that something which, *ex hypothesi,* is but a series of feelings, can be aware of itself as a series.'— *Exam.* 3d ed. p. 242. Which alternative is commonly accepted, there can be no doubt. But if it be admitted that 'the Mind or Ego is something different from any series of feelings,' how can the acknowledgment be described as a 'belief'? In postulating a belief, we are guilty of the inconsistency of supposing *ourselves* outside the series, forming a belief as to something different,— that is, our own identity as distinct from the series of feelings. We escape the inconsistency if there be knowledge of Self in every state, and if our conception of Personal Identity rests upon such knowledge.

In order to proceed we must assume the possession of MEMORY. We must have not merely a present experience, but recollections of past experiences. But how can a succession of feelings remember? By common consent the sensation ceases when the object no longer continues to make an impression on the nerves of sensibility. The recollection of the sensation, or the 'idea' of it, as Mr. James Mill and others name it, is quite different from the sensation. Under this admission, it becomes needful to call in the aid of Memory as an original power. An impression upon our sensitive organism may produce a sensation, but cannot continue or recall it. Sensation is 'Receptivity or Passivity.' Recollection is activity. In this we come upon a form of experience entirely different from sensation, and which sensation could not produce. If sensation ceases when the impression on the sensitive nerves is discontinued, development of a sensation is impossible. Professor Bain says that sensations possess the power of 'continuing as Ideas after the actual object of sense is withdrawn.'— *Emotions,* p. 17. But the Idea cannot at the same time be different from the Sensation, and yet a continuation of the Sensation itself. An ideal representation or recollection roust be 'reproduced by mental causes alone,' and in saying so we postulate Memory as a property of Mind.

There is, however, still another demand towards the construction of a theory. We have a regard to the Future, as well as to the Past. On this account, Mr. John S. Mill postulates the following psychological truth, 'that the human mind is capable of Expectation,— in other words, that, after having had Actual Sensations we are capable of forming the conception of Possible Sensations.'— *Exam.* p. 219. This makes provision for another form of experience quite distinct from Sensation.

But what is the effect of the introduction of these two postulates, Memory and Expectation? If these two powers are attributed to the series of Sensations, the theory is involved in self-contradiction, by assigning to sensations attributes quite different from those which can belong to them, according to the explanation given of their origin and essential character. If these powers are postulated as belonging to 'the human mind,' or as powers 'which we are capable' of using, a development theory is abandoned, and we are on the old ground of faculties.

Granting now as postulates, that 'the human mind' is capable of Memory, and also of Expectation, how can we account for the diversity of nature belonging to the forms of experience remembered and expected? Life is not made up of a series of Sensations merely. There are affections and emotions welling up from within; there are comparisons of things without and within, and reasonings leading to definite conclusions; there are regrets as to the past, and purposes as to the future. May we, in sight of all this diversity, now escape the necessity of adding to the number of our own postulates? In postulating Memory, have we not postulated a good deal more? Does not Memory imply attention and comparison, and do not these involve intellectuality, in complete contrast with mere receptivity? From this manifest and serious perplexity I see no satisfactory outlet. 'Every one of himself will readily perceive the difference betwixt feeling and thinking.'— Hume, *Treat. on Hum. Nature,* B. I. Pt. 2.

One of the most interesting attempts to complete the theory is that of Professor Bain, wrought out with great ability. He assigns Emotional, Volitional, and Intellectual characters to Feeling.— *Emotions and Will,* c. I. The substratum of life is thus regarded as Feeling, while Emotional, Volitional, and Intellectual activity are only modifications of Feeling. The first position is, that Emotion may be derived from Sensation. To establish this, it is urged that every Feeling has a physical side and a mental side, and that gradually the physical side may abate and the mental side increase, in which case an emotion exists. Hume felt a need for other materials. He said, 'The idea of pleasure or pain, when it returns upon the soul, produces the new impressions of desire and aversion, hope and fear, which may properly be called impressions of reflection, because derived from it.'— *Hum. Nat.* B. I. Pt. i. sec. 2. Next, 'Volitional characters' are assigned to Feeling on the following ground — 'Although the operations of the Will are conceived by us as something distinct from, or super-added to, the operation of Feeling proper, yet in every volition, rightly so named, the stimulus, or antecedent, is some feeling.' Finally, 'intellectual characters' are assigned to Feeling thus,— Since Sensations possess the power of continuing themselves as Ideas, 'this property of Persistence and also of recurrence in Idea, belonging more or less to sensational states, is their intellectual property.' Such an ingenious scheme of development cannot fail to gain admiration, but it assumes too much. Sensation has a physical 'stimulus or antecedent,' but the Sensation itself is 'in me.' Admitting next, that Feeling is the 'stimulus or antecedent' of a Volition, Feeling is then used in a sense different from Sensation. An assumption is thus made, to help the argument. And even then the Feeling supposed does not account for the possibility of Volition, which is 'something distinct from, or superadded to, the operation of Feeling proper,' and implies some power different in nature as its source. Finally, as 'recurrence in idea' is not persistence of a sensation, the recurrence needs some power other than Sensation to account for it. Besides, intellectual action is much more than mere reproduction of what has gone before. It gathers what Sensation cannot give, and thus originates conceptions which are far removed from all that sensitive organism transmits by the incarrying nerves. Nay more: when Sensation and Intellectual action are compared, with a view to decide their relations to each other, so far is Intellectual-Action from being a development from Sensation, that Intellect is required for the use of the Senses. So obvious is this last statement, that Professor Bain distributes the Senses on the basis of their relation to Intellect.

He says, 'Some of the senses are evidently intellectual in a high degree, as sight and hearing, others are intellectual in a much smaller degree, as Smell and Taste.'— Note in Mr. Mill's *Analysis,* 2d ed. I. 7. Taking, then, even the lowest of the senses, Intellect is involved in their use, and development up to Intellect is forestalled.

7. The final resort of a development theory is found in the Laws of Association. On this account, the theory is often named the Associational theory.

Mr. James Mill, following in the line taken by Locke and Hume, traces the relation between Sensation and Association in the following manner: The simplest element in experience is Sensation, the representation, copy, or recollection of the sensation is an Idea: and the connecting or combining of Ideas in the mind is association. This last is Association of Ideas, not of objects, nor of sensations. The name points to combinations by the exercise of recollection. The Laws of Association are Laws of Memory. So Mr. J. Mill says, 'Our ideas spring up, or exist, in the order in which the Sensations existed of which they are the copies.'— *Analy.* 1. 56; or I. 78.

The Laws of Association as given by Mr. John S. Mill are the following: '1st, Similar phenomena tend to be thought of together. 2d, Phenomena which have either been experienced or conceived in close contiguity to one another, tend to be thought of together. 3d, Associations produced by contiguity become more certain and rapid by repetition. When two phenomena have been very often experienced in conjunction, and have not in any single instance occurred separately either in experience or in thought, there is produced between them what has been called Inseparable, or, less correctly, Indissoluble Association, by which is not meant that the Association must inevitably last to the end of life — that no subsequent experience or process of thought can possibly avail to dissolve it; but only, that as long as no such experience or process of thought has taken place, the Association is irresistible. 4th, When an association has acquired this character of inseparability, not only does the idea called up by association become, in our consciousness, inseparable from the idea which suggested it, but the facts or phenomena answering to these ideas come at last to seem inseparable in existence.'— *Exam.* 219.

In this statement of the Laws of Association, the substitution of the term 'Phenomena' for 'Ideas' is an improvement, as embracing the remembrance of all mental facts. But this comprehensiveness is gained at the risk of embracing more than the facts of mind. The laws as given will be generally accepted, with this modification, that the third really embraces two distinct laws, and the fourth is not a law of Association in the same sense as the others.

The four laws of Association may be named, the Laws of Similarity, of Contiguity, of Repetition, and of Tenacity or Persistence. Hume named them, 'Resemblance, Contiguity in time or place, and Cause and Effect.'— See also Hamilton's *Reid,* p. 199, and Dissert. D * *.

Mr. Mill's fourth law transcends the limits of Association of the facts of internal experience. That external facts are often considered to be necessarily connected merely on the ground of mental association, is certain. But this tendency of mind is not an application of any law of association, but a tendency towards false inference, which needs to be constantly guarded against, as a source of error. It is a disposition to make our thoughts the measure of external existence.

The value of the Laws of Association as instruments for the development of mind now requires consideration. Is Memory sufficient to account for the origin of Intellect; or does the action of Memory presuppose Intellect?

The Laws of Association provide only for connecting together facts which pass through consciousness, and for constituting one of these facts a help for recalling the other. Nothing can 'recur' in consciousness which has not already passed through it. If there be in consciousness only Feelings, and provision for their association, the result can be nothing more than combinations of Feeling. If Memory spin its thread out of the stores of material treasured in the past; and if these stores contain nothing but feeling; the thread must be all of one fibre. Sensations as forms of passivity are not capable of activity. Feelings may afford materials for thought, but cannot themselves produce thought. Here also we are brought to a stand-still. For the sake of progress, we must pass over to the old ground of faculties, postulating Intelligence as an original possession.

The facts next requiring attention are those pointed at in Mr. Mill's fourth law. These facts being admitted as belonging to consciousness, and yet distinct from the normal action of the Laws of Association, have an important bearing on the origin and certainty of human knowledge. While Sensations and their Associations are concerned exclusively with our own experience, Observations and Inferences are concerned with external objects, as well as with facts belonging to experience. By observation, we recognise combinations and associations of external objects, and from such observation we draw certain inferences of our own. These inferences we hold to be true of the objects. We have thus a twofold aspect of association,— associations of mental phenomena, and of external facts. The difference between these two is very marked. Internal Associations, we originate in accordance with the Laws enumerated; External Associations we only recognise, and do not originate, except in the case of actions which are manifestations of our own personality. Taking, then, Associations of our own experience, and associations of external objects observed by us, the spheres are so distinct, that the combinations must be formed under different laws. The question now is,— How far can Internal Associations afford a criterion of external reality? This question is raised for the purpose of deciding, how far conceivability, or its opposite, is a test of external existence. On this subject, see Des Cartes' *Method,* Pt. IV., 'that all things which we very clearly and distinctly conceive, are true;' Leibnitz, *Meditationes de Cognitione Veritate et Ideis* (1684), ed. Erdmann, p. 79; Reid's *Intellectual Powers,* Essay IV. c. 3, with special reference to Hamilton's note, p. 377, Whewell's *Philosophy of the Inductive Sciences,* I. 54; Reply to foregoing, Mill's *Logic,* B. II. c. 5; Criticism of Mr. Mill, by Herbert Spencer, *Principles of Psychology,* c. II.; Mansel's Prolegomena Logica.

The essential points in a reply are condensed into the following paragraphs: —

Truth is recognised either by Intuition, lower or higher, or by Logical Inference; that is, either directly or indirectly. (Whether there are higher, as well as lower intuitions, is a question not essential to the discussion.) Observation is certainty. This is equivalent to affirming the certainty of known facts. Logical Inference from observed facts has validity. Observation is equally certain as to the relations of objects, as to their separate existence. An association, whether matter of experience or of external observation, is matter of fact. The recurrence of such associations in observation, is an additional fact known by the aid of Memory.

What, then, is the relation between Internal and External Reality? Perception is observation of an external object, the fact perceived being as certain as the fact of perception. Sensation, being an internal fact dependent upon an impression made on the sensitive organism, warrants an inference to the existence in the object of a property capable of making the impression. Associations, whether internal or external, being known as facts, warrant an inference to laws, or powers (if not both), competent to explain their origin. As observation of objects affords the materials for our conceptions of them, the external association of qualities in an object may have an exact counterpart in the conception of these qualities associated in the mind. If our observation of trees has uniformly involved the recognition of trunk, branches, and green leaves, these three characteristics will be associated in our conception of a tree. We could not on this ground, however, warrantably maintain the physical impossibility of any variation. The sight of a black beech gives external diversity, and introduces a new association. True, then, as it is in the history of mind, that external facts or phenomena answering to ideas constantly associated within, come at last to be regarded by us as in reality inseparable, such an inference from internal association to external reality is logically incompetent. The possibilities of existence are not restricted by the range of our conceptions. Conceivableness is not the test of truth; nor is inconceivableness the test of the false. As a test of *possible existence,* conceivability is the least reliable that can be used. The conceivable may be only what we have known; the inconceivable, nothing more than what we have never known. The tendency to employ inconceivableness as a test of truth has involved philosophical inquiry in confusion, and has led to the egregious assumption that our thoughts are the measure of reality.

Passing from facts to *principles,* we come upon another example of confusion. The mind's insight into self-evident truth has been confounded with conceivableness as a test of truth.

Insight into self-evident truth does not make mind the measure of truth, but indicates only the mind's power to recognise truths which are higher than facts. So insight into the self-contradictory does not erect the limits of mental power into limits of possible truth, but only illustrates the fact that there is in mind a power to detect the inherently false. The false is not identified with the inconceivable. It is by understanding the terms of a proposition, that we recognise it to be self-contradictory, carrying in itself the evidence of its own falseness. The test lies in the proposition itself, not in the power of conception belonging to this or that mind. Few things are more likely to mislead, than to represent the Inconceivable as the furthest removed from Truth. For this reason, the formula is open to serious objection, as a statement of the criterion of *a priori* principles of knowledge,— 'A necessary truth is a proposition the negative of which is *not only false but inconceivable.'*

The history of philosophic thought as to the knowledge of Self may be traced in the following line. DES CARTES makes the knowledge of self an essential element in all knowledge.— *Method* (1637), Pt. IV., Veitch's ed. p. 74; *Meditations* (1647), II., Veitch's ed. p. 24. He says,— 'I think, therefore I am; if I doubt, still I affirm my own existence; if I am deceived, still I exist.' LOCKE, tracing all knowledge to sensation and reflection, admitted the existence of *mind,* defining Person as 'a thinking intelligent being, that has reason and reflection, and can consider itself as itself.'— *Essay* (1690) II. 27, sec. 9. While holding that 'there is nothing in the Intellect which was not previously in Sense,' he did not expose himself to the point of the clever addition of Leibnitz, 'except the Intellect itself,' for he granted mental existence. HUME denied 'that we are every moment intimately conscious of what we call our Self, and maintained that we are only 'a bundle of perceptions.'— *Treatise on Human Nature* (1739), 1. iv. 6. The Scotch School followed, attacking the Sceptical Philosophy, and seeking to reconstruct the science of Mind on some better basis than that of Locke. But Reid spoke hesitatingly of the knowledge of mind. He said, 'The attributes of mind, and particularly its operations, we know clearly, but of the thing itself we have only an obscure notion.'— *Intellectual Powers* (1785), Essay v. c. 2. Stewart followed more decidedly on the negative side, saying of mind, that 'we are not immediately conscious of its existence.'— *Elements of the Philosophy of the Human Mind,* vol. I. (1792), Intro. Part I. In these statements, both authors were hampered by discussions as to the Essence of Mind. The French School, which sprung almost wholly from the Scotch School, became much more clear on the immediate consciousness of mind. Royer-Collard led the van, in the Lectures delivered in Paris in 1811, published by Jouffroy in his edition of Reid's Works, vols. iv. and v. MAINE DE BIRAN, an independent thinker, made it his chief concern to maintain our consciousness of mind as a cause or active force.— *Examin des Leçons de Philosophic de M. Laromiguière* (1809), Œuvres Philosophiques, edited by Cousin, 1841. After him, COUSIN himself followed on the same side, *Cours de Philosophie,* Leçons v. vi., Wight's translation; *History of Modern Philosophy,* Edinburgh, 1852, vol. i. p. 88 and p. 109; and also *Leçons sur la Philosophie de Kant,* Leçon VIII,, Henderson's translation, *The Philosophy of Kant,* London, 1854, p. 193. THEODORE JOUFFROY, Prof. of Mor. Phil. at Paris, took the same ground, in his Introduction to Stewart's Outlines. This introduction is translated by George Ripley of Boston, U.S., and is the first of the *Philosophical Essays* by M. Theo. Jouffroy, Edinburgh, 1839 (dark's series), see p. II and p. 56. The French movement is ably traced in Morell's *History of Modern Philosophy.* The German School, in its reaction against Hume, took a different course under guidance of the master spirit, Kant. In the development of a transcendental philosophy, Kant held that the Ego or Self is known in every conscious state; but such knowledge he considered a knowledge of mind only as phenomenon, giving nothing permanent. He even goes so far as to say that the Ego or Self as thus known 'is but the consciousness of my thought.' But the mind itself, the thing in itself (Ding-an-sich), as a permanent thing, is reached only by transcendental conception. This is the Mind as Noumenon, separated from every element of experience. The *cogito, ergo sum,*— I think, therefore I am,— of Des Cartes, gives only an empirical psychology, whereas beyond that we must seek a rational psychology. 'I *think* is, therefore, the only text of rational psychology, from which it must develop its whole system.' This double view of Self as phenomenon and as noumenon is so important that I subjoin detailed references: — *Kritik der Reinen Vernunft* (1781), Vorrede zur zweiten Auflage, note, *Werke,* Rosencranz, Th. II. Supplement ii. p. 685. A very important passage withdrawn from the latest editions, given by Rosencranz as Supplement xi., Th. II. 716. Another withdrawn passage, given by Rosencranz as Supplement xiv., Th. n. 730, and Supplement xxi., Th. 11. 774. And Des Zweiten Buchs der Transcendentalen Dialektik, Erstes Haupstück. Mr. Meiklejohn in his translation has wisely embraced all the passages in the text, admitting of the references being given to the pages, Kant's *Critique of Pure Reason,* p. xl. Introd., pp. 41, 81, 86, 95, 168, and 237. The progression of thought was by a transition to higher abstraction, with exception of a decided protest from JACOBI (1743 — 1819), 'The Faith-Philosopher,' as Ueberweg calls him, *Geschichte,* Th. III. 206. The theory of Jacobi is best gathered from his work, *David Hume, über den, Glauben, oder Idealismus und Realismus,* 1787. The elder FICHTE (J. G.) followed Kant with an Idealism, which made the Ego or 1 everything; but with him the Ego or I is not the individual, but universal reason. Thus the problem of Personality was abandoned for higher speculative efforts separated from the facts of consciousness. Fichte's *Wissenschaftslehre,* 1794; in the following year, SCHELLING took the same line, in his work entitled *Vom Ich als Princip der Philosophie, oder über das Unbedingte irn Menschlichen Wissen,* 1795. With both of these philosophers the End was not Kant's noumenon, or Pure Self, but The Absolute or The unconditioned, Das Unbedingte. HEGEL went to the opposite extreme, to seek a *beginning* in the universal, and thus we have the last use of Being and Determinate Being, Seyn and Da-seyn, *Wissenschaft der Logik,* 1812. With Hegel, Philosophy takes its rise at the utmost remove from facts; at the extreme opposite from Kant's commencement in the *Kritik d. R. V.,* 'all our knowledge begins with experience.' From that extreme, however, Hegel comes, through evolution' of thought, to self-consciousness. Later German thinking has returned upon Psychology. J. F. HERBART (1776 — 1841) insists that Philosophy must begin with the facts of consciousness. He gives primary importance to the *Ich, I,* 'with which word the proper self-consciousness of every one is indicated to himself;' and this Ich, I, 'exists, that is, is present, not merely in Itself, but also with the Not-I,— Nicht-Ich.'— *Lehrbuch zur Einleitung in die Philosophie,* 1813, sec. 124, Werke, by Hartenstein, I. 198. F. E.

104

Βενεκε (1798 — 1854) followed in the same line, insisting upon self-knowledge in self-consciousness, *Erkenntnisslehre,* 1820. See also, the younger Fichte (Immanuel Hermann), who regards each Personality as an eternal entity, *Das Erkennen als Selbsterkennen,* 1833, and *Zur Seelenfrage, eine philosophische Confession,—* Of the Problem of the Soul, A Philosophical Confession,— 1859, translated by Morell under the title, *Contributions to Mental Philosophy,* London, 1860; and Adolf Trendelenburg, *Logische Untersuchungen,* 1840. For the earlier stages of German thought, see Schwegler's *History of Philosophy,* translated by Dr. James Hutchison Stirling, with notes of the translator; for the later stages, see Ueberweg's *History of Philosophy,—* Theological and Philosophical Library, New York and London, edited by Professors Henry B. Smith and Schaff.

The philosophy which acknowledges immediate consciousness of Self, has been ably vindicated by Hamilton, *Metaph.* I.; very admirably by Ferrier, *Institutes of Metaphysic,* in which prominence is given to this as fundamental; by MANSEL, *Prolegomena Logica,* p. 137; and *Metaphysics,* p. 180; and in President M'Cosh's *Exam. of Mill's Philosophy,* p. 80. Dr. Shadworth Hodgson, *Time and Space,* London, 1865, raises 'the question how consciousness is related to, or distinguished from, Self-consciousness,' and affirms that self-consciousness is a later attainment, by reflection.— P. 168.

CHAPTER II
KNOWLEDGE OF MORAL DISTINCTIONS
(UTILITARIAN THEORY)

1. The Development theory, which seeks first to rise from Sensation to Intelligence, endeavours next, with the aid of Intelligence, to reach a knowledge of moral distinctions. The power to observe and reason about our Sensations being granted, the development theory undertakes to distinguish between right and wrong in action.

2. As the foundation of the intellectual theory is laid in Sensation, the foundation of the moral theory is laid in the pleasurable and painful experience characteristic of our Feelings. The Ethical Theory may be summarized thus: 'Actions are right

105

in proportion as they tend to promote happiness, wrong as they tend to produce the reverse of happiness.'— Mill's *Utilitarianism,* p. 9. In view of this, the theory is named 'The Happiness Theory,'— Eudæmonism (from ευδαιμονια, happiness),— Hedonism *(ηδονή,* pleasure). Of the two designations, the former indicates a view of happiness higher than the latter. Bentham thinks that 'the word happiness is not always appropriate,' because 'it represents pleasure in too elevated a shape.'— *Deontology,* I. 78.

In accordance with the Sensational basis, we must look first at pleasure and pain as opposites, then at different kinds of pleasure and pain, then at the reasons for seeking pleasure and shunning pain, next at the reasons for preferring one pleasure to another, and finally, we must consider whether the tendency or fitness of an action to produce happiness or misery, determines the rightness or wrongness of that action.

3. That pleasurable and painful feelings are experienced by us is matter of agreement. The range of facts with which we have to deal is also well defined. 'By happiness is intended pleasure and the absence of pain; by unhappiness, pain and the privation of pleasure.'— Mill's *Util.* p. 10. Pleasures and pains of all kinds are here included, whether connected with Sensations, Feelings, or Intellectual Activity.

4. The rise of pleasure, as connected with the functions of our life, admits of a twofold explanation. It is the natural accompaniment of our Sensations, or of the exercise of our energies. In the one case it attends upon our 'Passivity or Receptivity,' as in the warmth of the body, or the cooling influence of the breeze. In the other case, it attends upon our Activity, or Voluntary use of powers, as in the exercise of our muscles, or of our reasoning power. The former belongs to sentient existence; the latter to active existence, whether physical or intellectual, or both combined.

Besides these forms of pleasure, there is another, which does not here call for special note, namely, pleasure in the possession of objects of value.

Pain comes either through injury inflicted upon the Sentient organism, or through unnatural restraint upon the energies when brought into exercise. Pain is not merely a negation, or want of pleasure, but a positive experience, opposite in kind.

5. Pleasure being a form of experience naturally attendant upon the use of our sensibilities or energies, is not the end of their use. This is the obvious exposition of the previous paragraph. Pain being attendant upon the injury or restraint our powers is not the product of their natural use. Pleasure and pain are the index of the natural and the unnatural in the use of powers, of conformity with the law of their exercise, or violation of that law. As Feuchtersleben has said, 'Beauty is in some degree the reflection of health,' so pleasure is the symbol of natural exercise. Pleasure and pain are respectively as the smooth play or the irksome fretting of machinery, but neither is the end for which it is kept moving. Consciousness of simple pleasure and nothing more is unknown. A capacity or faculty whose function it is to produce pleasure and nothing more is unknown. Pleasure may thus be generalized as the common accompaniment of all natural exercise.

6. Pleasures differ in kind according to the capacities or faculties on whose exercise they attend, and they vary in quality according to the quality of mental exercise, of which they are the natural accompaniment.

In accordance with the first statement, we speak of the pleasure of the senses, of the affections, of the intellect, of the imagination. In accordance with the second, we speak of the pleasures of the senses as lower than those of the intellect, and sensualism is a term of reproach applied to the indulgence of the appetites, in neglect of the restraints of understanding and conscience. As the active transcends the passive, so does the happiness of activity surpass in value all the pleasures which spring from mere sensibility. And, as among the active powers, some transcend others, the attendant pleasures are graduated accordingly.

Mr. John S. Mill has insisted, with peculiar felicity, on the diversity of quality among pleasures. It is one of his highest distinctions as an expounder of Utilitarianism and a leader of thought, that he has given prominence to the superior quality of some pleasures in comparison with others. Thus he has dwelt upon the important fact, that 'a being of higher faculties requires more to make him happy . . . than one of an inferior type.' So also he points to the fact that those equally capable of appreciating and enjoying all pleasures, 'give a most marked preference to the manner of existence which employs their higher faculties.'— *Util.* p. 12. This is admirable, both as indicating the relations of pleasures to the faculties employed, and the superior quality of the pleasure, according to the quality of the faculty in exercise.

7. Pleasure, as agreeable to our nature, is a common object of desire. Pain, as disagreeable to our nature, is a common object of dislike.

The natural desire of pleasure stimulates to the use of empowers, gives zest to their continued employment, and contributes largely to mental development, and to continuance in a life of activity.

The natural aversion to suffering acts as a check upon unnatural use of power, and warns of the danger which attends upon an unhealthy state or undue action of any power.

That pleasure is agreeable, and as such desirable, is simple matter of fact, and needs no proof. 'What proof is it possible to give that pleasure is good?'— *Util.* p. 6.

8. Passing now from pleasure and pain as forms of experience, to the capacities or faculties upon whose exercise they attend, it is evident that the experience of pleasure or pain is largely dependent on use of our own faculties, that is, upon our own actions. That the experience of either is altogether dependent on our own actions cannot be affirmed, for there are both pleasures and pains experienced which are not determined by our own acts. For example, the pleasure of a bracing atmosphere on a clear morning, and the depressing influence of a thick, damp atmosphere, on a dull morning. But, that our pleasure or pain is dependent mainly on the use of our faculties, is admitted.

9. Actions may be classified according as pleasure or pain attends upon them. They may be described as pleasurable or painful actions. That pleasurable actions are agreeable to the agent, and painful actions disagreeable, is only another mode of saying that pleasure is agreeable, pain the reverse. That pleasure may be described as good, and suffering as evil, is equally obvious, but no additional meaning is thereby conveyed. Good and evil cannot here be taken in a moral sense for we have no

evidence of the presence of anything more than the agreeable or disagreeable; and moral quality belongs to actions, whereas neither pleasure nor pain is a personal action.

10. In actions classified as pleasurable, the action is not identified with the pleasure, but the pleasure as a passive experience, attendant on the action, and dependent upon it, is often described as the consequence of the action. It is the consequent, not the subsequent. It is dependent upon the action for its existence, but does not follow after the action when it is past. On account of this relation between action and pleasure or pain, the theory of moral distinctions based upon it is named the Theory of Consequences.

11. Passing from actions which have an exclusively personal reference, to actions which affect the experience of others, these actions also may be classified according as they produce happiness or unhappiness to others. Such happiness or unhappiness on the part of others may be either the incidental and undesigned accompaniment of our action, or it may be the direct and designed result of our conduct. In the former case, the experience of others is an attendant result of our action. In the latter, the experience of others is the contemplated end of our action. If that end be the happiness of another, the motive is benevolent, the act is beneficent, the result is a definite amount of happiness to the person concerned. If the end contemplated be the unhappiness of another, the motive is malevolent, the act is injurious, the result is a definite amount of misery to the person concerned.

In this description of these actions, we simply extend the application of agreeable and disagreeable to the experience of another, which we take to be an experience analogous with our own, and in accordance with this application, we describe our motive and act, as wishing good or doing good, wishing evil or doing evil, understanding that the terms good and evil here mean nothing more than agreeable and disagreeable.

12. Contemplating these characteristics of actions as producing happiness or unhappiness to ourselves or others, it is maintained by the upholders of the Utilitarian Theory of Morals, that actions are morally right as they tend to produce happiness, morally wrong as they tend to produce unhappiness. It is thus the usefulness of actions in securing happiness that determines their

moral character. On this account the Theory is named Utilitarian. For the different senses in which the term Utilitarianism has been used, see Prof. Grote's *Exam. of the Utilitarian Philos.,* Cambridge, 1867.

This theory, which was formally promulgated among the ancients by Epicurus, has appeared in a variety of forms in modern times. These are given in successive paragraphs, as a guide not only to the history of the theory, but also to its criticism.

13. Hobbes (1588 — 1679), in making happiness the standard, applies the term to personal happiness. 'Whatsoever is the object of *any man's appetite* or desire, that is it which he for his part calleth good; and the object of his hate and aversion, evil; and of his contempt, vile and inconsiderable. For these words of good, evil, and contemptible, are ever used with relation to the person that useth them; there being nothing simply and absolutely so; nor any common rule of good and evil to be taken from the nature of the objects themselves; but from the person of the man, where there is no commonwealth; or, in a commonwealth, from the person of him that representeth it, or from an arbitrator or judge, whom men disagreeing shall by consent set up, and make his sentence the rule thereof . . . . Of good there be three kinds: good in the promise, that is, *pulchrum;* good in effect, as the end desired, which is called *jucundum,* delightful; and good as the means, which is called *utile,* profitable; and as many of evil; for evil in promise is that they call *turpe,* evil in effect and end, is *molestum,* unpleasant, troublesome; and evil in means, *inutile,* unprofitable, hurtful.'— *Leviathan* (1651), Part I. c. 6, Molesworth's ed., vol. iii. p. 41. With Hobbes, personal appetite is a sufficient guide; anything is good as it happens to be desired. 'There is no such *finus ultimus,* utmost aim, nor *summum bonum,* greatest good, as is spoken of in the books of the old moral philosophers.'— *Ib.* c. XI. iii. 85. In studying the system of Hobbes, it is important to turn to chapters 14 and 15, on 'Laws of Nature,' said to be 'found out by reason.'

14. Paley (1743 — 1805) gives a higher form to the same theory, introducing the benevolent element, and reference to the Deity. 'Virtue is the doing good to mankind, in obedience to the Will of God, and for the sake of everlasting happiness.

According to which definition, "the good of mankind" is the subject, "the will of God" the rule, and "everlasting happiness" the motive, of human virtue.'— *Moral and Political Philosophy,* c. VII. (1785.)

15. Jeremy Bentham (1747 — 1842) propounded the theory of 'The Greatest Happiness of the Greatest Number' as the end determining the rightness of actions. The phrase was first used by Priestley. 'Nature has placed Mankind under the government of two sovereign masters, pain and pleasure. It is for them alone to point out what we ought to do.'— *Introduction to the Principles of Morals and Legislation* (1789), I. I, Works, ed. by Bowring, I. I. 'By the principle of utility is meant, that principle which approves or disapproves of every action whatsoever, according to the tendency which it appears to have to augment or diminish the happiness of the party whose interest is in question.'— *Ib.* 1. 2. 'When an action . . . is supposed by a man to be conformable to the principle of utility, it may be convenient, for the purposes of discourse, to imagine a kind of law or dictate.'— *Ib.* 1. 8. 'Of an action that is conformable to the principle of utility, one may always say, either that it is one that ought to be done, or at least that it is not one that ought not to be done. One may say also, that it is right it should be done, at least that it is not wrong it should be done . . . . When thus interpreted, the words *ought* and *right . . .* have a meaning; when otherwise, they have none.'— *Ib.* I. 10. The theory is presented less guardedly,— almost recklessly,— in the posthumous work (1834) *Deontology,* vol. 1. pp. 17, 24, edited by Sir John Bowring.

16. Mr. John S. Mill accepts Utilitarianism under the form of universal benevolence. He has still further refined and elevated the theory by introducing the quality of pleasures as an element in determining what is right, and by laying down the rule that a higher is always to be preferred to a lower. This is now the accredited type of Utilitarianism. 'The theory of life on which this theory of morality is grounded is, that pleasure and freedom from pain are the only things desirable as ends.'— *Util.* p. 10. 'Some kinds of pleasure are more desirable and more valuable than others,' p. II. 'Of two pleasures, if there be one to which all, or almost all who have experience of both give a decided preference, irrespective of any feeling of moral

obligation, that is the more desirable pleasure,' p. 12. 'From this verdict of the only competent judges, I apprehend there can be no appeal,' p. 15. 'If they differ, that of the majority among them must be admitted as final,' p. 15. Such judges 'do give a most marked preference to the manner of existence which employs their higher faculties,' p. 12. 'The ultimate end, with reference to and for the sake of which all things are desirable (whether we are considering our own good, or that of other people), is an existence exempt, as far as possible, from pain, and as rich as possible in enjoyments, both in point of quantity and quality,' p. 17. 'This being, according to the utilitarian opinion, the end of human action, is necessarily also the standard of Morality,' p. 17.

17. The criticism of Utilitarianism implies two things, first, criticism of its theory of life, and secondly, of its theory of morals. Any adequate refutation of it must show that the theory which makes happiness the sole end of life is not a theory of human life, and thereafter that the tendency of an action to promote happiness does not determine the moral quality of that action.

The following recent criticisms of utilitarianism are particularly worthy of attention,— Grote's *Exam. of Utilit. Philos.;* Lecky's *European Morals,* chap. i.; M'Cosh's *Exam. of Mr. J. S. Mill's Philos.* ch. 20; Professor Blackie's *Four Phases of Morals;* and 'The Law of Nature,' in Professor Lorimer's *Institutes of Law* (Edinburgh, 1872).

18. The end or final object of any being is determined by the nature of the being itself. That end must be according to the capacities and faculties possessed. A being of lower power must have a lower end of life, a being with higher faculties must have a nobler end of life. Even if happiness were the end of all life, still would it be a distinct happiness in each case, according to the different possibilities of each form of life. In acknowledgment of this, Mr. J. S. Mill has successfully, and with keenness of feeling not unreasonable, repelled the current allegation that utilitarianism lowers men to the level of the swine. 'The comparison of the Epicurean life to that of beasts is felt as degrading, precisely because a beast's pleasures do not satisfy a human being's conceptions of happiness. Human beings have faculties more elevated than the animal appetites.'— *Util.* p. II.

19. In a complex form of existence each power has its own end to serve according to its own nature. The ramification of nerves provides for sensitiveness over the surface of the body; heart, arteries, and veins provide for the circulation of the blood. The eye is for seeing, the ear for hearing, and the intellect for acquiring knowledge.

20. Sensitive organism has for its end varied forms of sensibility or sensation, and the pleasurableness of the sensation, though not the end itself, is connected with the end. Thus what we describe as the pleasures of the senses may be said to be component parts of the end which the senses serve. Such pleasurable sensation may belong to the lower forms of animal life in which sensation follows sensation, while a 'conception of happiness' is impossible.

21. Of the 'faculties more elevated' which belong to man, each must serve a higher end, according to its own nature. The end of intelligence is knowledge; of memory, recollection; of will, self-direction; of affection, such as love or sympathy, the good of another. If the end of each power is in harmony with its own nature, Intelligence, Memory, Will, and Affection being entirely different in nature from Sensibility, cannot all have the same end. To say, for example, that sensibility and intellect have the same end, is to contradict the only rule by which the natural end of a power can be decided. It is to say that Passivity has the same end as Activity, which is practically to enunciate the contradiction that Passivity and Activity are the same.

22. While each power has its own end determined by its own nature, it is possible for an intelligent being to use any one of his powers, merely for the sake of the pleasure attending on its use, and not for its natural end. The possibility of this is restricted to an intelligent being capable of forming a conception of happiness, and contemplating the voluntary use of means for a selected end. The lower animals experience pleasure in accordance with laws of their nature, which operate irrespective of any control from the animals themselves. So it is with the laws of our sentient nature. But an entire revolution of being occurs where intelligent self-direction is possible. In a being thus endowed, powers are capable of being used according to the conceptions and purposes of the being himself. It thus becomes possible to use a power, not only for its natural end, but for other

and subordinate ends, and even, in some measure, for ends contrary to its nature. Thus forming a conception of pleasure as an end, we may seek this end in the use of any one of our powers. Each one of them has a distinct form of pleasure associated with its exercise; ascertaining this, and being able to determine the use of our powers, we can bring them into exercise for the sake of the pleasure attending upon their use. But when such a thing happens it is not under the law determining the natural use of the power, but by special determination of our own. We cannot change the nature of the power, or alter the end which it naturally serves, but we often voluntarily employ a power for the sake of the attendant pleasure, and not for its own natural end. This is done when we employ the intellect, not for the discovery of truth, but for the pleasure which attends on the search for truth; or, when we cherish sympathy, not for the sake of relieving the sufferer, but for the luxury of feeling which we experience.

23. If a general conception can be formed of the end or final object of our being, it must be by reference to the higher or governing powers of our nature, and as these are intellectual or rational, the end of our being is not pleasure, but the full and harmonious use of all our powers for the accomplishment of their own natural ends. These natural ends admit of a threefold classification. As concerned with our own being, it is the end of life to secure the development and forthputting of all its energies; with other beings, their development and performance of their life-work; and finally and transcendently, with the Absolute Being himself, devotion to Him as the source of our being and the ruler of our destiny.

24. If the theory which makes happiness the sole end of human life be proved erroneous, the theory of moral distinctions built upon it loses its foundation. The insufficiency of the Ethical theory may, however, be still further shown when tested by the special facts which it professes to explain. Certain actions are commonly distinguished as right actions, and others as wrong. Certain other actions are as commonly regarded as actions which do not fall under this twofold classification. This broad distinction of actions requires explanation under a professed ethical theory.

25. All actions producing happiness are not regarded as moral actions. Dinner-eating is not as much a moral action as truth-speaking. Hearing music, studying a fine picture, and encouraging a fellow-man in trouble, are not all alike spoken of under the designations of actions morally right, though they are confessedly pleasurable. All morally right actions are agreeable actions, but all agreeable actions are not moral actions. Happiness is thus wider than morality. By selecting too general a characteristic, the moral quality of actions has been missed. So also with utility, if that be preferred, as the mode of expressing the principle. 'Some limit must be assigned to the principle, for it is obvious that we do not make everything a moral rule that we consider useful.'— Bain's *Emotions and Will*, p. 273. Professor Bain explains the limitation by making morality a matter of authority. Morality is 'utility made compulsory.' This is a change from a stronger position to a weaker, and, only exposing the difficulty, does not solve it. If only some utility constitutes morality, utility itself is not the test. If Authority determines that some utility is right, we still want the ground on which the decision is given.

26. All actions producing pain are not morally wrong actions. To scratch your fingers on a thorn-bush, to submit to the humiliation of confessing that you have done wrong, and to refuse help to a friend in suffering, are all painful actions; but they are not on that account wrong actions. In all these cases, the end of the action is something else than the pain experienced. The pain is only the attendant upon the action, as in opposite cases pleasure is an attendant.

Though men seek pleasure for its own sake, they cannot seek pain for its own sake. The law of our nature which makes pleasure-seeking possible, makes pain-seeking impossible. There are no actions which have pain as their end. If, therefore, pleasure be the end of life, it is impossible to go against it, and the classification of certain actions as morally wrong altogether disappears.

Pain may be endured as a means to an end, even as a means for securing happiness. The pain of a surgical operation for the sake of health, the pain of self-denial for the sake of moral training, are examples. This fact makes a further inroad upon the theory. Moral evil cannot be used as a means of moral good. In making the production of happiness the test of right actions, and the production of pain the test of wrong actions, moral distinctions are hopelessly confused, and even immoral men may gain a reputation for goodness.— See Plato's *Gorgias*, 499. That the painful may lead to the pleasurable, is proof that pleasure and pain are not by their own nature ends in themselves, but simply attendants on personal action. Of contraries, the one cannot produce the other.

27. A general rule of moral conduct cannot be founded on the distinction of quality amongst pleasures. As each power of our nature has its own natural end and its own attendant pleasure, it is impossible to determine the appropriate exercise for each power on the rule that a higher pleasure is always to be preferred to a lower. The lower powers, having their own natural ends, must have their appropriate exercise.

28. A general rule of moral conduct cannot rest upon a conception of the aggregate of pleasures available for man as an individual. Such a calculation of consequences is too perplexing to admit of certainty in our decisions, or application to the details of individual life. 'The good or evil effect of an action dependeth on the foresight of a long chain of consequences, of which very seldom any man is able to see the end.'— Hobbes's *Leviathan*, Pt. I. c. 6. Kant urges this difficulty, *Metaphysic of Ethics*, p. 10.

A wider generality still belongs to Utilitarianism when it makes the rightness of actions depend upon their tendency to promote the greatest happiness of the greatest number. The definition which might suffice to describe the end of true benevolence is impracticable as a statement of the universal rule of conduct. This generality must, however, be held as restricted to the happiness of the greatest number, which, on reasonable calculation, may be influenced by individual action. Anything wider is not essential to the system, for, as Mr. J. S. Mill says, 'It is a misapprehension of the utilitarian mode of thought to conceive it as implying that people should fix their minds upon so wide a generality as the world or society at large.'— *Util.* p. 27.

Apart, however, from the perplexity of attempting to use the rule, the method here taken for reaching a rule of life is unsuitable. Moral life, in harmony with all analogy, is a unity having consistency in all its parts. It therefore implies the exercise of a variety of powers, each one of which must have a law for its own guidance, rendering it impossible to reduce the laws of conduct to the simplicity of a single maxim. If unity be attainable, it is only in the general affirmation of the rightness of using our natural powers. The aggregate of pleasures can no more afford a definite rule of conduct than the aggregate of powers could decide a single line of action. As well attribute respiration, circulation, and nerve-energy to a single bodily organ.

29. A theory of benevolence is logically unattainable under a utilitarian system. Since Bentham's time, Utilitarianism has given prominence to benevolence, making 'The greatest happiness of the greatest number' its standard of rectitude. But in this it has amended its ethical form only by the sacrifice of logical consistency. If happiness is the sole end of life, it must be the happiness of that life to which it is the end. To make the happiness of others the end of individual life, is to leave the utilitarian basis, by deserting the theory of life on which it rests. Utilitarianism is in the very singular position of professing itself a theory of universal benevolence, and yet laying its foundations on the ground that personal happiness is the sole end of life. As long as it maintains that 'pleasure and freedom from pain are the only things desirable as ends,' the maxim must mean that these are the only things desirable as ends for each individual, and here its Moral Philosophy must end. To do good to others for the sake of our own happiness, is, however, compatible with the theory; but this is not benevolence, and whatever honour belongs to the propounder of such a theory may be fairly claimed for Hobbes.

30. To appeal to Civil or Social authority for the ground of moral distinctions is to confess the failure of Utilitarianism as a philosophy of morals. 'Morality is an Institution of Society, maintained by the authority and Punishments of Society.'— Bain's *Emotions and Will,* p. 257. If actions producing happiness or unhappiness, include more than actions regarded as right and wrong; actions punished by Society include less. This form of the theory puts 'positive good deeds and self-sacrifice' beyond 'the region of morality proper.'— *Ib.* p. 292. Utilitarianism is thus reduced to a mere fragment of an ethical theory. Besides, in this form Utilitarianism loses a philosophical basis for the fragment of a theory which is retained. It rests only on authority,

without a reason for 'moral enactments,' which are made to rest only on the votes of the majority. If it attempt a reason for its enactments, it falls back upon utility, which it nevertheless confesses to be too wide for its purpose. If it seek to explain why all utility is not enforced, it introduces the claims of 'individual liberty,' and thus points to rights superior to its own account of morality. And by trusting to the majority as the source of 'moral enactments,' it is reduced to the necessity of maintaining, either that no law is unjust, or that an unjust law is a constituent part of morality.

31. PROBLEMS.— (1.) How far can the agreeable in experience be shown to coincide with the right in action, and in what respects are they separated? (2.) Distinguish the desirable from the right. (3.) Take collectively the pleasures of scientific research, of truthfulness, of making money, and of paying debts, and ascertain how far the moral character of the actions is determined by the quantity and quality of pleasure experienced. (4.) How do the pleasure of self-approval, and the pain of self-condemnation, stand related to the ground of moral distinctions given by Utilitarianism? (5.) Distinguish between the functions of self-government and of civil government. (6.) Test the following: — 'The common dislike to utility, as the standard, resolves itself into a sentimental preference, amounting to the abnegation of reason in human life.'— Bain's *Emotions and Will*, p. 275.

CHAPTER III
CONSCIENCE
(UTILITARIAN THEORY)

1. The Utilitarian Theory, in making the criterion of right consist in a tendency to promote happiness, does not admit the need for a Moral faculty, as a power by which moral distinctions are recognised. The element of knowledge being allowed to fall out, the aim has been to account for the authority usually attributed to Conscience. It is admitted that a peculiar sacredness is commonly attached to moral distinctions, and a theory of the development of Conscience is constructed with the view of explaining this fact. Generally, under this theory, Conscience is represented as a form of Feeling, involving reverence for moral

distinctions, and impelling to their observance. Sometimes Conscience has been regarded rather as a restraining force, involving 'a pain more or less intense, attendant on violation of duty.'

On account of the view thus taken of the functions of this power, it is commonly named by Utilitarians, 'The Moral Sense.' This name has thus an entirely different meaning from that intended by Shaftesbury and Hutcheson, with whom Moral Sense was a power of Perception.

2. A theory of Conscience, in harmony with a development theory of Mind, has been propounded by Hartley, *Observations*, I. iv. 6.; and by Mr. James Mill, *Fragment on Mackintosh* (anonymous, 1835), p. 259; but most fully and definitely by Professor Bain, *Emotions and Will*, p. 283, and *Mental and Moral Science*, ETHICS, chap. III. The theory in its latest form is most deserving of attention.

3. Professor Bain's Theory of Conscience is the following: — 'Conscience is an imitation within ourselves of the government without us.' The proof of this is found, 'in observing the growth of Conscience from childhood upwards,' and 'its character and working generally.' 'The first lesson that a child learns as a moral agent is obedience . . . . The child's susceptibility to pleasure and pain is made use of to bring about this obedience, and a mental association is rapidly formed between disobedience and apprehended pain, more or less magnified by fear. The feeling of encountering certain pain' (both physical and moral) 'is the first motive power of an ethical kind that can be traced in the mental system of childhood.' . . . 'A sentiment of love or respect towards the person of the superior infuses a different species of dread,' which is 'sometimes a more powerful deterring impulse than the other.' . . . 'When the young mind is able to take notice of the use and meaning of the prohibitions imposed upon it, and to approve of the end intended by them, a new motive is added, and the Conscience is then a triple compound, and begirds the actions in question with a threefold fear.'— *Emotions and Will*, pp. 283 — 6.

4. The philosophic thought of Germany has for the most part been separated from the Sensational or Development Theory. Some few of the more recent writers, however, have embraced it. Of these, Schopenhauer may be taken as an

example. He was born in Danzig, and was Professor of Philosophy (Privatdocent) in Berlin, and afterwards in Frankfurt-on-the-Maine, where he died in 1860. After saying that many would be surprised if they knew of what their Conscience is composed, he suggests that the elements may be computed thus — 'one fifth, fear of man; one fifth, superstition; one fifth, prejudice; one fifth, vanity; one fifth, custom.'— *Die beiden Grundprobleme der Ethik,* 1st ed., Frankfurt am Main, 1841, p. 196, 2d ed., Leipzig, 1860.

5. Such descriptions as those of the two preceding paragraphs may be allowed to contain a considerable measure of truth, the first bearing on associations commonly attendant on the moral training of early life, and the second on the heterogeneous combination of motives which often sway men, when they profess to have the approval of Conscience for their conduct. But both fail to provide a theory of Conscience, as a power authoritative for self-guidance, and even supreme in authority, as Conscience is generally allowed to be. Either there must be a power discovering a sovereign law of conduct; or, the reality of Conscience must be denied.

6. Schopenhauer gives only a gathering of unreasonable and unworthy motives which may operate within the mind of one who fancies himself doing right. That such a combination may exist, under shelter of an appeal to Conscience, and with some degree of support from the moral sentiments, will be generally admitted. But when Schopenhauer grants that men thus swayed would be surprised were the true analysis of their motives presented to them, he practically admits that no one could imagine such a state of mind entitled to be regarded as a genuine exercise of Conscience.

7. Professor Bain's treatment of the question is altogether more interesting, as more obviously facing the difficulties connected with development of a power such as Conscience. The solution proposed has, moreover, the advantage of logical consistency with the phase of Utilitarianism adopted, according to which utility enforced by punishment is the test of morality. On the other hand, it suffers from being manifestly out of harmony with the broader and more attractive basis, according to which the tendency to produce happiness is the ground of moral excellence in human conduct. Professor Bain gains the element

of authority, but only by the surrender of a large part of the territory of morals. Still more to its disadvantage is the consideration, that an internal authority which is only an imitation of external government, has not the evidence of its truth in its own nature, but depends upon the sufficiency of the warrant for the external authority to which it appeals.

8. As a history of early experience, the theory in its first part accounts only for training in obedience, as an enforced necessity. It points only to the use which parents can make of certain 'primitive impulses of the mind,' such as fear, love, and prudence, in order to secure obedience. But it ignores the fact, that at a very early stage children distinguish as to lightness and wrongness in the commands issued. There are some commands which children resent as unjust, and which they are forced to obey only at the cost of injury to their nature. If this discrimination be possible on the part of children, it is clear that something more is required for their training than force and fear.

9. The full strain falls upon the third stage in the alleged development of Conscience, 'when the young mind is able to take notice of the use and meaning of the prohibitions imposed upon it, and to approve of the end intended by them.' What Professor Bain has said in reference to an *a priori* theory, holds with equal force here,— 'There can be no such thing as a standard overriding the judgment of every separate intelligence.'— *Emotions*, p. 262. Human thought cannot be kept in continual subjection to authority. To accept as right what we have been always commanded, or accustomed to do, is continued childhood. Every separate intelligence must find sufficient reason for accounting certain actions right, and others wrong. This cannot be found either in the authority of parents or in past practice. It must be recognised by personal intelligence, on evidence either of fact or principle. It is certainly true, as Dr. Bain says, that, 'wherever an agreement is come to by a large or ascendant party, there is a natural tendency to compel the rest to fall in with that.' But so much the more obvious is it, that every man must seek a standard satisfying to his own Reason, and act upon that. This Dr. Bain practically admits in the quotation last given, and Mr. Mill has powerfully argued for such unrestrained freedom of thought, in his work on *'Liberty.'* Such a standard, if

found, may lead to a doctrine of righteous disobedience to external authority, and a reversal of earlier practice.

10. The theory must fall back on utility as the basis of personal assent to moral distinctions, and in doing so it owns the failure of its attempt to develop Conscience by means of authority. Either 'every separate intelligence' must find for itself a law of nature, marking off some actions as right, others as wrong, or it must continue under the trammels of authority. If the former, the failure is admitted; if the latter, the escape is not effected. Professor Bain admits that 'the grand difficulty' is to account for 'the self-formed or independent conscience,' 'where the individual is a law to himself.' 'But,' he adds, 'there is nothing very formidable in this apparent contradiction,' 'when the young mind is sufficiently advanced to be able to appreciate the motives, the utilities, or the sentiment that led to their imposition — the character of the conscience is entirely transformed; the motive power issues from a different quarter of the mental framework. Regard is now had to the intent and meaning of the law, and not to the mere fact of its being prescribed by some power.'— *Emotions,* p. 288. The difficulty here seems much more formidable than Professor Bain allows. The situation of the theory is briefly this,— Utility is the basis of moral distinctions; but some limit must be assigned to the principle, for we do not make everything a moral rule that we consider useful. Utility made compulsory is the standard of morality; Morality is thus an institution of society; Conscience is an imitation of the Government of society; Conscience is first fear of authority, and then respect for it; but, 'even in the most unanimous notions of mankind, there can be no such thing as a standard overriding the judgment of every separate intelligence;' the individual must therefore emancipate himself from authority, in order to be 'a law to himself;' to this end he must recognise the intent and meaning of the law; for this purpose he must fall back on Utility. It is not, however, all utility, but only Utility made compulsory, which affords the basis of morals, and it is Society which determines what shall be made compulsory. How can every separate intelligence emancipate itself? How can it find to its own satisfaction a rule of life so essentially superior to the authority of Society, as to warrant independent action in opposition to the teaching of Society?

CHAPTER IV
DUTY OR OBLIGATION
(UTILITARIAN THEORY)

1. On a Utilitarian Theory, the problem concerning moral obligation wears this form:— If tendency to produce happiness determine the rightness of an action, how can we rise above the agreeable and desirable to find philosophic warrant for a doctrine of personal obligation? Utilitarianism meets its last and severest test in the attempt to distinguish between the desirable, which is the optional; and the dutiful, which is the imperative.

2. That happiness is by our nature desirable, is a fact which neither constitutes a law of personal obligation, nor obviates the necessity for having one. It cannot constitute a law of action, for the desirable has power only to attract, not to command. Besides, the desirable may often be the unattainable. The dutiful is not only the possible, but the binding. Neither can the desirability of happiness obviate the necessity for a law of obligation in the guidance of life. All pleasures are desirable, but all cannot be enjoyed at once; of pleasures, some are higher in quality, some lower, but the higher cannot always be preferred to the lower, therefore the quality of pleasure does not of itself afford a sufficient rule for selection. If man must sometimes surrender a higher enjoyment for a lower, and yet rigidly restrict lower pleasures for the sake of higher attainment and action, we need to discover the ground of these necessities. Analysis discovers a *physical necessity,* since man must eat, as well as think; rest, as well as work; and an *intellectual necessity,* since man must concentrate his attention in order successfully to guide his efforts, and must therefore do some things, and leave others unattempted; but, within the possibilities of human effort, there is still another necessity, since of the things which a man can do, he recognises some as binding upon him in a sense in which others are not, and this is *moral necessity.* If, to perform the high functions of his life, he must deny himself some pleasures; and if, as a member of society, he must surrender his own pleasure for the good of others, there is a law of Self-denial and there is a law of Benevolence. Utilitarianism must, therefore, supply a basis of obligation in order to make good its claims as a Philosophy of Morals.

3. The extreme difficulty of discovering a basis for moral obligation under this theory has led to great diversity of opinion among its upholders. Bentham makes the cleanest cut through the difficulty by simply denying that there is such a thing as duty. 'It is, in fact, very idle to talk about duties; the word itself has in it something disagreeable and repulsive.'— *Deontology,* ι. 10. 'The talisman of arrogance, indolence, and ignorance, is to be found in a single word, an authoritative imposture . . . . It is the word "ought," "ought or ought not," as circumstances may be . . . . If the use of the word be admissible at all, it "ought" to be banished from the vocabulary of morals.'— *Ib.* pp. 31, 32. And yet, he has not advanced thirty pages, before we find the following,— 'Every pleasure is *prima facie good,* and ought to be pursued. Every pain is a *prima facie* evil, and ought to be avoided.'— *Ib.* p. 59. This posthumous work — *Deontology* — is so unguarded as to warrant the opinion that Bentham's memory would have been more honoured by withholding it from publication.

4. Mr. Charles Darwin attempts to surmount the difficulty by reducing its dimensions. 'The imperious word *ought* seems merely to imply the consciousness of the existence of a persistent instinct, either innate or partly acquired, serving him (man) as a guide, though liable to be disobeyed. We hardly use the word *ought* in a metaphorical sense when we say hounds ought to hunt, pointers to point, and retrievers to retrieve their game. If they fail thus to act, they fail in their duty, and act wrongly.'— *The Descent of Man,*— 'Moral Sense,' I. p. 92. The quotation is preceded by these words,— 'Thus at last man comes to feel, through acquired and perhaps inherited habit, that it is best for him to obey his more persistent instincts.' And this quotation is preceded, two pages earlier, by these words,— 'The wish for another man's property is, perhaps, as persistent a desire as any that can be named,' I. p. 90. Neither a good morality nor a doctrine of personal obligation can rest on this basis.

5. Professor Bain meets the difficulty by making external authority the source of personal obligation, and restricting obligation to 'the class of actions enforced by the sanction of punishment.'— *Emotions,* p. 254. This, at one sweep, cuts off from the area of personal obligation the whole class of right actions. 'When a man does his duty, he escapes punishment; to

assert anything more is to obliterate the radical distinction between duty and merit.'— *Emotions,* p. 292. On the contrary, to assert the duty of right actions is to preserve this distinction, for duty binds to the performance of an action, merit belongs to the person on account of having fulfilled his duty. But to restrict moral obligation to the avoidance of wrong actions,— to say that it involves only restraint upon mean and cruel deeds, but does not make noble and beneficent deeds binding upon men,— is to give up the grandest part of morality, and to confess failure at a vital point in the theory. For a Utilitarian theory there is the further disadvantage of a surrender of its claims as a theory of benevolence,— in this form it ceases to be a theory inculcating 'the greatest happiness of the greatest number.' But even within the restricted area the theory fails to establish a doctrine of moral obligation. It only points out how evil deeds are restrained by society, not why a man ought to refrain from such actions. If to escape this difficulty we fall back upon utility, everything in the form of obligation is lost, since that which is to be explained is the selection of some utilities as those which are to be enforced.

6. The fullest appreciation of the difficulty is to be found in Mr. John S. Mill's *Utilitarianism.* He keeps strictly to the view which recognises the foundation of morals in the tendency of actions to promote happiness, holds to the benevolent interpretation of the theory, and finds no limitation of it, except that afforded by the quantity and quality of pleasures. He therefore shuns the reference to external authority as the source of obligations. His nearest approach to it, is the acknowledgment that the question as to the comparative excellence of pleasures is to be decided by the votes of competent judges, from whose decision there can be no appeal, p. 15. But he does not elevate such judges into the position of authorities determining personal obligation. They are only competent witnesses recording the results of their experience.

7. Mr. Mill complicates the question of Obligation by his mode of stating it. He says, 'The question is often asked, and properly so, in regard to any supposed moral standard, What is its sanction? What are the motives to obey it, or, more specifically, what is the source of its obligation? Whence does it derive its binding force? It is a necessary part of moral philosophy to provide the answer to this question.'— Chap. iii.

p. 39. The more specific statement is exact, but the two earlier forms of the question apply to topics quite distinct. Sanction and Motive are both essentially different from Obligation. *Sanction* is a confirmation of the moral character of an action, which follows it in experience. *Motive* is that which induces or impels a man to do an action, whether that action be right or wrong. Both of these belong to moral philosophy, but not to that part of it now engaging attention. *Obligation* is the binding of a moral agent to do that which is right, whether he incline or not; and to refrain from doing a wrong action, however much he incline to do it. The question is, Can a standard of Happiness have the binding force of moral law? Happiness is agreeable; to secure it is desirable; but how is it dutiful or binding on me to seek it for myself, or to promote the happiness of others even at the sacrifice of my own?

8. Mr. Mill finds 'the source of obligation' in personal feeling. The following are the most definite statements: 'The ultimate sanction of all morality is a subjective feeling in our mind,' p. 42; 'The internal sanction of duty, whatever our standard of duty may be, is one and the same,— a feeling in our own mind, a pain, more or less intense, attendant on a violation of duty,' p. 41; 'This feeling, when disinterested and connecting itself with the pure idea of duty, and not with some particular form of it, or with any of the merely accessory circumstances, is the essence of Conscience,' pp. 41 — 2. It is unfortunate that the term *Sanction* is the one employed in these passages. That such a pain as that described is a sanction of morality is uniformly admitted. But it is not admitted that 'the source of obligation' can be found in anything personal, far less that it can be identified with this sanction.

Looking at the merits of the theory, it is worthy of notice that in seeking an internal source of Obligation, Mr. Mill selects Pain; as in seeking an external source, Dr. Bain selects Punishment. Both point to restraint on wrong actions.

The statement that 'the internal sanction . . . is a pain attendant on violation of duty,' presupposes a doctrine of duty, but does not supply it. The knowledge of duty cannot originate out of a pain which is consequent on violating our duty. Still less can duty itself originate from such a source. The knowledge of duty, and painful feeling because of neglect of duty, are so different, that the one is knowledge of binding force as to what is to be done; the other is experience of disturbing force consequent upon what has been done. The question, therefore, remains, what is 'the pure idea of duty' connected with this feeling? 'Binding force' over a person must come from a source superior to the person. If so, it cannot come from his own feeling, nor even from his own knowledge. The knowledge of obligation must be knowledge of 'binding force,' applying to him, as one subject to moral law. Obligation must be a condition of the life of a moral being, even though unacknowledged by the man himself.

9. Identification of Obligation with 'the conscientious feelings of mankind,' involves the serious difficulty of admitting that those who have no such feelings thereby escape obligation. This difficulty is met by Mr. Mill in the following manner: — 'Undoubtedly this sanction has no binding efficacy in those who do not possess the feelings it appeals to; but neither will these persons be more obedient to any other moral principle than to the utilitarian one,' pp. 42, 43. This defence of Utilitarianism is unavailing, because of the essential difference between obligation and obedience. The transition from binding authority to binding efficacy, shifts attention to a new subject, and leaves the difficulty standing. Obligation is requirement of obedience; Obedience is acknowledgment of obligation. The real difficulty is in answering this question,— If a man do not acknowledge or feel his obligation, is he on that account free from obligation? To answer in the affirmative is to admit that Utilitarianism is incapable of attaining a doctrine of moral obligation. A man who has no conscientious feelings to restrain him from telling falsehoods, is not thereby released from obligation to the law of truthfulness.

10. The theory which makes 'the greatest happiness of the greatest number' the test of moral action, loses all its value, if it be without a scientific basis for moral obligation. If there be one thing which specially commends the theory to our admiration, it is the aspect of universal benevolence which it wears. But, in order to be accepted as a sound theory of Benevolence, it must establish on a philosophic basis a doctrine of unvarying obligation to act benevolently. Mr. Mill puts the question thus,— 'Why am I bound to promote the general happiness? If my own happiness lies in something else, why may I not give that the

preference?' Mr. Mill answers, 'If the view adopted by the utilitarian philosophy of the nature of the moral sense be correct, this difficulty will always present itself, until the influences which form moral character have taken the same hold of the principle which they have taken of some of the consequences — until, by the improvement of education, the feeling of unity with our fellow-creatures shall be (what it cannot be doubted that Christ intended it to be) as deeply rooted in our character, and to our consciousness as completely a part of our nature, as the horror of crime is in an ordinarily well-brought-up young person,' p. 40. This is an admirable passage. But it fails to meet the scientific demands upon an Ethical Theory. It concerns obedience, not obligation; and vividly portrays the need for renovation of nature before the law of benevolence can become the general rule of life among us. But the difficulty of attaining uniform consistent benevolence in practice is not the subject engaging attention. The philosophic difficulty of constructing a theory of morals is one thing; the practical difficulty of rendering uniform obedience to the requirements of morality is quite another thing. Doubtless, it is beyond the power of Moral Philosophy to make men obey the law; but it is the part of Moral Philosophy to show that there is a moral law to be obeyed. Mr. Mill's answer is insufficient because of the wide separation between theory and practice. That the practical difficulty of personal conformity with the law of benevolence 'will always be felt until the influences which form moral character have taken hold of the principle' is certain. But the question is, what obligation rests on the person who would form his character aright, to accept this principle of benevolence as the rule of conduct? It is certain that Christ intended the feeling of unity with our fellow-creatures to be deeply rooted in our character; but it is no less certain that in order to secure the fulfilment of his intention, Christ proclaimed the principle of benevolence as a law for Humanity. And, in order to establish a philosophy of benevolence, Moral Philosophy must show that the principle of benevolence is a law of natural obligation. If we are to escape the admission that Selfishness is dutiful, we must pass Mr. Darwin's view, that persistent desire is the ground of obligation. If we are to maintain that morality requires a man to keep his promise, even though he is not forced to do so, we must pass Professor

Bain's view, that external authority is the source of duty. And now, if we are to avoid the position, that a man is freed from obligation by simply disowning it, we must pass Mr. Mill's view, that personal feeling is the source of obligation. Has, then, Utilitarianism no answer to the question, What is the source of Obligation? 'Why am I bound to promote the general happiness?' Must Philosophy, before attempting an answer, wait until the improvement of education has rooted in the character of all men a feeling of unity with their fellow-creatures? If so, on what ground must education proceed? On Prudence, which means only Self-interest? or on Natural Law? The Intuitional Theory gives its answer thus,— The standard of morals has in itself the authority of law, binding on every intelligence capable of understanding and applying it. A man cannot live and escape obligation, however much he violate it. But, the standard of Happiness cannot be the standard of morals, because the agreeable, or desirable, does not in itself possess 'binding force' to determine the action of moral beings.

PART II
IMPULSES AND RESTRAINTS
BELONGING TO THE NATURE OF
MAN

CHAPTER I
IMPULSES TO ACTION

1. There are certain forces belonging to human nature which so operate as to impel us to act. By means of these Impulses, activity is made a law of our nature.

2. These Impulses have been denominated 'principles of action,' 'motives,' 'active powers,' and 'springs of action.' 'Principle,' signifying a commencement, may apply to the origin of activity, as well as of knowledge; but it is better that it be kept for the latter application, and it is so reserved here. 'Motive' is ambiguous, being applied to external objects which attract, as well as to internal forces which impel. 'Active Powers,' the favourite title of Reid and Stewart, does not adequately discriminate these forces from the intellectual powers.

3. Some Impulses belong to our physical nature, and are experienced by us in common with the lower animals. They are not acquired, but are essential conditions of animal existence, concerned with the support of the physical frame and the continuance of the race. They are hunger, thirst, and sex. In these, appears man's affinity of nature with the brutes. These Impulses are commonly named Appetites. In a rational nature, they are warrantably gratified only in accordance with an intelligent regard to their appointed ends. Deflection from this is surrender of rational self-government, and assimilation to brute life.

4. The larger number of Impulses are of a superior order, as is shown by their dependence upon intelligence for their rise in consciousness.

5. Various forms of classification have been proposed. Dr. Reid gives a threefold division,— mechanical, animal, and rational.— *Active Powers*, III. i. I. This is a mixed division, as mechanical impulses are animal. It has been objected to by Stewart *(Philos. of Act. and Mor. Powers,* Intro.), who classifies

thus: — Appetites, Desires, Affections, Self-love, the Moral Faculty. Dr. Thomas Brown arranges by reference to their relation to time, Immediate, Retrospective, and Prospective.— *Lect.* 52. For Professor Bain's classification, v. *Emotions and Will,* chap. II.

6. Difference of psychological nature among the Impulses affords a philosophic ground of classification. On this basis Impulses may be divided into three classes,— Desires, Affections, and Judgments;— craving powers, giving powers, and persuading powers. These indicate respectively, the emptiness of our nature, the fulness of our nature, and power of discrimination in our nature for self-guidance. All these forms of impulse may be blended in a single mental state, but they cannot be merged in each other, or lose their distinctive features.

7. DESIRE is craving,— a force impelling us to draw into our possession what is fitted to give satisfaction. It primarily affords evidence that our nature is not self-sufficient. Every desire involves three things,— (1.) consciousness of want; (2.) consequent restlessness of nature; and (3.) longing for satisfaction. These three particulars indicate the origin, attendant sensibility, and essential characteristic of the impulse so denominated. Appetites are a class of desires, belonging to physical existence. They are distinguished from other desires, as being periodical, and becoming quiescent by means of satisfaction. Mental Desires are continuous in exercise, seek continuity of gratification, and are dependent upon some degree of intelligence for their exercise. Stewart distinguishes the following mental desires,— Desire of knowledge, of society, of esteem, of power. *(Outlines of Mor. Phil.)* Though the Desires seek self-satisfaction in contrast with the satisfaction of others, they are not selfish, that is, do not seek their end by the injury of others. Where selfishness appears there is unnatural desire, associated with the natural or normal. Our Desires are the forces which specially expose us to the risk of selfishness. On this account, every exercise of desire calls for rigid application of self-government.

8. Affection is inclination towards others, disposing us to give from our own resources what may influence them either for good or ill. In practical tendency, the Affections are the reverse of the Desires. Desires absorb; Affections give out. Affections

presuppose a recognition of certain qualities in persons, and, in a modified degree, in lower sentient beings, but not in things, for the exercise of affection presupposes in the object of it the possibility either of harmony or antagonism of feeling. Affections take the form of Love or Hate (Antipathy), according as the objects of them are esteemed, in any sense, good or bad; and the form of Reverence or Pity, according as the object is esteemed either superior or inferior in nature and experience. Desires invariably seek what is accounted a personal gain. But affections are of two classes, seeking either the benefit or the restraint of others. In the latter class, affections have an element of self-protection, which is of great moral significance.

9. Judgments of two distinct classes take rank as impulses, namely, Judgments of Prudence, concerned with self-interest or expediency; and Judgments of Rectitude, concerned with rightness in actions and dispositions, leading to judgments of obligation and responsibility.

For the difference between these two classes of judgments, as impulses to actions, see Reid's *Act. Powers*, III. 3. That Conscience performs the function of what the Scotch School have called 'Active Powers,' is commonly held; but, on any theory, this is possible only by means of a judgment bearing on present circumstances.

Judgments do not simply and of themselves perform the function of impulse, but these two classes of judgments have associated with them certain dispositions whose impelling force operates with the judgments. These dispositions are, desire of personal advantage (often called, self-love) with expectation or hope, and reverence for moral law, with devotion to the Deity as Moral Governor. Without the judgments, the attendant dispositions are not experienced. The judgments, therefore, are properly regarded as the origin of impelling force. On the other hand, without the attendant disposition, the judgments would fail to perform the part of an impulse. The presence of these dispositions depends not upon the circumstances in which a man is placed, but upon the degree of intellectual energy bestowed upon the question how far duty or interest is involved. This, therefore, establishes the intellectual origin of the impulse. Kant's *Metaph. of Ethics*, p. 60, and p. 120. It is at this point that there lies the explanation of what appears the singular utterance of Mr. Mill, in objecting to the saying 'that my conscience prevails over my desires,' when he adds,— 'as if conscience were not itself a desire — the desire to do right.'— *Exam.* p. 567.

10. All these impelling forces are original powers of our nature, not to be accounted for by any process of development. Desires and Affections, as inferior to Judgments, may be said to lie in the line between sensation and intelligence. Yet, so far are they from being stages of development towards intelligence or intermediate forces by means of which intellect may be evolved, that physical desires are dependent on our organism, while mental desires presuppose intelligence as the condition of their experience. Neither continuance of a particular feeling nor growing intensity of it, nor combination of various feelings can account for Desires or Affections.

11. Problems.— (1.) Granting that Judgments are formal expressions of Truth, can they be at the same time Impulses to action? (2.) If a Moral judgment awaken reverence for moral law, is the judgment in that case the spring of action, or the reverence, or both together? (3.) Granting that some judgments are impulses to action, should judgments of obligation, when viewed in this relation, be held to constitute a class distinct from judgments of rightness?

CHAPTER II
ETHICAL CLASSIFICATION OF NATURAL IMPULSES

1. As Moral Philosophy is concerned with moral action, it must afford an explanation of the origin of our actions, as well as of our knowledge of their moral quality. It must determine the Ethical value and relations of the Natural Impulses.

2. Impulses to action must themselves be active. In so far as they come under control of the Will (v. *infra.* Part III.), their exercise may possess moral quality, that is, may come under regulation of Conscience.

3. As Desires and Affections may spring into exercise irrespective of control of the Will (v. Part III.), they may be, in their rise, mere natural forces, possessed of no moral quality. Desires, craving self-satisfaction, are not in themselves selfish, affections, inclining towards the good of others, are not in

themselves benevolent; affections, inclining towards resistance of others, are not in themselves malevolent.

4. A Desire or Affection which is merely natural, and not moral, in its rise, thereafter takes rank as a moral action, since its continuance depends on the Will, and is liable to the application of moral principle. Desire which is not in itself selfish, may become so in its indulgence; affection not in itself benevolent, may wear this moral character in its exercise; such affection as hate, which is not in itself malevolent, may become so in the manner of its operation.

5. A Judgment of expediency, regarded merely as a proposition, has no moral quality; but, when accepted as an impulse to action, stimulating the desire of personal advantage, it immediately comes under the dominion of moral law. Thus a judgment of expediency may assume the form of an impulse to neglect or to transgress moral law, in which case it is itself wrong, and the consequent action must wear a similar character.

6. A moral judgment, regarded merely as a proposition affirming the application of moral law, has in itself no moral quality; but, regarded as an impulse capable of awakening reverence for the law, and devotion to the Lawgiver, it is not only morally right, but is the only Impulse which, from its very nature, is necessarily right, requiring reference to nothing beyond itself for its warrant. In order, however, that a judgment may legitimately be credited with this warrant, it must be recognised as involving an application of pure moral law. See p. 28, sec. 12.

7. By reason of the sovereignty of Moral Law, and the distinctive character of the Moral Judgment as an impulse to action, all other impulses are morally subordinate to the Moral Judgment, which alone among the impulses has uniform, unquestionable title to sway the conduct.

8. The Natural Desires and Affections, as Natural Impulses, are dependent upon a moral judgment for the determination of the moral quality of their exercise, in respect of the circumstances and degree in which they influence our conduct.

9. Amongst the subordinate Natural Impulses, Affections occupy a position superior to desires, when both are regarded from a moral point of view. This Ethical superiority rests primarily on a natural superiority, but ultimately on the fact that

moral principle demands self-denial in submission to its authority, which imposes more restraint upon desires than upon affections. In practice, Self-denial is only the negative result attending on the acknowledgment of the supremacy of moral law. It is restraint in one direction, consequent upon activity demanded in another.

10. Problems.— (1.) Is Hate not by its nature malevolent? (2.) If Hate is not in itself malevolent, by what addition is it turned into a malicious force? (3.) Granting that Desire is inferior to affection, if a desire be a natural attendant on an affection, does the former in that case take equal ethical rank with the latter?

CHAPTER III
RESTRAINTS UPON ACTION

1. Diversity of character among our natural impulses, in itself implies restraint upon some of the number, in order to action of others. The most obvious examples are found in the contrary affections — Love and Hate, Reverence and Pity. A further restraint is involved in the subordination of impulses to moral law.

2. Besides the restraint upon activity, arising (1.) from the natural laws of exercise, and (2.) from the application of moral law, there are certain natural forces whose primary, though not exclusive, function it is to restrain from action. These are Emotions, of which the chief are Wonder, Grief, and Fear.

3. Emotion is agitation of feeling, attended by more or less physical disturbance, and always implies a sense of weakness. The Emotions, in common with the Impulses, imply movement of our inner nature; but Desires and Affections are movements towards their objects. Emotions are movements from their objects.

4. Their restraining power is experienced with great diversity of degree, and at their height they attain an overwhelming force, paralysing the other energies.

5. Emotions, like desires, are concerned with Self, and are marks of the weakness of our nature. But they differ completely in function, the Desires craving satisfaction, the Emotions shunning injury.

6. The Emotions are in close relation with Intelligence. Fear, the lowest of them all, may be experienced in some form by every sentient creature, but in its higher forms it is dependent on the exercise of intelligence. If the lower animals are often subjects of fear from which man is delivered by his intelligence, it is no less true that the animals escape many forms of fear to which men are liable.

7. Emotions in their rise are naturally independent of the Will, and in their exercise may reach a paroxysm, ungovernable by the Will. In all their ordinary exercise, however, they are subject to the laws of self-government. In harmony with the common laws of activity, the measure of control possible under excitement may be increased.

8. Wonder, in filling the mind, throws an arrest for a time upon the voluntary direction of activity; Grief dulls the mind, abating proportionately its interest in things around; Fear is capable of putting a restraint upon powers, both of intelligence and of action.

9. Besides their inherently restraining power, Emotions are naturally fitted for amalgamation with the Impulses. When acting in combination with an Impulse, the Emotion which restrains in one direction, lends its force to intensify the power of impulse urging in another direction. This law of combination holds good, however, only when the Emotion is experienced in moderate degree. As it rises towards full energy it absorbs consciousness, and the possibility of amalgamation with an Impulse ceases. Fear, when moderate in degree, will give force to the desire of safety; Wonder will quicken curiosity; Grief will stimulate reflectiveness. But as Emotion rises in intensity, the stimulating force gradually abates. At the maximum of force, Fear paralyses, Wonder stupifies, Grief deepens into the listlessness of despair.

10. Problems.— (1.) Is Wonder greatest in mind when it is the child of ignorance or of knowledge? (2.) Can the Emotions be proved to afford evidence of the greatness of our nature, while they are at the same time essentially connected with its weakness? (3.) How does the emotion of Fear stand related to the affection of Reverence? (4.) Is Grief capable of proving in any way an elevating power, though its immediate effect is depressing?

PART III
THE WILL
CHAPTER I
ITS NATURE AND RELATIONS TO OUR OTHER POWERS

1. Will is a power of control over the other faculties and capacities of our nature, by means of which we are enabled to determine personal activity.

It is to be carefully observed that Will is control of our own powers, *not of external things.* Edwards has quite overlooked this, in his definition,— 'Will is that which chooses anything.'— *Freedom of Will,* I. I. And again, he extends its application to '*things* present and absent.' Locke had said, *Essay* II. 21, sec. 15, with more accuracy, '*Volition* is an act of the mind knowingly exerting that dominion it takes itself to have over any part of the man, by employing it in, or withholding it from, any particular action. And what is the *Will,* but the faculty to do this?' So Reid makes Will 'a power to determine in things which he conceives to depend upon his determinations.'— *Active Powers,* II. I. From the time of Kant, the doctrine of the Will has generally had the leading place in the Ethical systems of Germany. Next in importance in the treatment of the Will, is the literature of America, which has distinct Treatises on this subject by Edwards, Upham, Tappan, Whedon, Hazard, Bledsoe, and Day.

2. Will is a power distinct from all the other powers already named. Intellect is knowing power, Will is controlling power. Affection is inclination towards another person, Will is guidance of our own activity. Desire is craving of what we have not, Will is use of what belongs to us as part of our own nature. Emotion is excitement of feeling in contemplation of an object, Will is energy from within, directing us in our relations to external objects. Affection, Desire, and Emotion, are all concerned with external objects, Will is concerned with the management of affections, desires, and emotions. Intellect, besides being occupied with the objects and occasions which awaken affections, desires, and emotions, is capable of making these exercises of feeling themselves the matter of observation,

but it is the function of Will, under fixed laws, to determine in the case of all these, including Intellect, the time, manner, and measure of exercise.

Most important of these distinctions is that between desire and will. These have often been identified. Their distinction is thorough-going, as indicated above. This has been insisted upon by Locke, *Essay* II. 21; by Reid, *Act. Powers*, II. 1, Works, 531; by Stewart, *Act. and Mor. Powers*, App. p. 471, Works, vi. p. 343; by Upham, on the *Will*, c. v. p. 84. Des Cartes identified Desire and Will, *Principles of Philos.* XXXII. So also did Priestley, *Philosophical Necessity'*, p. 35. Edwards said, *'Will* seems to be a word of more general signification, extending to things present and absent. *Desire* respects something absent . . . I cannot think they are so entirely distinct, that they can ever be properly said to run counter.'— *Freed. of Will*, 1. I. Dr. Thomas Brown said, 'These brief feelings, which the body immediately obeys, . . . are commonly termed Volitions; while the more lasting wishes, which have no such direct termination, are simply denominated Desires.'— *Cause and Effect*, 1. 3, 3d ed. p. 51.

3. Will is an essential and prominent feature of Personality. A person is a Self-conscious Intelligence, capable of self-determination. If Intelligence is needful to make knowledge of Moral Law possible, Will, or power of self-determination, is needful to make obedience to that law possible. Power of self-determination is thus essential to the nature of a moral being. Kant says of man that 'his will' is his 'proper self,' *Metaph. of Ethics*, 3d ed. 71. It is power of control over our whole nature. 'The immediate object of every act of will is to move some portion of the body, or to influence mental activity.'— *Freedom of Mind in Willing*, p. 13, by Rowland G. Hazard, New York, 1864. The author, however, gives a definition too wide, when lie says, 'Will is the power or faculty of the mind for effort,' p. 24.

4. Will holds a double relation to Intelligence, (1.) a relation of *superiority* in respect of control; and (2.) a relation of *dependence* in respect of need for guidance in the government of the subordinate powers. The former is the common relation of Will to all other powers of personal activity. The latter is a special relation subsisting between Will and Intellect, by reason of which self-control in human experience is a Rational Self-control.

Reason is the 'legislator and governor of Will.'— Kant, *Metaph. of Ethics,* p. 18. The term 'governor' must, however, be interpreted in harmony with legislation or discovery of law, which is the proper function of intelligence.

Intellect has superiority of teaching power, without controlling power, Will has superiority of controlling power, without teaching power. The grand distinction of man as an active being is recognised when the harmony of these two is such as to secure unity of force, and unity of result.

6. To all the powers lower than Intelligence, Will holds only the single relation of superiority in respect of control, without any dependence in respect of authoritative guidance. These lower powers afford occasion for the exercise of Will, but Will is not dependent on them for a rule of action. This singleness of relationship is consequent upon the natural inferiority of the affections, desires, and motives to Intelligence, and their dependence upon it for exercise. These impulses are in their nature insufficient to afford a rule of conduct; Will, or power of self-direction, therefore, needs a rule of guidance. On the subjects of this and the preceding paragraph, see Upham on the *Will,* Part I. chaps, ii. and iii.; Tappan, *The Doctrine of the Will,* chaps, iv. v.; Hazard, *Freedom of Mind in Willing,* Book I. c. iii.

6. Consequent upon the superior relation subsisting between Will and Intellect, in comparison with that subsisting between the Will and affections, desires and emotions, the Will may be represented as standing between the higher power and the lower powers, to maintain proper action, that the higher may guide the lower, and the lower not override the higher. In this view, Intellect may give law to the Will, the lower powers never can.

Kant has represented this relation by saying that the Will stands between the sensory and the reason.

7. Intellect, in affording the law of conduct, is constantly and closely connected with the sensibilities, thereby providing for completeness of control on the part of the Will, when executing moral law.

8. The lower powers, such as the affections and the desires, may operate without check from the Will; for, the

relation between Will and Impulse is not such that Will must control, but only such that it may control.

PROBLEMS.— (1.) Distinguish between willing, choosing, and preferring. Edwards on the *Will,* l. I, criticised by Tappan, *Doctrine of the Will,* p. 73; Hazard on *Willing,* p. 177. (2.) What forms of choice lie within the sphere of Will, and what beyond? (3.) Interpret the term *Desire,* when a form of action is said to be its object, *e.g.,* I desire to write,— I wish to speak with you. (4.) Can a rigid line of separation be drawn between a sphere of thought and a sphere of action?

CHAPTER II
THE WILL: ITS EXERCISE

1. An act of Will, directing present activity, is named a Volition, from the Latin *volo,* I will. 'Voluntas est, quæ quid cum ratione desiderat.'— Cicero, *Tusc. Disput.* iv. 6.

2. Volitions are distinguished from each other according to the nature of the power over which control is exercised. Thus the volition may involve personal determination in the direction of affection or desire,— of observation or reflection.

3. An exercise of pure will is unknown in consciousness. We may will to think, or to sympathize with one in suffering, or to restrain our fears, but we cannot will to will. This is a simple interpretation of the nature of Will, as indicated in the previous chapter, sec. I. 'A mere Will without any motive is chimerical and contradictory.'— Leibnitz, *Fourth Paper, Letters of Leibnitz and Clarke,* p. 93. Reid states it thus,— 'Every act of will must have an object. He that wills must will something.'— *Active Powers,* Essay II. I.; Hamilton, 531. 'Volitions never exist independently of motives.'— Upham, *The Will,* sec. 136, p. 213.

4. Volitions may have different degrees of volitional force, according to the measure of control exercised on an existing impulse. There may be simple *consent* of the Will, that is, Volition in simple accordance with an existing Impulse. And there may be *deliberate determination* of the Will, that is, Volition in accordance with a distinct decision of the Intellect as to what is right or wrong in action, or,— beyond the moral sphere,— as to what is prudent or advantageous. Deliberate determination may lead either to exercise of an existing impulse,

or to resistance of the impulse so as to provide for its expulsion from the mind. Consent of Will may be without deliberation; Resistance by the Will never can. Diversity of degree in volitional force depends on the degree in which Intellect has regulative power in guiding our actions. 'Rational actions require preliminary effort to design the plan, or the series of efforts by which the end maybe reached.'— *Causation and Freedom in Willing,* by Rowland G. Hazard, p. 13, London, 1869 — two letters of great ability, addressed to Mr. John S. Mill, worthy of the earlier work from the same pen.

5. Volition is not uniformly the spring of our actions. There is a spontaneous, as well as a volitional, origin of activity. There are forms of activity provided for by the constitution of our nature, independently of our choice; as there are others which can be originated only by means of personal choice. That 'internal principles and motives operate in a uniform manner,' as Hume maintains,— *Liberty and Necessity,* Essays, II. 103,— is beyond doubt.

6. Volition is the origin of activity only in so far as actions are regulated by our intellectual powers. It is only the intelligent being which can contemplate, devise, and execute a form of activity purely subjective in its source. What we originate is achieved, in respect of plan, by means of thought; in respect of force, by means of will. Only such action as owes its form to intellectual as well as volitional power is properly named Self-originated. See *Causation and Freedom in Willing,* by Rowland G. Hazard.

7. Volition fulfils its function in other cases by the control of activity which it does not originate. The origin of activity is then spontaneous; only its continuance is under sway of the Will. Thus the current impressions received through the senses, are not voluntary in origin, but only in continuance. So it is with the desires, affections, and emotions, in so far as they are dependent on the sensory. What I see in walking, is seen because I have an organ of vision, and also intellectual power capable of acting spontaneously in harmony with this organ. What I feel in consequence of what I see, is just as plainly spontaneous. But concentration of attention upon any one object is voluntary, as implied in the previous paragraph. In so far as a man does not originate his own activity, he is the creature of circumstances; in so far as he originates his actions, he is the master of circumstances.

8. Volition is concerned with the continuity of every action, whether Will be or be not competent to originate the action or actually involved in its origin. Or, to indicate the position as regarded from the opposite extreme, the Will is capable of terminating all normal forms of personal activity. Otherwise, action ceases to be personal, and becomes abnormal. Sensibility, contrasting with activity, follows a different law. Continued agitation of feeling, despite efforts of Will, involves nothing abnormal. As Cicero has said,— 'Quæ Græci πάθη vocant, nobis *perturbationes* appellari magis placet, quam *morbos.*'— *Tusc. Disput.* iv. 5. Continuance of excitement, even when we long to escape from it, is in accordance with our nature,— is agitation, not disease.

9. In so far as the Will cannot originate all actions, and cannot altogether prevent the rise of impulses, it has only a restricted control. Within these natural limits, however, the control exercised by the Will is rational self-control, inasmuch as the exercise of intellectual power is constantly under command of the Will, for the guidance of our activity.

10. A Rational Self-control is adequate self-control of all personal activity. It is adequate in range, inasmuch as it applies to continuance of activity on the part of all our powers. It is adequate in guiding power, inasmuch as it has been shown that Reason is competent to supply a moral law, or law of guidance sufficient for the direction of all forms of activity, and Will is capable of operating in harmony with Intellect. See above, Part I. chap. iii. Truth superior to personality is the one requisite for harmonious self-direction of the life. Such truth, Reason is competent to recognise; and the exercise of Reason, Will is competent to command. Any disturbance of this relation between Reason and Will is a breach of the normal condition of human nature.

11. The question as to the Freedom of the Will is obviously concerned with the laws which regulate the exercise of the faculty. But this question is so universally regarded as the chief matter of dispute affecting the Will, that it is desirable to assign to it a special chapter. Its extreme difficulty is a further reason for distinct treatment, since it is, as Hume avers, 'the most contentious question of metaphysics, the most contentious science.'— *Human Understanding,* sec. 8, Essays, II. 110.

12. Problems.— (1.) Trace the effects to Ethical Science arising from the identification of Reason and Will. (2.)

Distinguish between knowledge voluntarily acquired, and that acquired involuntarily. (3.) Can Will originate an exercise of Affection? (4.) Are there any circumstances in which love or pity may be matter of command? (5.) How can there be various degrees of force belonging to volitions? Give examples and interpret them, so as to discover the law or laws which determine volitional force. (6.) Does strength of Will vary among the individuals of the race?— Hughes, *The Human Will,* ch. x., London, 1867. (7.) Is Will a faculty capable of development?

CHAPTER III
THE FREEDOM OF THE WILL

1. The question as to the freedom of the Will, being essentially concerned with the laws regulating the exercise of this power, is exclusively a question of Psychology, to be determined by analysing the facts of consciousness. This statement settles the method to be followed, and thereby shuts off for the present the Metaphysical questions necessarily and closely connected with this subject. The area of discussion is thus narrowed to the fundamental problem. The correlative metaphysical problems are not thereby abandoned, but merely separated and delayed.

The philosophic nature of the problem is vital to the whole discussion. If it be accurately represented as a question concerned exclusively with the operations of mind, the form of the discussion at least is fixed. Hume, as a defender of Necessitarianism, with a 'reconciling project' on hand, held 'that men begin at the wrong end of this question concerning liberty and necessity, when they enter upon it by examining the faculties of the soul, the influence of the understanding, and the operations of the will.'— *Human Understanding,* sec. 8, Essays, II. 108. He would have us begin with 'the operations of body and of brute unintelligent matter.' Kant, in his renowned defence of Freedom of Will, denounces in the severest terms those who 'regard it as a mere psychological quality.'— See Kant's *Metaphysic of Ethics,* 3d ed. p. 135, where will be found some of Kant's strongest language. But it is to be observed that in deciding it to be a psychological question, or question concerning the laws of mind, nothing further is decided. More especially it is not thereby affirmed that the essential nature of the Will's freedom can be fully explained, and this is the point at which Kant pours out his fury. The first demand is a careful elucidation of the facts involved, without which there can be no thorough discussion of the subject. What explanations of the facts may be possible, is an after question.

2. The problem as to the freedom of the Will is further seen to be a Psychological one, by reference to the powers with the regulation of which the Will is concerned. As already shown, an exercise of pure will is impossible,— preceding chapter, sec. 3. If then it is the function of Will to control the Intellect, and the Impulses and Restraints natural to us, the question as to its freedom in doing so, is purely a question as to the power belonging to Mind. It is a problem which inevitably raises collateral questions as to the laws which regulate Intelligence and the lower powers of mind. Without answering these, no solution can be reached.

The nature of the question is misunderstood, and even perverted, if it be made a question as to 'liberty of indifference.' 'In things absolutely indifferent there is no foundation for choice, and consequently no election nor will.'— Leibnitz, *Fourth Paper, Letters of Leibnitz and Clarke.* p. 93, and again p. 167.

3. The problem as to the freedom of the Will is, from one point of view, only a special aspect of the wider problem as to the measure of control which the will exercises over the other faculties and capacities of our nature. This wider problem having in part engaged our attention, the facts already ascertained must be taken into account as essential to the settlement of this final question. What is the power of Will, depends for its answer in great measure upon what is the relative power of Intelligence on the one hand, and of Impulses, such as desires and affections, on the other hand. Has the Will controlling power over the other faculties, or have the other faculties controlling power over the Will? This is not the whole problem; it is only one aspect of it; yet, it is that aspect which has been most prominent throughout the discussion, even to the overshadowing of the question concerning the nature of Will itself.

4. The problem may be viewed apart from these relations, and then it wears the form of a question concerning the essential nature of the Will itself. Thus considered, the question comes to be this,— Is the nature of the power of will such as to make

freedom an essential characteristic of its exercise? In other words, Is Will a self-determining power? And ultimately, Has the Mind power of self-determination?

5. These three phrases,— The Will is free, the Soul is free, and the Person is free, with their correlative negations, are, on either side, only three forms of expressing the same thing. The following authors consider it of importance that liberty should be attributed to the person or agent, not to the faculty: — Locke, *Essay*, II. 21; Edwards, *Freedom of the Will*, I. 5; Reid, *Act. and Mor. Powers*, iv. iv. 5, Works, 611, Stewart, *Dissert.*, Note DDD, and *Act. Powers*, App. I. Hazard defines Will thus,— 'The power or faculty of the *mind* for effort.'— *Freedom of Mind in Willing*, p. 24.

6. On account of the relative form of the problem having mainly engaged attention, the discussion has turned upon the comparative determining force of thoughts, volitions, and dispositions, as all three have a bearing on activity. The question has thus become very largely one as to the determining force of MOTIVES. For if it can be shown that Motives determine or cause Volitions, the question of freedom of Will is settled in the negative, by a direct application of the law of Causality. On this ground, it has been tacitly assumed that it holds true conversely, that if the Will is free, in the sense of being superior to motives, it must be so by superiority to the law of Causality also, although such a view really violates the nature of the problem, and that to the extent of making it irrational.— Cicero, *De Fato*, XI. For whatever be the nature of the problem, it certainly does not stand thus. Is a Volition an uncaused event? Are there facts in consciousness which cannot be attributed to any cause? Hume identifies the idea of necessity and of causality, *Hum. Understanding, Libert. and Necess.*, sec. 8, Essays, II. 96. And yet, so far is there common ground, that he says, 'It is universally allowed that nothing exists without a cause of its existence, and that chance, when strictly examined, is a mere negative word, and not any real power which has anywhere a being in nature.'— *Ib.* II. p. 110.

7. Dealing with the relative aspect of the problem, we have to compare the determinative force of motives and volitions; not merely their power over our activity, but their influence over each other, so as to decide, whether motives determine volitions,

or volitions determine motives, or whether both statements may be in some sense true. If the last possibility were established, it would then become needful to distinguish the different senses in which the word 'determining' had been employed, and what bearing this diversity of usage had on the chief question as to the freedom of Will.

8. The first requisite here is a satisfactory explanation of the nature of Motives, by which they may be sharply and unmistakeably distinguished from Volitions. Edwards gives the definition thus, 'By *motive* I mean the whole of that which moves, excites, or invites the mind to volition, whether that be one thing singly, or many things conjunctly.'— *Freedom of the Will*, Pt. I. sec. ii. This is objectionable on many accounts. We are dealing with the comparative force of *mental powers*, but this applies as well to things or external objects. And since it is admitted that external objects awaken in us such impulses as desire and affection, there is no need for the wide popular use of the term, which would reckon money and place as motives to action. More serious, however, is the objection that the definition begs the question in dispute. If the law of mental activity be that motives excite to volition, further philosophic investigation is useless. The matter is settled on the necessitarian side. The will is not free. The object awakens the motive, the motive excites the volition, and the action is the result. The object, together with sensibility of nature, which makes me liable to its influence, is the cause of my action. Such a theory might have some fair claim to acceptance if it applied to an irrational nature, but is quite inadequate where motives must be classified as rational and irrational. Motives so different in nature must be regulated in their exercise by different laws.

It must at least, then, require a scientific process to prove that the single law of mental exercise is, that motives excite to volition. We need first to know exactly what motives are, before we proceed to ascertain what effects they produce. Take the three terms, 'that which *moves, excites,* or *invites* the mind.' The last may be thrown out, as it points to the influence of the object, which is really represented in the mental movement with which we are to deal. The other two terms will serve the end, or Belsham's expression 'moves or influences the mind in its choice' (*Elements of Philos.* 228), if we take motive to mean, an internal force which moves or excites the mind towards a single definite line of *action*. Hunger, love of fame, sympathy with a sufferer, may suffice as examples. Motive is an internal force; Hamilton says, 'a mental tendency' *(Reid's Works, 608)*, which impels to action, either internal or external. The action may be confined to the mind itself, or it may pass over into the external sphere, this makes no difference. As several such impulses may unite their force, it is legitimate to speak of the whole as the motive force in the case. Reid used motive in the sense of 'a thing that is conceived'— *ens rationis,* and so was led to hold that motives 'may *influence* to action, but they do not act.'— *Act. Powers,* IV. iv. I, Works, 608. This is untenable; see above, Part II. chap. ii. sec. 2. Motives are likened to weights by Leibnitz, *Letters between L. and Clarke,* Fifth Paper, 157,— defended 165,— defended after the death of Leibnitz, by Thummig, quoted by Hamilton, *Reid's Works,* 611.

In contrast, 'The faculty of the *Will* is that power or principle of mind by which it is capable of choosing.'— Edwards, *Freedom of the Will,* I. I. To this must be added, 'Choosing forms of activity or actions,'— not things. Motive is impulse to act; Will is power of determining whether to act or not to act; and, in the event of acting, whether to act in this way or in that. The whole dispute concentrates on these two points; What is motive, and what is will?

9. A classification of motives, or natural impulses which urge to action, is the next requisite for an adequate treatment of the problem. This classification has already been given, Part II. c. i., under which they have been presented in three groups,— Desires, Affections, and Judgments. Between the two first and the last a clear line of separation runs, warranting their classification as Dispositions and Judgments. The distinction of these two is broadly marked. The one class includes forces which impel, only by their own inherent strength as feelings; and are non-rational. The other class includes only forces which are rational as well as impelling, and which impel by reason of their rational character, thereby constituting a specific kind of motive. The difference between these two is so great that the impelling power of the latter can be experienced only in a rational nature, whereas impulses of the former class may belong to natures of a lower type, and may be experienced by them in a large degree,

though not always to the full measure of human nature. The one is recognition of a rule of life, as a rational motive, the other is experience of disposition as motive-force. Upham, in a very interesting passage, proposes a classification of motives into personal and moral.— *Treatise on the Will,* II. sec. 133, p. 207. The distinction is important, but the designations are unfortunate, as moral motives are pre-eminently personal.

10. These two classes of motives have common relations to the Will, but they have at the same time relations so different as to set them in opposition to each other, disposition influencing Will in one way, the understanding in another. This has been indicated so far in Part III. c. i. sec. 4. sec. 5, and it is a consideration of vital importance. Both have some influence in determining the exercise of the Will; both are under some control of the Will as to their own exercise, but only rational motives provide a rule to the Will for its guidance, in addition to fulfilling the function of impulse.

11. Both rational motives, and lower motives, including desires and affections, have some influence in determining the exercise of Will. Both Intelligence and Disposition are capable of spontaneous action, and in accordance with this law of their activity, both afford *occasion* for the exercise of Will. As already stated (Part III. c. ii. sec. 3), an exercise of pure Will is impossible. The Will is thus dependent upon the other energies of our nature for the primary condition of its exercise. Motives do so far determine the Will, as to fix the direction and form of the volitions. This, however, establishes nothing as to power or force to control the Will; though it does discover a measure of exercise on their part independently of Will.

12. The rational motives and the lower motives, being quite distinct in nature, are capable of restricting each other in action. While spontaneous action both of Intelligence and of Disposition is recognised as fact, unrestricted exercise of each motive power, until it exhausts its energy in fulfilment of its end, is not similarly recognised. That dispositions may rise to a force equivalent to ascendency in consciousness, is a well-known fact, afterwards to be considered, but such ascendency is not recognised as a uniform law of their exercise. For example, desire of honour may arise simultaneously in the minds of a number of associated persons, when a question of precedence is

to be settled. But the law of activity applying to this disposition is not such as to make it impossible for one to give way to another, and inevitable that all be swayed to the last by the desire of pre-eminence. Men are not forces which, being set in motion, must move on with a velocity proportioned to the single motive power, until they dash against each other. Sir W. Hamilton, criticising Reid, says,— 'If motives "*influence* to action," they must co-operate in producing a certain effect on the agent; and the determination to act, and to act in a certain manner, is that effect.'— *Reid's Works,* 608. To 'influence' and to 'determine' are not synonymous; and so far are they from being necessarily consequent, that it is granted, in case of conflicting motives, that determination is, at least in some cases, contrary to influence. 'Human choice is *affected* by such stimuli, not determined by them.'— Kant, *Metaph. of Ethics,* 3d ed. 161. There is, then, in human nature some moderating power, distinct from an impulse such as desire, which may interfere with the law of exercise belonging to desire itself, so as to put restraint upon it. On the other hand, if each man exercise his own judgment in estimating carefully the qualifications of each of his associates, and in comparing them with his own, the law of intellectual action is not such that judgment must sway, so as to make it impossible that men should be influenced by a desire of precedence. There is thus a moderating force, distinct from intelligence, which may interfere with its exercise, so as to put a restraint upon its action. The higher and lower motive forces of our nature are so different as to fit them for performing the part of counter-checks upon each other. A law of their exercise is this,— That the action of motives of the one class involves a check upon motives of the other class. This counter-check, however, being consequent upon their own nature as contrary to each other, discovers nothing as to the action of Will.

13. The higher and the lower motives, by reason of their diversity of nature, and antagonism in action, are placed in different relations to the Will. The higher motives, as rational, that is, capable of discovering reasons for conduct, may be of the nature of rules or moral laws. They may therefore be both sufficient and authoritative as guides for the conduct, even to the restraint of the lower motives. The lower motives, on the other hand, are only forces seeking distinct ends, without being able to

afford a reason for doing so, much less to take the place of moral law. While sufficient to urge on towards the attainment of their own ends, they are neither sufficient nor authoritative as laws for the guidance of personal action. This is only an exposition of that fundamental law of moral life, that the Reason rule the passions. From this it might be argued, as Kant has done, that the law which requires personal control, implies the power of personal control, for Moral Law cannot itself be an expression of injustice, by demanding the impossible. The argument is irresistible, I think; for, as it seems to me, the alternatives are,— moral government of free agents by law intrusted to themselves for application, or, government *ab extra,* through means of human sensibilities, to the sacrifice of human personality,— similar to the government of the horse by corn and whip-cord — a government modified only by the reason and kindliness of the roaster. But I do not use the argument from moral law to human freedom, for in prosecuting a psychological investigation, we are at present concerned with evidence, not with argument in support of our position.

14. There is, in personal experience, control over both the higher and lower motives additional to that which they exercise over each other, and that is personal control, implying freedom of self-government. We have seen that these two classes of motives, as they come into play, naturally act as counter-checks upon each other. But this does not exhaust the measure of control exercised over our thoughts and dispositions. It only indicates a very small part of it. Granting now spontaneous action of both thought and disposition, and natural restriction of the one by the other, there is besides, government of both so as to determine the manner and measure of their exercise. Take the case already supposed, desire of pre-eminence, with its possible restraint, and even mastery. By the exercise of intellect, facts are observed, compared, and classified, and subsequently a course of reasoning is prosecuted in order to determine present duty. This process is not explained either by the influence of the desire, or by spontaneity of the intellect. The explanation is not found in the desire of honour, for that is a motive to seek only its own end, and, according to the law established above, sec. 12, it can act only as a check upon such exercise of intellect as would tend to its own restraint. The explanation is not found in spontaneous

action of the intellect, for while there may be a spontaneous recognition of facts, there can be no spontaneous prosecution of arguments. The laws of intellectual activity, as known to us in consciousness, directly contradict the supposition. Attention, the first essential act in the process, is a distinct exercise of personal power; and thereafter, arguments do not follow by fixed law, but by personal effort, so that if the reasoning be fallacious, we have the blame,— if it be correct, we have the praise of it. The occasion of the desire has not been of our own arranging,— the desire of honour has arisen spontaneously and naturally; but we are conscious of personal volition in putting our intellect to use, and keeping it in exercise while we prosecute the investigation. Mr. Mill says, 'To be conscious of free-will must mean to be conscious, before I have decided, that I am able to decide either way.'— *Exam.* 564. No. That would not be consciousness of free-will, but only conviction of possessing such a power. To be conscious of free-will must mean to be conscious in deciding that I am deciding.— M'Cosh, *Intuitions,* 2d ed. 266; Mansel, *Metaph.* 363; *Battle of the Two Philosophies,* 35; Hazard on *Causation,* 132, Alexander, *Moral Causation,* 12.

Turn now to the desire itself. That receives a check, consequent upon the voluntary exercise of the intellect. The concentration of attention on the question of duty withdraws so much from the strength of the desire, which for the time is held in subjection. And, as the exercise of attention is the result of personal effort, so by consequence is this temporary subjection of the desire. In this sense it is correct, in describing freedom, to say, as Mr. Mill has done, that the will, as free, is 'capable of acting *against* motives,' *Exam.* 576, but this does not mean that the will is capable of acting without motives; and still less that a man 'can do different things while the motives remain the same.'— Hartley on *Man,* I. 507.

Suppose now that the decision of duty in the case is, for the suppression of the desire of honour in the circumstances, how is submission possible? How can a natural desire be suppressed, while the opportunity for gratification continues? The view of the opportunity is sufficient to awaken the desire; the desire itself is natural,— we may say, in the circumstances, inevitable. Is, then, its continuance equally inevitable? Certainly not. Its suppression by personal determination is in accordance

152

with familiar laws of mind. To *transfer* the attention from the prospect of honour to the question of duty is to put the desire under restraint; to *concentrate* the attention upon duty, awakening thereby the reverence for moral law, is to remove the conditions requisite for the continuance of the desire. In reversal of the law of its rise, we have the law of its departure. In this manner, man throws off a strong ambition, and maintains the dignity of a moral being. In this way it is that he becomes master of circumstances by being master of himself. By the opposite course, though still through the exercise of intelligence, man may concentrate attention on the object or opportunity for gratification. Such concentration throws open the mind to the full influence of the object, voluntarily placing the whole nature under its sway. In such a case the motive develops according to the single law of its own exercise. Its influence will be according to the sensibility of the nature. And if, when at its maximum, the motive determine action, volition first gave to motive its force.

It is in our consciousness of self-control for the determination of activity, that we obtain our only knowledge of causality. Each one knows himself as the cause of his own actions. In the external world we continue ignorant of causes, and are able only to trace uniform sequence, as Hume and Comte have insisted. But in consciousness we distinguish between sequence and causality. We are conscious of our own causal energy, by knowing the origin of our activity in self-determination. 'This was illustrated, though inconsistently, by Locke, *Essay* 11. xxi. sec. 5. It was held by Maine de Biran, *Nouvelles Considérations,* p. 363; and Cousin, *Cows de l'Histoire de la Philosophie,* second course, L. xix.; transl. *Hist. of Modern Philosophy,* ll. p. 206; and Mansel, *Prolegomena Logica,* 139; and is generally held by those who adopt the libertarian side. It is, however, rejected by Sir W. Hamilton, *Metaph.* H. 390; *Reid's Works,* 866; *Discussions,* 612; and in this he finds a supporter in Mr. Mill, *Exam.* 357. Regarding the question from the point of view afforded by the movement of the limbs, on which Maine de Biran had dwelt, Hamilton argues thus: 'Between the overt act of corporeal movement of which we are cognisant, and the internal act of mental determination of which we are also cognisant, there intervenes a numerous series of intermediate agencies of which we have no knowledge; and consequently we can have no consciousness of any causal connexion between the extreme links of this chain.'— *Metaph.* ll. 391. That the management of brain, nerve, and muscle is not matter of consciousness, is admitted; and consequently that we have no consciousness of causal connexion between volitions and the movements of these organs. But we are conscious of the sensation of movement, and we are conscious of observing the movements. How, then, does the case stand? I will to move my arm, and both by sensation and observation I recognise the consequent movement. This is not direct consciousness of the causal nexus, but it is consciousness of the *originating* force of the whole, the efficiency of which is tested by direct experiment, and confirmed by results within our own consciousness. According to Hamilton's theory, it is *origin* of existence we need to recognise in order to reach causality; and here we have consciousness of the origin of our activity. But the question is really to be settled elsewhere. Obscurity hangs over the intermediate stages in the case of bodily movements. But in the use of our mental powers — in the government of understanding and desire, for example,— it is otherwise. Everything is within consciousness. By exercise of Will, we bring the intellect into use, and by continuance of volitional energy we prosecute a course of reasoning. We are conscious of the fact of control, and in immediate connexion and-dependence, we are conscious of the controlled exercise of mind. It is in this control of mental power that we have direct knowledge of the exercise of causal energy. 'Intelligence endowed with will is causality.'— Kant, *Metaph. of Ethics,* 3d ed. p. 64 — 70. In the management of bodily organs the area of knowledge is widened, but our knowledge is immediate only so far as volition is concerned, and is only mediate so far as the next act is concerned. On this subject see Chalmers's *Sketches of Mental and Moral Philos.* c. IV. sec. 27, ed. 1854, p. 161; Hazard on *Causation and Freedom in Willing,* p. 7; and a valuable passage in Cairns's *Treatise on Moral Freedom,* p. 222.

15. Freedom of Will, as known in consciousness, is control over the whole nature by means of the control we have over the understanding. The intellect is continually at command for guidance and impulse, our best dispositions are all in harmony with it, and our evil dispositions, which are out of

harmony with it, can be grappled with in earnest moral conflict. So far from freedom of will being out of harmony with reason, and in violation of its fundamental principles, it is possible only in the possession and use of reason, and is preserved in its natural force only by the continuous government of reason in the sphere of personal activity. The understanding must be able to compare motives with some standard of judgment or rule of conduct,— must be able to go forward in thought, and forecast the form and tendencies of different actions, in order that there may be any real choice or self-determination in action. Intelligence is essential to the exercise of Will. 'A false relish may frequently be corrected by argument and reflection.'— Hume, *Essays,* II. 227; *Prin. of Morals.* In this close union of intellect and will for the control of all the powers of our nature, lies the explanation of Kant's tendency to identify the Will with the Practical Reason. The two powers are certainly distinct, but their united action is essential. Their union in our nature provides for the possibility of personal freedom; their union in self-government secures freedom in practice.

16. The negative aspect of freedom of Will, presenting the lower alternative open to man, is government by the passions in disregard of the reason, with use of the understanding only as servant to the lower propensities. This is the possibility of a two-sided nature, in which Will stands between, with the power of giving to either the ascendency. For freedom of Will is not merely power to act or to refrain, but power to accept impulse in action, from the lower as well as from the higher side of our nature. Where this lower alternative is the one more commonly preferred, there is subjection of the kingdom of mind to Mob-Rule, *v.* Plato's *Republic.* Such a life leads down into the abyss of wilful baseness, where the grand elements of human personality are at length broken up by what is nothing less than moral suicide.

17. As freedom of action is attainable through rational control of the whole nature, the key to the exercise of such freedom is found in the power of attention. This is the key to possible superiority over circumstances and dispositions, and also to the possibility of uniform guidance by the reason. The ruling type of human freedom, as recognised in consciousness, is discovered in the control exercised over attention. Intellect exerts

its governing power only as we put it to use for this end, and that means attention. Objects, when contemplated by us, touch our sensibility, and awaken dispositions which have the force of motives. This being the law of our experience, we weaken or strengthen these lower motives according as we direct our attention. Our experience under contemplation of objects is the product of natural constitution, and is not subject of volition; but the continuance and increase of such sensibility, with attendant dispositions, are elements of experience constantly under our own control, according as attention is bestowed upon the object, or withdrawn from the object, and concentrated upon another.

18. As the possibility of personal freedom is provided for in the full command we have over our intellect, and as freedom is practically realized when intellect is used as the power guiding our conduct, moral freedom becomes an established attainment by means of successful conflict with the clamant dispositions. 'It is Conscience which preserves the might of the Will.'— Trendelenburg, *Naturrecht*, p. 56.

19. In proportion as the government of Intelligence over the life is voluntarily established, definite lines of moral action are preferred with uniformity, as occasion arises. The laws of moral conduct being definite, and applicable to the several powers which we possess, the lines of action which they mark out are no less certain. As perfect moral freedom is realized, consistency of moral action is attained, with such diversity, in the form of actions, as circumstances may require. The law being one, the Will is in full harmony with it. According to the accuracy of the estimate we have formed of a man's moral character, will be the accuracy of our anticipations as to the manner in which he will act in given circumstances. The possibility of forecasting probable lines of moral action is not an argument against freedom of will, but a proof that such freedom is in accordance with moral law, that is, in harmony with Reason. See Upham on the *Will*, chapters III. and VI.

20. Behind and beneath these inquiries as to control of intellect and dispositions, and as to the manner in which such control is carried through to its practical result in forming the external actions, there is a deeper and far more perplexing question,— How does the Will regulate itself? If it can use intelligence to restrain disposition, or if it can stimulate

disposition, so as to hold the understanding in check, such use of other powers implies an inherent and superior power in itself. How is this power brought into exercise? How can Will regulate the forth-putting of its own energy? It is when we thus withdraw from the relations in which Will acts, to consider Will in itself, that we encounter the most serious difficulty. At this point we pass beyond the facts of consciousness, as Kant maintained — *Metaph. of Ethics,* 3d ed. p. 71,— and enter the region of hypothesis and inference, where philosophy may be constrained to own its weakness.

21. Proper treatment of the question requires careful appreciation of the source of its difficulty. The question itself is concerned with the power of pure will, but, as already recognised, ch. II. sec. 3 of the present Part, an exercise of pure will is unknown in consciousness, consequently the source of the difficulty is that we control our other powers without being conscious how power of control lies always at command, or how it is brought into use as occasion requires. The real state of the case is this,— We use our power, knowing well to what end we exert it, but without knowing how we bring it into use. The power itself is unique, but such ignorance of the manner in which we use a power has many analogies in the history of mind.

22. Of legitimate hypotheses there are three available forms,— (1.) constrained action, under dominion of some controlling power, distinct from the Will itself; (2.) spontaneous action, according to an inherent and invariable law of energy operating within the Will itself; or (3.) free action, admitting of variation within a sphere where alternative courses are equally possible.

23. The hypothesis of *constrained action* of Will is invalidated on the ground of inconsistency with the recognised facts of consciousness. Of these facts, the following are the most important, that Intelligence and Disposition are controlled,— that we are conscious of personal control over these powers, so that their exercise is in the direction of our volitions,— and that we praise or blame ourselves as the authors of the consequent actions. To prove that these are only suppositions and not facts, has been found too hard a task for the supporters of the hypothesis of constrained action. If we cannot plead the testimony of consciousness as to the manner in which Will is

brought into exercise, we have its clear testimony as to the fact of the Will's control over the other powers of mind. Whatever be the law of its own exercise, Will is free from the dominion of intellect and disposition. It is not controlled by them, but controls both. The strongest motive does not determine the Will; but the Will determines what motives shall be allowed to gain strength. As to 'the strongest motive,' see Reid, *Act. Powers,* Essay IV. 4,— Works, 610; Stewart, *Philos. of Act. and Mor. Powers,* II. App. 1,— Works, VI. 351; Upham on the *Will,* sec. 138; Tappan, *Review of Edwards,* 21; Hazard, *Freedom of Mind,* Book II. c. x.

24. The hypothesis of *spontaneous action,* according to an invariable law operating within the Will itself, is invalidated by the facts of consciousness. The facts indicated in the previous paragraph are inexplicable on this supposition. While the fact of control over intellect and disposition is obvious, it is equally clear that the control is not so uniform as to favour belief in a law of spontaneity as characteristic of Will. So far from every disposition being uniformly gratified or checked as it arises, there are great variations in the measure of control maintained. Inasmuch as intellect is brought into use, sometimes as guide and encourager of dispositions, sometimes as their restrainer, there is no such uniformity in the manner of control, as to harmonize with a law of spontaneity in Will, similar to that which applies to the dispositions themselves when uncontrolled.

25. The hypothesis of *free action* as the law of exercise for the Will itself, is the only one which harmonizes with the facts of consciousness. Relative freedom in the sense of freedom from control of intellect and disposition on the part of the Will, being established by simple analysis of the facts of consciousness; controlling power on the part of the Will over both intellect and disposition being recognised in exercise within consciousness; a theory of the Will is completed only by maintaining that this power is distinct in nature from any other known to us, and that freedom of action in adopting available alternatives, is the law of its exercise.

26. That we should exercise a power without being conscious of the manner of its exercise; and that, on account of the absence of such consciousness, we should be unable to complete a philosophy of its action, are not singular facts, but facts which are sustained by numerous analogies in the history of

mind. A whole series of examples is afforded by the control which the mind has over the body in executing the determinations of the Will. We determine to walk, and we execute our intention, without knowing how the feat is accomplished, or being able to complete a philosophy of it, either physiological or mental, any more than we can complete our philosophy of volition. So it is with our use of the various senses. So it is also, coming into the department of mind, with the marvels of memory. We recall the experience of the past, so that we have no doubt of the accuracy of our recollections, and we have the laws of association to guide us in some degree as to the manner in which facts are classified in order to be readily remembered; but how we put in operation and employ the power of memory so as to recall past events, is what no philosophy has been able to explain, because consciousness yields no testimony. So is it, in like manner, with our recognition of first principles of truth and rectitude. The control of our bodily organs is a mystery of our life, which Physiology has only made more mysterious. The wonders of memory are altogether perplexing. But when we penetrate as far as Will, discerning the internal power, which has sway over all other powers, making self-determination possible, a scheme of self-government rational, and formation of moral character a reality in personal progress; we reach the inner mystery of human life. The results of the exercise of Will we know; we are besides familiar with the work of self-control itself; but we cannot explain how the Will comes into action in accordance with the peculiar law of its own exercise. As pure volition is unknown, a philosophy of Pure Will is impossible. Beyond the psychological analysis which discovers the subordination of the understanding and dispositions to the Will, the utmost that can be attained is that Will is the ultimate power of mind, in harmony with Intelligence, to provide for government of all the special and subordinate forces of human nature. In accordance with this view, Kant describes the Will as the man's 'proper self,' and indicates the closeness of its union with intelligence by describing its laws as 'the laws of his intellectual will.'— *Metaph. of Ethics,* 3d ed. p. 71.

27. Kant passes beyond the acknowledgment of our ignorance of the manner in which Will operates, to maintain that man exists in two states, a sensible and a cogitable; in the former

of which he is subject to physical law, in the latter of which he is superior to it. The distinction is drawn with great clearness and power in the Grundlegung,— *Metaph. of Ethics,* pp. 70 — 73. The theory is a bold one, having much to commend it as a speculative suggestion, but it is altogether untenable if it mean anything more than man's superiority to physical laws, and his inability to give a complete explanation of this superiority by means of the operations of his own Will. This theory of the cogitable world, as distinguished from the sensible world — the world of human causality, in which man acts as a thing-in-itself, and the world of experience, in which man is a mere phenomenon,— does not make 'the smallest pretence to know anything of the laws obtaining' in the cogitable world, 'excepting only the formal condition of them,' namely, 'their autonomy, which alone can consist with freedom,' p. 72. But, in so far as it makes experience only phenomenal, it reduces the sensory too far, and separates it from true union with the higher nature of man. The doctrine of freedom of will claims no such severance from the sphere of experience, and makes no such affirmation of the merely phenomenal nature of that sphere. In so far as the theory makes the cogitable world 'a mere idea, negative of the sensible world,' and represents reason as 'cogitating herself into a supersensible state;' and declares that 'the notion of a cogitable system is a mere station which reason needs for a fulcrum to lift itself out of the mass of appearances, and cogitate itself as sui-active,' it attempts the impossible, and offers the form of an explanation, where the reality is unattainable.

28. Equally untenable are the representations of the later Transcendentalism, which makes human reason a manifestation of Universal Reason, and speaks of Will as containing 'the element of pure indeterminateness, or the pure reflection of the Ego (I) to itself,' and as 'passing over from indistinguishable indefiniteness to Determinateness.'— Hegel, *Philosophie des Rechts,* sec. 5, sec. 6, pp. 16, 17. As Dr. J. Hutchison Stirling puts it, 'Undevelopedness gives free will.' . . . 'Will is the undeveloped universal.'— *Lects. on the Philos. of Law,* III. As already seen, the knowledge of pure will is impossible; consciousness of its exercise there is none, and consequently knowledge of transition from indeterminateness to determinateness is impossible. The theory, not only transcending

an empirical Psychology, but breaking connexion with it, is without a solid foundation, and thereby fails to establish its claim to be regarded as a philosophy of Will. Accordingly, as the younger Fichte has remarked, Hegel has no place for a doctrine of freedom of will in the individual.— Im. Hermann Fichte, *System der Ethik,* vol. II. Part i. sec. 19, p. 81. As a dialectic scheme of universal existence, Hegel's system is certainly the grandest production embraced in the history of philosophy. And yet, as a pure Dialectic, Spinoza's system, based on the radical conception of one great Substance, source, and explanation of all existence, maintains a closer harmony with the conditions of thought, if not with the characteristics of finite Personality.

Problems.— (1.) Analyse and interpret current phrases which make actions the objects of Desire, such as, 'I desire to write;' or, 'I wish to speak with you.' (2.) Critically examine the doctrine that freedom of Will must imply will to will. 'The soul determines all the free acts of the will in the exercise of a power of willing and choosing.— Edwards, *Freedom of the Will,* II. i. (3.) State the law of causality, and distinguish between its application to external facts, and to the facts of mind. (4.) Does freedom of Will require us to 'define a cause, without comprehending, as a part of the definition, necessary connexion with its effect'?— Hume, *Essays,* II. III. (5.) Critically examine the following,— 'I ask my consciousness what I do feel, and I find, indeed, that I feel (or am convinced) that I could, and even should, have chosen the other course if I had preferred it, that is, if I had liked it better; but not that I could have chosen one course while I preferred the other.'— Mr. Mill's *Exam. of Hamilton's Philos.* 3d ed. p. 566.

CHAPTER IV
NECESSITARIANISM

1. The Necessitarian doctrine, in denying freedom of will, does not altogether refuse a place to freedom. But the only liberty which it acknowledges is liberty of acting as we will, denominated freedom from constraint or coaction. 'I say that a thing is *free* which exists and acts by the sole necessity of its nature.'— Spinoza, Letter 62, *Life, Corresp. and Ethics,* by R. Willis, M. D., p. 393. 'By liberty we can only mean a power of

acting or not acting, according to the determinations of the Will.'— Hume, *Essays,* II. 110. By freedom or liberty in an agent is meant, 'being free from hindrance or impediment in the way of doing or conducting, in any respect, as he wills.— Edwards, *The Will,* Part 1. sec. 5.

2. Such liberty being attributed to man, the upholders of the scheme have a double objection to the name Necessitarianism, as descriptive of their theory, *first,* because it seems to convey that they have no place for liberty, and, *secondly,* because it seems to imply that they really hold that men are constrained in their actions; both of which they deny. Thus Mr. Mill, as an upholder of the theory, speaks of it as 'the falsely-called Doctrine of Necessity,'— preferring 'the fairer name of Determinism,' and says, that the word Necessity 'in this application, signifies only invariability.'— *Exam.* p. 552. Determinism is an unsuitable word, because on both sides a doctrine of determination of will is held, the dispute being between self-determination, and motive-determination. And still more to complicate matters, there is a sense in which libertarians may say, that volitions are determined by motives; see preceding chapter, sec. 10. The doctrine itself Mr. Mill states thus,— 'A volition is a moral effect, which follows the corresponding moral causes as certainly and invariably as physical effects follow their physical causes. Whether it *must* do so, I acknowledge myself to be entirely ignorant, be the phenomena moral or physical; and I condemn accordingly the word Necessity as applied to either case. All I know is that it always *does.'— Ib.* p. 562. These modifications, then, being obviously accurate in themselves, are to be carefully regarded in criticising the theory.

3. The distinctive features of Necessitarianism or Determinism are, *negatively,* the denial of freedom in willing to act; and *positively,* the presentation of a theory of Will, professedly adequate to account for all the facts of consciousness which bear upon the direction of human conduct.

4. The Necessitarian theory, on its negative or critical side, rests upon an application of the law of causality. It urges that every event follows a cause: that this holds true in the sphere of mind as well as of matter; and so applies to volitions as well as sensations. At this point there is no divergence of opinion. Indeed, most libertarians go further than necessitarians here, and

do not halt, like Mr. Mill, at the statement that the effect 'certainly and invariably' *does* follow its cause, but advance to the position that it *must* do so. Liberty of indifference and liberty of caprice are repudiated, and are not to be set to the account of libertarianism, any more than a doctrine of constraint is to be charged against necessitarianism. These are the extremes; taken in the heat of conflict, to be abandoned in calmer mood. That every volition must have a cause, is a necessity freely admitted. To Hume it is granted, according to his demand, that a cause has a 'necessary connexion with its effect.'— *Essays* II. III. This does not, however, touch the question in dispute.

Spinoza was a necessitarian in logical consistency, as the author of a dialectic which rests on the existence of only one substance. In his view, 'men deceive themselves when they suppose they are free,' and this because, though conscious of their own acts, they are ignorant of the causes by which these acts are determined.— *Ethics,* Part II. prop. 35.

5. The Necessitarian theory not only insists upon the application of the law of causality within the region of mind, as to which all are agreed, but further insists upon an *interpretation* of the law in accordance with the analogy of the physical world. Looking from the effect backwards to the cause, it maintains that the law of causality warrants the affirmation, not only that an adequate cause has acted, but also *how* it has acted. Looking from the cause forward to the effect, it maintains, on warrant of the law of causality, not only that the cause has produced the effect, but that it was *necessitated* to produce that effect. But this is something more than an application of the law of causality. With the law, it carries an interpretation founded on knowledge gathered in a particular sphere. It is an argument from matter to mind, and as such needs to be vindicated on the basis of facts, not merely proclaimed on the authority of a general law.

No mere statement of the law is sufficient to establish the theory, and obviate the need for an appeal to the facts of consciousness. To say that the same cause acting in the same circumstances will produce the same effect, is a most accurate statement, but is of no value in the attempt to prove that matter and mind, in so far as they do act, must act in a manner exactly analogous. The statement concerns only the amount of force or power in the cause, and not the mode in which the cause operates. It is merely that the same produces the same, which ultimately is nothing more than this, that the same is the same. To say of two forces that they will cause the same velocity or produce the same amount of heat, is only equivalent to saying that the two forces are the same. This is shown to be the case, equally when the measurement is applied to the cause, and to the effect. The same sympathy will lead to the same help; the same selfishness will lead to the same neglect. No doubt. The same is the same, whether you measure from the one end or from the other. But the whole matter in dispute lies beyond this. The theory must, therefore, be tested by an examination of the facts of consciousness, with the view of ascertaining the laws of exercise applying to mental causes or forces. And when we thus pass from the physical to the mental, we at once recognise a complete difference in the laws of exercise governing the forces of the two spheres. There is so much which is common to both. Effects 'certainly and invariably' follow their causes in both spheres. In both, causes are as invariable in their nature, and as certain in their results. But there is an essential difference between the mental and the physical. Circumstances do not so 'certainly and invariably' determine causes in the mental, as in the physical sphere. Or, to put it in another and more positive form, there is in the mental world an adjustment of forces, which is not found in the material world, except when man interposes to make the adjustment. This difference is so broadly marked, that there is in the sphere of mind at once less certainty, and more certainty as to results. There is less certainty, so far as circumstances contribute to the result; and more certainty, so far as the nature of the operating force is concerned. Physical action (so called) depends mainly upon attendant conditions; mental action depends mainly on internal nature. As to circumstances or attendant conditions, it is more certain that friction will produce fire, than that provocation will produce anger. On the other hand, considering the nature of the efficient cause, it is less certain that steam will produce locomotion, than that volition will produce action. Thus, in the mental world, if you take such forces as love, pity, and reverence, a single distinct and uniform effect 'certainly and invariably' follows from the action of each of the three; but their exercise depends upon something more than the circumstances fitted to call them forth, and still more obvious is it that such circumstances afford no exact criterion of the measure in which these forces operate in mind. These are facts which go to show that causality in mind is not exactly analogous with causality in matter.

6. Passing now the controversial use of the law of Causality made by necessitarianism, we come to its constructive use, in forming a theory alleged to afford an adequate explanation of the facts of consciousness, so far as these are concerned with personal action. In this part, the theory deals specially with the laws regulating the exercise of natural and acquired motives, as carrying a complete explanation of volitions. Necessitarians 'affirm as a truth of experience, that volitions do, in point of fact, follow determinate moral antecedents with the same uniformity, and (when we have sufficient knowledge of the circumstances) with the same certainty, as physical effects follow their physical causes. These moral antecedents are desires, aversions, habits, and dispositions, combined with outward circumstances suited to call those internal incentives into action. All these again are effects of causes, those of them which are mental being consequences of education, and of other moral and physical influences.'— Mr. Mill, *Exam.* p. 561. In following through this theory of volitions, there is no need for raising the question as to the possibility of the development of our natural powers, already discussed in Part I. Div. ii.

7. The Necessitarian theory accounts for the rise of distinct motives in consciousness, by affirming that there are 'outward circumstances suited to call those internal incentives into action.' This is ground common to both theories. It has been always admitted that personal experience is thus far determined for us. But these 'internal incentives' are awakened not by any physical energy which objects exert over us, but by natural sensibility, *connected with observation.* It is granted, then, that we have an example of necessity, not even of volition (certainly not of free-will) in the rise of motives. Whether it be possible by voluntary determination to provide for the awakening of natural or acquired dispositions, need not at present detain us.

8. The Necessitarian theory explains the continuance and influence of motives in consciousness by the constitution and acquired tendencies of the mind within which they arise. Mr.

Mill refers to 'education and other moral and physical influences.' Edwards points to 'the particular temper which the mind has by nature, or that has been introduced and established by education, example, custom, or some other means.'— Pt. I. sec. ii. Here too is matter of agreement, but here also the point of divergence is reached. It is granted that what a man is by nature, he is by necessity, that is, without personal choice. And as men differ somewhat in constitution, it is granted that, independently of personal choice, there may be some diversity in the natural force of dispositions, as they come into play. Thus far it is held on both sides, that there is determination without choice. Beyond this, the controversy begins. Libertarians distinguish between a man's nature and his character, maintaining that the one is made for him, and the other he makes for himself. This, however, may be passed, while we consider the point of more immediate importance here, viz., the laws which determine the progressive strength of motives. Libertarians admit the accuracy of the Necessitarian theory, in so far as it points to a man's nature and acquired tendencies as contributing towards an explanation of the strength of a motive. But they affirm that, after making full allowance for the outward circumstances, for the nature of the man, and for his acquired tendencies, the answer is incomplete. They urge, that the influence of *observation* or *attention,* so essential to our experience, is omitted; and that the solution of the question as to the strength of any motive, whether great or small, depends largely on the account given of personal observation. In absence of any philosophy of this, Libertarians affirm that the solution of the problem as to the laws which determine the development of motive force, stands unfinished in the scheme of Necessitarianism. Edwards arranged admirably the points of consideration, when he indicated these three,— 'the nature and circumstances of the *thing viewed;* the nature and circumstances of the *mind that views;* and the degree and manner of its *view.'* But the last named is very imperfectly examined; see *Freedom of Will,* i. II. 2. The incompleteness of its treatment is apparent in these statements of the general result,— 'The Will always is as the greatest apparent good is,' and 'the Will always follows the *last* dictate of the understanding.' Still more perplexing is the statement of Hobbes,— 'Will is the last appetite in deliberating.'— *Leviath.* I. vi., Works, vol. III. p. 49. The term

'Deliberation' is, however, used in a very wide sense; see p. 48. A psychological investigation of the part which the understanding performs in connexion with the increase of motive force in the mind, is, in the view of Libertarians, an obvious want in the opposite scheme.

9. Necessitarianism encounters difficulties, arising from its own nature, in attempting to construct a harmonious theory of moral government, and to interpret the moral sentiments common to men. With a statement of each of these difficulties, I conclude the subject of the Will.

10. Necessitarianism has difficulty in accounting for the consciousness of Moral Responsibility, and for the justice of personal liability to punishment. The following is an outline of Mr. Mill's view of the subject: — 'Responsibility means Punishment. When we are said to have the feeling of being morally responsible for our actions, the idea of being punished for them is uppermost in the speaker's mind.' This may mean expectation of punishment, or 'knowing that we shall deserve' it. The former, as expectation of responsibility, is not consciousness of it. That which may be, deemed to require the free-will hypothesis is 'the belief that we ought to be' accountable; 'that we are justly accountable; that guilt deserves punishment It is here that issue is joined between the two opinions,'— *Exam.* p. 571. On the theory of Necessity (we are told), a man cannot help acting as he does, and it cannot be just that he should be punished for what he cannot help. Not if the expectation of punishment enables him to help it, and is *the only means* by which he can be enabled to help it?'— *Exam.* 573. 'There are two ends which, on the Necessitarian theory, are sufficient to justify punishment: the benefit of the offender himself, and the protection of others.'—*Ib.* 576.

11. A philosophy of the moral sentiments, including self-approbation and self-condemnation, shame and remorse, is peculiarly difficult under the necessitarian hypothesis. Remorse may be taken as the example. Priestley treats of it thus,— 'A man, when he reproaches himself for any particular action in his past conduct, may fancy that if he was in the same situation again, he would have acted differently. But this is a mere deception, and if he examines himself strictly, and takes in all the circumstances, he may be satisfied that, with the same inward

disposition of mind, and with precisely the same views of things as he had then, and exclusive of all others which he has acquired by reflection since, he could not have acted otherwise than he did.'— *Illust. of Phil. Necessity,* p. 99; see also Belsham's *Elements,* p. 406. It is at least an awkward escape from a theoretic difficulty to maintain that the whole human race is deceived. The philosophic question is this,— What power belongs to us as intellectual beings? Have we such power, that a man can attain to accurate views of the moral quality of an action before he perform it, as well as after the action is done? The negative cannot be maintained on a utilitarian theory of morals, any more than on an Intuitional theory.

12. Problems.— (1.) On the theory that knowledge of causality is only knowledge of sequence, can an appeal be consistently made to the law of causality itself, as sufficient warrant for a theory as to the origin of a new form of existence? (2.) Granting moral distinctions as common to Intuitionalism and Utilitarianism, can these afford any rule of conduct in harmony with a Necessitarian theory of volition? (3.) Are Rewards and Punishments means of government, employed to determine the strongest motive; or are they the consequences which naturally and justly follow voluntary conformity to moral law, or violation of it? (4.) On the basis of the necessitarian theory, work out an explanation of the common opinion, as expressed by Mr. Mill, 'That whoever cultivates a disposition to wrong, places his mind out of sympathy with the rest of his fellow-creatures.'— *Exam.* 572. (5.) If men are governed by contrivances for awakening the strongest motive, how has it come to pass that rewards are less employed for this end than punishments?— *The Battle of the Two Philosophies,* p. 49. (6.) In view of the need for protecting common rights, what is the difference between these two cases: 'It is just to punish so far as is necessary for this purpose, as it is just to put a wild beast to death (without unnecessary suffering) for the same object'?— *Exam.* 578.

PART IV
MORAL SENTIMENTS

1. Besides the Affections and Emotions already described in Part II., there are other dispositions of mind, which have as their objects, moral actions considered in themselves, or persons regarded as agents acting within the moral sphere. These are properly named 'Moral Sentiments,' and are experienced only through means of the exercise of our moral nature, distinguishing between right and wrong.

2. These Sentiments afford illustrations of the common law of mind, that all exercise of the intelligent nature is accompanied by an experience of sensibility. Intelligence directed on moral distinctions, is thus attended by a particular order of sensibility.

3. The moral sentiments differ in their psychological character, according as the judgment on which they attend, applies merely to an action in itself considered, or to the agent whose action is observed, or to self as the agent. These sentiments may thus wear the character of mere feeling, or of affection, or of emotion. The name 'moral sentiments,' therefore, is not to be regarded as indicating exact similarity of psychological character in the dispositions grouped under it, though they agree in these two characteristics, that they are of the nature of sentiment or feeling in contrast with intelligence; and that they attend upon moral judgments. They harmonize with these judgments, as sentiment can harmonize with thought, and they support the judgments as attendant sanctions.

4. In accordance with their functions, the natural ground of classification is obtained by reference to the distinct moral judgments which they accompany, as these judgments refer to the actions or to the agent,— and, in the latter case, to another person or to self.

5. In harmony with the twofold division of moral quality, as right or wrong, moral sentiments appear in double form, as pleasurable or painful, each sentiment of a pleasurable kind, because of approval, having its contrary, in case of a judgment of condemnation.

6. Viewing a moral action simply in the light of the judgment pronounced upon it, we experience a sentiment of

beauty or deformity, as the judgment is favourable or unfavourable. There is a moral beauty, varying in degree, according to harmony with moral law, and the simplicity or complexity of the action. There is in like manner a moral deformity, awakening, more or less powerfully, a sense of aversion or dislike.

7. Consequent upon a judgment approving an action, and the attendant sentiment of the beautiful, there is admiration of the agent. With the opposite judgment, and its attendant feeling, there is disrespect to the agent. These dispositions are of the nature of affections, analogous to love and hate. They accordingly have impelling power, as all affections have. Admiration of an agent in successive cases, leads to a judgment of general approval as to his character, attended by love and trust. Disrespect to an agent, in like manner, in consequence of its recurrence, conducts to dislike and distrust. 'A generous and noble character affords a satisfaction even in the survey; and when presented to us, though only in a poem or fable, never fails to charm and delight us.'— Hume, *Essays,* II. 195, *Dissert, on the Passions,* sec. 2.

8. Moral sentiment assumes a distinct type when the judgment on which it depends is concerned with our own conduct or character. Such sentiments, however, follow the analogy of those already described.

As the sense of beauty or deformity is dependent upon a judgment concerned with the action only, either sentiment is as natural in contemplation of our own action as in contemplating the action of another person. To shun experience or acknowledgment of either sentiment, simply because the action happens to be our own, is suppression of natural sentiment, possible only by shunning the approval or disapproval of conscience.

9. As there is a judgment of approval on ourselves when we have done a right action, there is a sentiment or pleasurable feeling of self-approbation attendant on the judgment. This sentiment, being experienced in consequence of the decision that there has been conformity with moral law, is in natural harmony with the teaching of conscience. It is thus, according to its essential relation with our moral judgments, a sanction of these judgments, and a natural reward of right action. Its experience is

often described as 'the testimony of a good conscience,' meaning an approving conscience.

10. The frequent recurrence of judgments of self-approval, if sufficiently tested by strict moral law, warrants a favourable judgment as to personal character, attended by a more enduring sentiment of self-esteem. Such self-esteem is in full harmony with Conscience. It is in nature wholly distinct from Pride, which is an immoral sentiment, the attendant of falsehood and self-deception. Self-esteem because of continuous observance of moral law, is in perfect harmony with a true humility, springing from habitual recognition of the limits of all our powers, for humility is not, as Hume makes it, 'a dissatisfaction with ourselves, on account of some defect or infirmity.'— *The Passions,* sec. 2; *Essays,* II. 191. Humility as a virtue is at the opposite extreme from humiliation or mortification, whether as the result of our own conduct or that of others. Self-esteem is an essential feature of a soundly working moral nature. The loss of it betokens moral disorder.

11. As there is a judgment of condemnation pronounced by us upon ourselves when we have done a wrong action, there is a sentiment of dissatisfaction with ourselves, which involves us in the experience of great uneasiness. This is often termed the accusation of an evil Conscience. In its more active form it is designated Shame, which, as it becomes intensified, is named Remorse. This sentiment, as a restraining force, wears the character of Emotion. This restraint it exercises in harmony with the authority of Conscience, so as to prevent continuance in immorality. This emotion, in common with others, is liable to gain ascendency, and overleap the barriers of personal control. It may thus urge to recklessness in complete surrender of self-government.

12. As continuance in immoral conduct leads to the loss of self-esteem, and to an intolerable experience of self-reproach, there is a struggle of the nature to escape its misery. And, if this attempt be made while the cause of the suffering continues in operation, it is carried through under shelter of false reasoning and excuses, which blunt the sense of shame, and prepare the way for shamelessness, in wilful defiance of moral distinctions.

13. Moral sentiments which are in harmony with Conscience, are by consequence in harmony with our whole

172

moral nature. Disregard of such sentiments, indicates some form of moral disorder.

14. Moral sentiments being essentially dependent on the moral judgments, rise spontaneously along with these judgments, and in accordance with them. They are not dependent on our Will, either to occasion or prevent their rise, except in so far as the judgments themselves depend upon our Will.

15. This law of the rise of moral sentiments, by which they depend upon preceding judgments, makes the moral sentiment of no value as a standard for deciding the moral character of actions. Everything here depends upon the validity of the moral judgment with which they have taken their rise. A sentiment of self-satisfaction will attend a judgment of self-approbation, whether that judgment be correct or not. The sole test of the moral value of sentimental experience is found in the test of the moral quality of personal actions,— clear recognition of moral law.

16. Problems.— (1.) Explain how one man can boast of an act, which another man regards with shame. (2.) In what combinations of experience may Shame instigate to action subversive of its own natural end? (3.) In Adam Smith's theory of Moral Sentiments, what is the value of his reference to a disinterested spectator in attempting to secure a test of sympathy?

PART V
DISORDER OF OUR MORAL NATURE

1. The preceding investigations have repeatedly brought into view evidence that our moral nature is in a condition of disorder. Stated generally, the result is, that our nature does not work in full harmony with the dictates of the governing power.

2. The evidence of moral disorder may be summarized under three divisions:— (1.) insubordination of lower motives, as in the gratification of natural desires in opposition to the guidance of Conscience; (2.) the action of impulses which are in their nature condemned by Conscience, such as envy, selfishness, cruelty; (3.) the experience of moral sentiment of a kind which can have exercise only in a nature disordered, and as a check upon the increase of moral disorder,— the sentiment which according to its degree of strength is named self-disapprobation,— shame,— remorse.

3. The disorder of our moral nature, of which the evidence is so distinct and abundant, has been all but uniformly acknowledged by philosophers. The explicit character of the general acknowledgment may be inferred from the following examples. The Socratic doctrine that Virtue is knowledge, and that no one is voluntarily evil, κακο ζ εκων ουδει ζ, may seem adverse to an admission of disorder, and so in form it is, for it implies the presence of adequate motive power for well-doing. But in reality it involves a very full acknowledgment of disorder, since it is supported on the ground that all men seek their own good, and that they excuse their folly by reference to some form of deception of which they have been the victims. Plato says, 'Virtue is the health and beauty and well-being of the soul, and vice is the disease and weakness and deformity of the soul.'— *Repub.* IV., Jowett's Transl. II. 276. The disorder he explains in the following manner. First distinguishing the parts of our nature as rational, concupiscent, and irascible, he says, 'Must not injustice be a kind of quarrel between these three — a meddlesomeness, and interference, and rising up of a part of the soul against the whole soul, an assertion of unlawful authority, which is made by a rebellious subject against a true prince, of whom he is the natural vassal — that is the sort of thing; the confusion and error of these parts or elements is injustice and

intemperance, and cowardice and ignorance, and in general all vice?'— *Ib.,* Jowett, IV. 275. See also the misery of a corrupt soul, as described in the *Gorgias.* Aristotle says, 'We are more naturally disposed' towards those things which are wrong, and 'more easily carried away to excess, than to propriety of conduct.'— *Ethics* III. I. The testimony from modern philosophy is equally explicit. Des Cartes says, 'With respect to seemingly natural impulses, I have observed, when the question related to the choice of right or wrong in action, that they frequently led me to take the worse part.'— *Medit.* III., Prof. Veitch's Transl. p. 39. I need not mention in detail Hume's representations of human vanity in sec. II. of his *Dissert, on the Passions.* In illustration of the fact 'that an opposition of passions commonly causes a new emotion in the spirits, and produces more disorder than the concurrence of any two affections of equal force,' he says, 'Hence we naturally desire what is forbid, and often take a pleasure in performing actions merely because they are unlawful. The notion of duty, when opposite to the passions, is not always able to overcome them; and when it fails of that effect, is apt rather to increase and irritate them, by producing an opposition in our motives and principles.'— *Dissert, on the Passions,* sec. VI., Essays, II. 218. Adam Smith's whole theory is a testimony to moral disorder, in the acknowledgment of the continual need for going out of self, in search of a disinterested spectator, in order to avoid bias. Mackintosh, in remarking that 'many passions prevail over' the moral sentiments, says, 'The prevalence itself . . . is perceived to be a disorder, when seen in another man, and felt to be so by the mind disordered, when the disorder subsides.'— *Dissert,* sec. VI., Remarks on Butler, Whewell's ed. p. 153. Comte says, 'We roust regret that even in the best natures, the social affections are so overborne by the personal, as rarely to command conduct in a direct way.— *Philos. Positive,* B. vi. c. 5; *Sociology,* Miss Martineau's Tr. II. p. 131. In accordance with this statement, Comte proceeds to speak of 'the radical imperfection of the human character,' II. p. 133. With these as representative witnesses to the fact of moral disorder, testimony need. not be extended in proof of its general acknowledgment.

4. As the fact of moral disorder appears conspicuously in the abnormal action of the desires and affections, and in the existence of dispositions, having the influence of motive forces,

which are antagonistic to the authority of conscience and to the harmony of our nature, the extent of the disorder may be computed on these data. Having regard to the difference between Intelligence and Disposition, the question may be considered from the two opposite points of view afforded by these sides of our nature. For this purpose, it is not needful here to reproduce the evidence in support of the position that the conscience discovers to us moral law, and has in this respect competent authority in the government of our life.— Part I. div. i. chaps, iii. and iv. Assuming this, our investigation must take the form of an inquiry, how far the conscience, and our intellectual powers generally, are affected in nature or action by the moral disorder existing in the mind; and, on the other hand, how far natural dispositions are influenced by this disorder.

5. Our Intellectual Powers are not so influenced by moral disorder as to render them uncertain guides in the recognition and application of moral truth.

Taking first a general view, the contrast between Intellect and Disposition is such that neither abnormal action of natural dispositions, nor the action of unnatural dispositions, produces an essential change upon intellect. Cognitive power, that is power of sight or knowledge, is so different in nature from the power of disposition, that each produces distinct results according to its own nature; in the one case, knowledge; in the other, movement or excitement of mind, exercising impelling or restraining force. It is no part of the function of cognitive power to produce sentiment, neither is it of sentiment to provide knowledge. This is a simple exposition of the difference of the two classes of powers.

When, however, we consider the laws which regulate the action of these two sides of our nature, we find that they do not operate singly, but conjointly, and in such a manner as to influence each other. What then is the nature and possible extent of this influenced? It is such that they may mutually stimulate or restrain each other, but not such that either can change the nature of the other, or the laws of its exercise. Affection in its ardour can greatly restrain the action of intellect, a fact commonly known under the designation of 'the blinding power of love.' Intellect in full exercise, takes the government of affection, and thereby keeps it in check. These are the laws which regulate the joint action of the two sides of our nature, and their bearing on the question under discussion is obvious. The intellect is by its nature the governor of disposition, but disposition in its development may break away from its control. Abnormal action of natural disposition does involve a check on intellectual action, so long as such abnormal experience continues; but when this experience passes off, intellect has free play, and at all events continues unchanged in nature and function. Unnatural desires, however their presence in consciousness may be accounted for, do in point of fact follow the same laws of exercise as the natural in respect of conjoint action with intellect. Envy as well as affection, cruelty as well as sympathy, can restrain intellect or be restrained by it; but in any case the laws of intellectual action continue undisturbed.

Looking now at the distinct forms of intellectual power finding exercise in consciousness, observation, understanding, and reason, the distinct law of intellectual action becomes apparent in a variety of applications.

Observation.— Disposition in any of its forms, normal, abnormal, or unnatural, has not stopped observation, nor perverted it, nor imposed upon it new laws of exercise. Whatever be the disorders in our nature, it has not ceased to be intelligent. Whatever be the medium or instrument of knowledge, all rests ultimately on consciousness, and that is by its own nature indisputable.

Reasoning.— As the facts of observation supply the materials for reasoning, the laws of thought, which supply the tests of accuracy, are equally undeniable with the facts, making rational power a guide to certainty. Whatever we feel or desire, makes no difference as to the nature of a fallacy or of a logical argument.

Reason.— The recognition of self-evident universal truth, that is, truth of principle as distinct from truth of fact, if it be admitted on the testimony of consciousness as characteristic of the mind, implies power of such a nature, that neither the moral character of our dispositions, nor the degree of force they may severally attain in particular cases, supplies an element of experience whose interpretation carries in it, as a consequence, the loss of this power. The nature of our dispositions may go far to determine how often the first principles of morals are overlooked by us, or what measure of consideration and application they have when recognised; but in saying so, it is admitted that the power of recognition remains.

These considerations are enough to show that the disorder in our nature does not so influence our intellect as to prevent the recognition and application of moral law. The evil is in consciousness, and the knowledge of it as evil is present also, but the conditions on which these two forms of experience arise are quite distinct. This conclusion is adverse to the Socratic doctrine, that knowledge is Virtue. There is a knowledge of vice, and a practice of it, while its true character is fully known.

If we distinguish between the power and the authority of Conscience, as in the famous sentence of Butler, 'Had it strength as it has right, had it power as it has manifest authority, it would absolutely govern the world;'— *Sermon* II.,— it is needful to bear in mind that its impelling force is not one which operates directly upon other motives, so as to measure its strength with theirs. Its power is simply such as belongs to the discovery of truth, which, in its own nature, has the authority of law. But here, as in all intellectual action, there is attendant sentiment, which is of such a nature as to exercise direct impelling force. Recognised moral law awakens reverence, which acts as motive force, and as a direct check upon dispositions which are immoral in character. When we speak of want of power in Conscience, it is not want of teaching power, which leaves the mind uncertain as to the fundamental distinctions between right and wrong, but want of reverence for moral law, a want which is inevitable if the teaching of conscience do not receive attention. Under this condition, with co-operation of the law of custom as it influences thought, and the law of habit as it influences practice, the mind may become regardless of moral law.

6. As the disorder of our moral nature is not such as to hinder the knowledge of moral distinctions, or to prevent their application in the guidance of life, it does not offer an obstacle to the construction of a philosophy of man's moral nature, and of moral distinctions themselves. On the contrary, the disorder of our nature is such that the character and extent of the disorder are clearly recognised by us. There is no man who regards selfishness as equally deserving of admiration when witnessed, and of self-approbation when practised, as benevolence, however

frequently he may be conscious of the recurrence of both. Whatever difficulty there may be in rendering submission to moral law, that difficulty is recognised only by means of our knowledge of the law itself. This is the interpretation of moral conflict under a conviction of present duty, and also of the formation of moral character on the model of clearly recognised virtues.

Dr. Wardlaw, in his *Christian Ethics* (4th ed. London, 1844), has taken up a position which involves the denial of the possibility of Ethical Philosophy, because of the disorder of our moral nature. He argues that, because of this, we are unfitted for philosophizing on moral questions, and that our nature does not afford the requisite materials for an ethical philosophy. Man is 'both the investigator, and, in part at least, the subject of investigation. In each of these views of him there is a source of error; the *first* arising from the influence of his depravity on his character as an investigator; and the *second* from the disposition to make his own nature, without adverting to its fallen state, his standard of moral principles, and his study in endeavouring to ascertain them,' p. 37. It must be conceded to Dr. Wardlaw that moralists have not given that amount of consideration to the extent and influence of moral disorder, which their admission of the fact clearly required. But, on the other hand, Dr. Wardlaw has gone to the opposite extreme of constructing a theory of this disorder which the facts of consciousness do not sustain. Moral Philosophers generally have not affirmed that our whole nature is in itself the standard of moral excellence, so that thoughts and impulses are all equally good in themselves, and authoritative as guides of conduct. The reverse of this is affirmed in every system of Ethics until you descend as far as Mandeville. But, on the other hand, Dr. Wardlaw takes an untenable position when he insists that man is incapable of investigating moral questions 'from the bias which, on all such subjects, the moral state of the heart unavoidably imparts to the operations of the intellect; — a bias which attaches uncertainty and inconclusiveness to all human inquiries and decisions concerning them,' p. 38. He has no sooner penned this declaration than he is constrained to modify it by saying that our conclusions on moral subjects 'are not, without great caution, to be depended upon.' But, if caution is sufficient to make them reliable, the position is abandoned, and it is granted that certainty and conclusiveness may attach to human decisions concerning moral truth and personal obligation.

7. The power to direct attention, exercised by us in our decisions on other subjects, is equally available for guidance of thought and action where moral distinctions are concerned. But this power is the condition which provides for the exercise of Will.— Part III. ch. iii. sec. 14. The moral disorder existing in our nature is, therefore, not such as to unfit for obedience to moral law. It certainly involves the frequent experience of evil dispositions, when circumstances favour their rise, and consequently such influence over our thoughts of a disturbing or blinding nature as disposition can exert. But in the possibility of self-directed attention, a clear battle-ground is provided in consciousness, over which conflict with unnatural propensities may be waged. To what extent such conflict is undertaken, and to what extent successfully waged, in personal history, depends upon the degree in which regard is commonly given to moral law, and the reverence habitually cherished for it.

8. How moral disorder originated in human nature, is a problem which philosophy is incompetent to solve. To distinguish between the normal and the abnormal is simple enough by analysis of the facts of consciousness. But the problem of the origin of abnormal experience and action, is a historical not a psychological one. Philosophy can only bring out and set in array the facts which prove the disturbance of the balance originally established among the powers. But the problem thereby started, being insoluble by philosophic methods, can be answered only by direct Revelation.

9. The more urgent practical question is,— How is moral disorder to be escaped, and the original balance of our nature restored? This problem really involves two very distinct questions,— What are the laws of mind in accordance with which successful conflict may be maintained with dispositions recognised as wrong? And, second, How shall such a moral victory as this be raised into a uniform aim of the life, until it is completely realized? To the first question, Philosophy offers a reply by pointing to moral law as the rule of life,— to the law of attention, as providing for the control of dispositions by the Will,— and to the law of habit, as establishing ascendency so far as attained. These are the laws of moral progress; and, in their

reversal, appear the laws of moral deterioration. But, in so far as we need an answer to the question, How is a reigning motive power to be secured under sway of which the moral agent shall not weary of his irksome task, and abandon it in despair? Philosophy is again constrained to bear testimony to its insufficiency for solving the problem which it has itself raised. How to battle with dispositions adverse to the harmony of our nature, may be readily determined; but how to restore motive power which has been lost, is a question which transcends philosophy. On this subject, see the very able Essay of Principal Shairp, 'The Moral Dynamic:' *Studies in Poetry and Philosophy,* p. 348.

10. Problems.— (1.) How far does the disorder of the moral nature contribute to the explanation of the diversity of moral decisions? (2.) Is there any sense in which an exercise of natural disposition could be represented as abnormal, without being by consequence immoral? (3.) Under what conditions may an evil influence be said to become ungovernable? (4.) Are there, in human nature as known to us, any latent mental forces morally evil in character, which are so related to the controlling power in mind, as to give them inevitably the ascendency, when they arise in consciousness?

METAPHYSIC OF ETHICS
PRELIMINARY

1. Besides the questions which concern the moral nature of man, there is a still higher range of inquiry belonging to Moral Philosophy. It is concerned with the origin of our existence, specially considering our nature as moral beings,— the relation in which we now stand to the source of our existence,— the interpretation which such relation may afford of the system or order of things in which we find ourselves existing,— and the destiny which awaits us.

This is a region of inquiry properly denominated Metaphysical, because the character of the inquiry transcends the sphere of investigation connected with the nature we possess, that is to say, transcends the psychological. This, though a common use of the term Metaphysic, is different from Kant's use, according to which metaphysic is applied to *a priori* knowledge, as contrasted with knowledge through experience. But *a priori* knowledge is recognised in Consciousness, and is discovered in accordance with definite laws of mind, as truly as the knowledge gathered by experience. The one is transcendental, the other empirical, yet these are two branches of Psychology. But a psychology which discovers *a priori* laws of life, cannot be the halting-place of Ethical inquiry. It only gives deeper interest to that sphere in which we seek an answer to the question as to the origin of our nature.

2. Objection may be made to such inquiry, and this on two quite distinct grounds. *First,* that the *a priori* forms of knowledge, upon which we must greatly rely in attempting to prosecute further inquiry, are only mental conditions, regulative of our own thought, and not assertive, or capable of being regarded as criteria of truth. This is Kant's position in the *Critique of Pure Reason,* from which he is led to maintain that the idea of God, as of the soul and the universe, is merely regulative. From this self-created difficulty, he seeks escape, by maintaining in his Ethical system, that we, as free agents, belong to a cogitable world, above consciousness. The objection has no force beyond the theory out of which it arises, and has not sufficient force even within that theory. To those who reject the regulative theory of the ideas of Reason, and hold that Reason

discovers self-evident truths, the objection loses all force. But, even within the theory, if ours is a phenomenal experience, regulated in accordance with the ideas of God, the soul, and the universe, the question is still legitimate, How is the origin of such life as ours to be explained?

The *second* form of objection to the higher metaphysic comes from the theory which denies the possibility of discovering causes. It is urged that as in observation we recognise nothing more than the succession of facts, and never attain to a knowledge of causes, we cannot reach a knowledge of the cause of our own existence, or of the existence of the universe. To raise the question concerning the origin of our own existence, seems to Comte to attempt inaccessible heights,— an attempt which belongs only to the earliest stages of intellectual evolution, not to the more advanced. But to shun a question is not to lay it. At best, these heights are declared inaccessible, only because it is alleged that solid footing cannot be discovered by which to reach their base. But if, as has been maintained, each intelligence has a knowledge of self as the cause of personal actions, we have a clear approach to the base of the heights; and besides, we have both impulse and warrant for attempting to scale them.

3. As the problem concerns the explanation of personal existence, it can take its rise only from the facts of that existence, which must determine the line of speculative inquiry. Psychology must itself be the basis of a legitimate Metaphysic. Speculation which begins with definitions, or abstract conceptions, not with the facts of experience, separates itself from the only ground of certainty. However ingenious, and logically consistent, it is only conjecture, not metaphysics, or legitimate philosophical speculation.

4. The problem concerning the origin of personal existence is only part of the one great problem as to the origin of the universe. To isolate ourselves from the system to which we belong, is impossible; and so is it, to detach the problem of personal life, from the wider question concerning finite existence generally. The problem concerning the origin of finite existence is one. All sciences culminate at length on a common eminence, where, in one way or another, the scientific mind concerns itself with the question as to the origin of Known Being. The natural

distinction between physical and mental sciences, becomes of no account in view of the common intellectual demand coming, not from the special facts, but from the minds which have been classifying these facts. It is thus true, as Sir W. Hamilton has insisted, *Metaph.* I. 30, that intelligence raises the grand question as to the existence of 'an Intelligent Creator and Moral Governor;' but the acknowledgment is pushed too far when Sir William affirms 'that the class of phenomena which requires that kind of cause we denominate a Deity is *exclusively* given in the phenomena of mind.'— *Ib.* 26.

5. As metaphysical inquiry seeks an explanation of the origin of known existence, and of its continuance under government of laws recognised in the several departments of science, the ultimate test of all metaphysical speculation must be found in the facts from which the inquiry takes its rise. Merely to *start* from facts is not a sufficient security for the accuracy of subsequent speculation. This security is found only by careful *return* upon the facts out of which the metaphysical problems arise. These, then, are the two fundamental canons of metaphysical speculation: To start from facts in search of the solution of the problems to which they give rise; and to return to the facts for test of every solution proposed.

6. A view of the breadth of existence to be explained may be readily secured by separating existence into three divisions, material, intellectual, and moral. The validity of these divisions need not now be insisted upon. It is enough for the present purpose that reference be made to the characteristics of mind as traced in the Introduction. If any prefer to divide existence into inorganic and organic, with the addition, in case of the human race, of the peculiar mental or spiritual features belonging to it, there is no reason why such a classification should not be adopted.

7. The various theories propounded in explanation of the order of things in which we exist are, The Theistic, or a Self-sufficient First Cause; the contrary of this, which in its negative form is Atheistic, in its positive form Materialistic, making Self-existent Matter the source of all; The Pantheistic, presenting in a variety of forms the theory that God is All; and, lastly, The Polytheistic, that there are many God's. The last need not detain us, as it is not vindicated on philosophic grounds.

CHAPTER I
THE EXISTENCE OF GOD

1. The solution of the problem of finite existence is found first in a Self-sufficient Being, Infinite and Eternal, who is First Cause, or source of all existence besides.

2. The problem concerning the origin of being is first consciously raised in the search for satisfaction as to the source of personal existence, and of all existence recognised around. This problem is the expression of a purely intellectual demand. Its solution is not directly required by the practical necessities of life. There is, therefore, no reason to conclude that men uniformly grapple with the question, Does God exist? Acknowledgment of the Divine existence is, indeed, closely allied with the requirements of personal life. But deliberate testing of the grounds on which this acknowledgment is made, is a logical and metaphysical exercise on which there is no evidence to conclude that men uniformly enter. The raising of the question is evidence of the prevalence of philosophic thought. Confirmation of this appears in the fact that the formal discussions of the subject occur in treatises more or less philosophic in character.

3. The first and most conspicuous fact connected with all forms of existence whose origin we seek to have explained is, that all are finite and restricted. That limited and restricted existence is not self-sufficient is evident. To say so is merely to present an amplification of the first statement. For, to say that a being is limited, either in the measure of existence, or in the range of its powers, is to say that it is not self-sufficient. The intellect must raise the question, How has it been so limited? or, Whence has it the laws of its existence? And these questions arise, because their solution is not seen in the being itself. This is the root of the problem. When, further, it is said of any being that it is restricted, it is meant that there is other existence so related to this as to lend some help to its action, as moisture and heat contribute to the growth of a plant, or to impose a check upon its action, as resistance of the atmosphere wearies the runner. It is to be observed further, that it is in the highest order of finite being that restriction is most apparent. The more numerous the forms of effort the more the points of restraint. Whether, therefore, we

recognise change of form and condition actually occurring, or merely limitation of being, we equally need an explanation of existence.

4. The logical alternatives open to us in seeking a solution of limited and restricted existence are two: — An infinite regress of finite causes; or, A self-sufficient, eternal first-cause. The four theories which have been offered come under the sweep of this duality of logical alternative. The Theistic doctrine, as a deliberate acceptance of the one alternative, stands in logical opposition to all the other three, which either accept the opposite alternative, or fail to deal with the essential features of the problem.

5. The regress of finite causes, each one of which shall be adequate to account for the measure of existence previously recognised, is logically the nearest solution, and meets the first demands of a logical process, under the law of Causality. To postulate a cause simply adequate to produce known existence, satisfies the immediate claim of intelligence. Accordingly, the truth of the conclusion may be accepted, merely as implying conformity with the laws of thought, though there be no means at command for verifying the supposition as to the existence of such a cause. The conclusion is thus of only a general nature, such as this,— In the cause there must be at least sufficient power to produce the effect. To this conclusion there can be no logical exception. Still, what is thus accepted, logically, but only hypothetically, is not conclusive. The intellectual requirement which raised the first question, now raises another as to the existence of this hypothetical cause, and so must continue as long as, in strict conformity with logical rule, only limited existence is postulated. In this line, therefore, there is no logical landing-place which can be conclusive, and no logical warrant for stopping. Besides, as the second stage in the process is only hypothetical, and there is no discovery of actual existence, by the contemplation of which we should have required to raise a fresh question, there is nothing better than a logical ground for procedure. As, then, it is impossible for us to continue the process to infinity, so is it impossible to rest in the belief that the history of existence has been progressively, what the order of thought must be regressively. And for these reasons, *First,* Logical consistency in reasoning cannot be identified with reality

of existence. *Second,* As individual thinkers differ in the measure of their knowledge of the various forms of existence, and each one logically postulates a cause adequate only to meet the measure of his own knowledge, the logical result is distinct in each case. The line of thought is essentially connected with the individuality of the thinker, and has no further hold upon reality than that obtained in the facts from which the intellectual process takes its rise. *Third,* An infinite succession of finite causes involves a hypothesis of infinity, without even so much as a hypothetical basis on which to support it. At each stage in the logical process, there is at least the hypothetical basis of a definite amount of existence on which to postulate a sufficient cause. When the intellectual process is stopped, we have warrant for affirming merely our inability to continue the process for ever, and similarly our inability to affirm that at some stage we should reach a logical halting-place. If, to escape the discomfort arising from the want of any solution of the problem, we suggest an infinite regression of finite causes, the suggestion is not only gratuitous, but we raise a new problem. On what ground are we to affirm infinity of existence? We have made an affirmation without trace of logical warrant. Our difficulties in carrying through an intellectual process bear witness to the limits of our thought, but provide no foundation for a hypothesis as to existence.

6. In postulating a self-sufficient cause, infinite in power, and eternal in duration, we postulate more than is logically sufficient to account for known existence. If, therefore, there be any warrant for this affirmation, it cannot be obtained by a logical process. It cannot be logically competent to reason from finite existence to infinite,— from restricted existence to that which is self-sufficient.— Hamilton's *Discussions,* p. 15. If we rest somehow in the acknowledgment of a Self-sufficient Being, it cannot be as the conclusion of a discursive process. Attempts at demonstration, whether starting from the most general conceptions, such as being, or extension *(a priori* in form); or starting from the facts of experience *(a posteriori* in form), are equally unsuccessful, however great the ability which they discover. Either the whole question is assumed in starting, or the Infinite is not reached in concluding. Kant has clearly shown this, and has thus rendered special service to the Theistic

doctrine.— *Critique of Pure Reason,* Transc. Dialec. II. III., Meiklejohn's Transl. p. 359. To begin, as Clarke did, with the proposition that 'something has existed from eternity,' is virtually to propose an argument, after having assumed what is to be proved.— *Demonstration of the Being and Attributes of God.* p. 8. Gillespie's form of the *a priori* argument, starting with the proposition, 'Infinity of Extension is necessarily existing,' is liable to the same objection, with the additional disadvantage of attributing a property of matter to the Deity.— *The Necessary Existence of the Deity.* The argument from Design is admirable as an inference from the character of the effect to the nature of the cause, but it pre-supposes the truth that there is a first cause. The argument of Des Cartes, as of Anselm, from the clearness of the idea of God, to the certainty of his existence, is incompetent, because we cannot lay down the canon that our thoughts are the criterion of reality, or that every clear idea must have its counter-part in an existing object.— Des Cartes, *Meditation,* III., and *Principles of Philos.* Pt I. xiv.; Anselm's *Proslogium;* for substance of the argument, see Ueberweg's *Hist.* I. 383. As Kant has said, we cannot allow reason 'to persuade itself into a belief of the objective existence of a mere creation of its own thought.'— *Pure Reason,* Meiklejohn, 359. Some ideas are creations of our own thought; for example, the idea of a centaur. Knowing this, we are aware that it is incompetent to reason from the thought to the thing. But, can we distinguish between thoughts which are of our own creation, and thoughts which are not? If so, the relations of thoughts to things may vary, and we may be aware of the difference. Even if the clearness of our thought of God be no argument to the reality of the Divine existence, still the idea remains as a fact to be accounted for. I can explain, by simple combination of the attributes of different beings, how the idea of a centaur has been formed. But how shall we account for the idea of God within us? How has this conception been formed? Des Cartes has a strong position here. 'By the name of God I understand a substance infinite, eternal, immutable, independent, all-knowing, all-powerful, and by which I myself, and every other thing that exists, if any such there be, were created. But these properties are so great and excellent, that the more attentively I consider them, the less, as I feel persuaded, can the idea I have of them owe its origin to myself alone.'— *Medit.* III., Prof. Veitch's Transl. p. 45. See Plato's *Republic,* B. VI.; Jowett, II. p, 351; and the elder Fichte's *Way of the Blessed Life,* translated by Dr. Smith, p. 48. Still, it is not the idea or conception of God which proves the reality of the Divine existence, though the presence of such a conception requires to be explained. Logical processes are insufficient for reaching this high truth. Thus far Comte is correct in speaking of inaccessible heights; but the mind is not restricted merely to observation and logic for the discovery of truth. There is in the nature of reason itself, provision for the recognition of higher truth.

7. The reality of the Divine existence is a truth so plain that it needs no proof, as it is a truth so high that it admits of none. It is not the clearness of the idea or conception of God, which proves his existence, for it is not a conception so clear to the mind of all men, as it was to Des Cartes, but often a conception rather vague, because not analytically examined. But there is certainty of belief in the Divine existence, supported by reference to finite existence, thereby explained. This is an intuitive belief, while that of infinite regress of finite causes is a logical belief. This is a belief so fundamental to human life, that men accept and apply it without question. When, advancing beyond this, the problem of finite existence is faced, the fact of the Divine existence is at once regarded as the adequate solution. It is only when an attempt is made to prove it, that doubt is felt to arise; and then, it is to be observed, the doubt attaches to the argument, not to the fact. In no region of inquiry more than here is there need for analysing doubt in order to decide upon its source. For, doubts concerned merely with the validity of accredited arguments, are to be discounted, when we seek a correct measure of doubt as to the true solution of the problem of finite existence. See Augustine, *De Vera Religione,* 72.

8. Intuitive belief in the Divine existence, contemplated in its radical form, is belief in a Supreme Being. It is acknowledgment of a Being who controls our destiny, and that of all finite existence. The conception may be vague, and indeed is certain to be indistinct until some analytic process is voluntarily attempted. But that some reference to a Supreme Being is natural to man, is a conclusion established by the testimony of history (see Cudworth's *Intellectual System),* and is

supported by the most recent inquiries regarding uncivilized life. On the last-named subject see specially, Tylor's *Primitive Culture,* 2 vols., 1870. An outline of the results I have given in the Appendix to *third* Edition of *The Philosophy of the Infinite,* 1872. To represent the religious beliefs of savage tribes as the result of logical processes, is the least satisfactory suggestion which can be made. On the admission that the belief is natural to the human mind, it is possible to find a general harmony of ascertained facts. The conception, being vague, may gather around it additions suggested by the circumstances of the people. These additions may accordingly be different in the history of different tribes, and may even fail in self-consistency. But it is the common original idea of a Great Ruler which is the explanation of the common features of belief and religious practice throughout the world. In harmony with this view, it is obvious that the idea of God becomes more comprehensive and self-consistent in all its features, as a people advances in intellectual activity.

9. The belief in the Divine existence, which is first accepted simply as a determining force in practical life, is afterwards accepted as the only adequate solution of the problem of finite existence. As already suggested, the raising of this problem belongs to a period of philosophic thought. And in seeking a solution of it, the existence of a sell-sufficient First Cause is accepted as adequate, and as the *only* adequate solution. The inquiry as to the origin of known existence thus becomes the test of the harmony of our belief with recognised facts. What is thereby accepted has new significance, being no longer a vague belief,— no longer personal experience of the force of some natural impulse,— but a clear discovery of the fitness of this belief to meet all the demands of intellect in its search for causes. It is thus that the natural belief comes to have associated with it a fuller, clearer conception of the nature of the Supreme Being. In this way, also, the conception receives its true scientific place and application. From these considerations, it appears that the legitimate use of a discursive process, is not in an attempt to reach the fact of the Divine existence as a logical conclusion, but in testing the harmony between the belief and the facts of existence. This latter use of the reasoning process is in accordance with the scientific methods followed in all

departments of investigation. When the mind makes inquiry as to the existence of a Being, Self-sufficient and Supreme, it is certainly more in accordance with the limits of logical proof, that it should advance from belief to confirmatory evidence, than that it should attempt to pass, by its own strength, from restricted existence to the transcendent grandeur of Infinite Being.— Mahan's *Nat. Theol.*, 1867.

10. Belief in the Divine existence is confirmed as the range of discovery extends our knowledge of the universe. With this belief given, the argument from design rises into a conspicuous place as an argument confirmatory. And as the harmony of the universe becomes more manifest in the correlation of forces, and the relation of mind to action, the confirmatory argument gains in proportion. Here also it is that the contradictions and insufficiency of conflicting theories become most apparent. To account for the order of the universe is the grand perplexity of every theory which attempts a philosophy of finite existence from any lower point of view than that recognised in the existence of an intelligent First Cause.

11. The whole of the earlier conclusions in Moral Philosophy, as to personal obligation and responsibility, find an ultimate resting-place in the recognition of the Deity as moral ruler, source of moral good. 'There is no teaching more mischievous than that which makes human belief in God the first regenerating power in human society, and God himself second.'— *Essays, Theol. and Lit.,* by R. H. Hutton, I. 5, London, 1871. Any theory of existence lower than the Theistic, leaves the essential features of our moral nature unexplained. The tendency under such a theory is to depreciate the facts of moral life which give character to the great problem of experience. Evidence of this appears in all the development theories of moral nature. We have seen obligation reduced to the strongest proclivity, and responsibility to punishment. Such representations fail in their appreciation of the facts to be explained. On the other hand, relying on the basis of necessary truth, we have seen in the nature of moral law, the source of personal obligation, and of individual responsibility. These correlated doctrines of Ethical science may be admitted to have logical consistency and coherence in systematic form, and yet may be regarded as wanting in living practical force. But when

that which springs from necessary laws of morality finds its resting-place in the government of a Supreme Ruler, the vital relations of the whole order of moral truth, law, and activity, become apparent on the grandest scale. If oughtness spring from the application of law, it is seen to be enforced by the Sovereign Ruler; and if responsibility for personal conduct flow directly from obligation to act, we discover now the Judgment Seat before which the response must be given. Even if Responsibility mean liability to punishment, narrow as this view is, it finds coherence only in the acknowledgment of a Judge, vested with authority and power to inflict what is due. If we venture further to gaze upon the complications and terrible mysteries of life, and attempt to rise above the dead level where we speak only of the imperfection which necessarily clings to finite existence; if, with the instincts of moral life, we venture to anticipate that Justice shall triumph, and the loftiest characteristics of man gain ascendency in his life, the rational warrant for such expectation is found only in the recognition of the Supreme One, ruling in absolute justice and purity over the hosts of intelligent creatures.

12. Belief in the Divine existence harmonizes with the religious instinct of our nature. That men reason themselves into religious feeling, is a proposition which could not claim serious attention. But that men recognise religious feeling to be reasonable, and that all the more clearly in proportion as they reflect profoundly on the higher relations of life, is a position more in harmony with the facts of experience. At the same time it must be allowed that reasoning of this kind is more the exercise of disciplined minds than of men generally, and partakes somewhat more of the character of philosophic thought than of what might fitly be called religious thought. Religious instinct seems, therefore, the term to describe the source of that widespread religious life which appears in our world under a multitude of forms. When subjected to analytic investigation, it is distinctly marked by two prominent features, *first,* the sense of dependence on higher power which is the spontaneous experience of a nature sensible of its inherent weakness, and subjection to governing forces in the universe, and, *second,* reverence of feeling for the perfection belonging to the Absolute Being. These two are the essential elements of the religious instinct, swayed by the fundamental belief in the Divine

existence. The harmony of faith with such feeling is complete. Only in such faith can a harmony be found. Without it there is the saddening, crushing sense of hopeless subjection to inexorable forces which in mystery sway the universe, regardless of intensest human emotion. Without this faith, a capacity of reverence is a fountain of disappointment, finding no higher object towards which it may direct its force than is discovered among men of wide experience and lofty disposition who die by our side. But with faith in Deity, dependence rises to trust, attended by peace the most profound which the human spirit can reach, and by reverence which finds in an object of infinite excellence an exhaustless source of satisfaction, attracting towards the loftiest attainment.

CHAPTER II
THE MATERIALISTIC (ATHEISTIC) THEORY

Having indicated the nature and value of the first logical alternative which lies open to us in seeking to account for the origin of finite existence, I pass to the consideration of conflicting theories, taking first the opposite extreme, in the form of a thoroughgoing contradiction of the Theistic doctrine. The other two theories,— the Pantheistic and Polytheistic,— as they do not involve a thoroughgoing contradiction, are mixed theories, and as such are wanting in self-consistency.

1. A purely Atheistic theory, being merely negative, proves nothing. Merely to utter a denial of the Divine existence is always possible; but such a denial is of no scientific value. Nor is there any logical worth in a plea of ignorance as to such a transcendent fact as the existence of an absolute but invisible ruler. We have seen that to argue from thought to existence is unwarrantable; much more unwarrantable is it to reason from ignorance to non-existence. Equally impossible is it to argue legitimately against the existence of an object merely on the ground that no such existence is visible. Though one avenue of knowledge be closed against us, it does not therefore follow that other means of information are not open. A plea grounded on invisibility is only a specific form of the illegitimate argument from ignorance to non-existence.

2. The negative worth of an Atheistic doctrine is to be tested by its success in assailing the theistic position. Success here can be attained only in one of two ways. Either it must be shown, first, that the theistic doctrine is insufficient to account for recognised facts; or, second, that a charge of self-contradiction can be established. These are the two available lines of criticism. But a doctrine that an Absolute First Cause is the source of all dependent existence is beyond reach of a charge of insufficiency. To repel this charge, however, is not to advance any argument for theism. No theory is established by simply rebutting a criticism. A charge of self-contradiction is equally powerless against the theistic doctrine, for, while the whole extent of being is embraced, the line runs clear between dependent being on the one side, and Absolute being on the other. All finite existence is regarded as dependent; and the Absolute Being, as the one source of all finite existence. Whatever may be said of other theories, Theism stands clear of the charge of self-contradiction.

3. No argument is logically competent against Theism on the ground that it postulates a cause more than sufficient to produce the effect. Such an argument, based on what has been named the law of parsimony — the Scholastic, 'entia non sunt multiplicanda præter necessitatem'— must be final against a logical process which would infer infinity of being from the fact of finite existence. Hence it is that by mere logical methods, no other course is open than that of taking successive stages of logical progress, through a regress of *finite* causes. But, in saying so, we merely indicate the law which determines the order of legitimate thought, and do not establish anything as to the facts of existence. If however the fact of Divine existence is matter of natural belief, not demonstrated by logical methods, objection is incompetent on the ground that the cause of existence is more than sufficient to produce the effect. That the sum of being, or even of power, is not discovered in the energy exercised at a given moment, is one of the most familiar truths even of ordinary experience.

4. The theory which criticises the Theistic doctrine, and meets it with direct contradiction, must in turn endure criticism, by subjecting to scrutiny a theory of finite existence which shall account for the facts on ground lower than Theism. In order to

take rank as a theory of the universe, and thus rise above mere Scepticism, it must pass over from the negative form into a positive.

5. In meeting this demand, the theory becomes Materialistic. The explanation of the universe is alleged to be discovered in its material substance, and this substance is eternal. But such a theory is insufficient as an explanation of the most commonly recognised facts. Without touching the multitude of complex questions involved in any theory which would attempt to explain the present condition of the universe, with unorganized matter as its sole cause or source, there are two considerations which are fatal to its logical claims, *first,* unorganized matter is inadequate as the cause of the various forms of organized existence. *Second,* we recognise in our own consciousness a form of existence higher than the material. Explanation of the higher by the lower is achieved only by the reversal of Logic.— See Huxley 'On the Physical Basis of Life,' *Lay Sermons,* p. 132; *As regards Protoplasm,* by Dr. J. Hutchison Stirling.

6. The perplexity of the problem under a Materialistic theory is not lessened but increased, when duality of origin is assigned, by introducing Force in addition to Material Substance. Duality of existence, with co-eternity of duration, involves perplexity sufficient to bar logical procedure. This duality of existence implies diversity of nature and mutual restriction; and these two, diversity and limitation, raise anew the problem which they were meant to solve. The explanation needs to be explained. Again, matter and force are postulated primarily to account for motion, but in accounting for motion, they are proved insufficient to account for existence. That which needs to have force exerted upon it in order to be moved is not self-sufficient, and the same is true of the force which needs matter on which to exert its energy.

7. Materialism not only fails to reach a primary source of finite existence, but, at the opposite extreme, it fails to harmonize the complex facts of known existence. Intelligence may be taken as the highest of these facts, with which to test the adequacy of the materialistic doctrine. Intellect starts the problem, and the solution must at least carry an explanation of such powers as belong to the investigator. Let us say that matter and force

conjointly produce intelligence, or that one of the two is competent to originate this high type of being. How can thought interpret and accept the possibility? Either the cause need not be adequate to produce the effect, and we are reduced to Hume's maxim, 'Any thing may produce any thing,' which is a mere utterance of Scepticism, or avowal of absolute ignorance, amounting to an abandonment of the problem, in face of the natural demands of intelligence; or, there is that in the cause which is competent to produce the effect, in which case force is more than material, it is intelligent; a Personal Intelligence is the fountain of dependent personality, and the Materialistic position is abandoned.

CHAPTER III
THE PANTHEISTIC THEORY

1. This theory, That God is all,— το παν,— has appeared in a variety of forms. The common intellectual aim of the theory is to maintain, not only unity in the source of finite existence, but absolute and eternal unity of all existence. That there is a changeable, a fluctuating, even an evanescent existence, is freely admitted, but the imperfect and transitory are only phenomenal,— the mere varying manifestations of the one abiding, unchangeable Being,— the surface swell on the unfathomable and untroubled ocean of existence.

2. The theory wears a materialistic or spiritualistic type, according to the point of view from which the facts are regarded. From the lowest point of view, matter itself is of the very nature of the Deity. In this form, the theory is only a higher phase of materialism. From the highest point of view, the Deity is the spiritual substance pervading all things; and, in activity, Deity is the spiritual force operating through all things. In this type of the theory, matter in all its forms, and intellect as existing under the trammels of finite personality, are the occasional broken discoveries of the grandeur of absolute being, which must itself for ever continue undiscovered.

Akin to this in thought, but quite apart from any formulated philosophic theory, is the poetic perception of life and intelligence in all forms of existence. But quite distinct in thought, while often approximating in expression, is the theistic view, that God discovers himself in all, and makes known the greatness of his nature to all his creatures who look with the eyes of intelligence on the face of nature, on the relationships of social life, and on the mysteries of the soul, which is constituted observer of all that lies within its restricted ken.

3. The special difficulty of a Pantheistic theory is, to connect the facts with the doctrine by any competent philosophic process. It first presupposes a conception of Deity, such as belongs to the Theistic doctrine; and secondly, a theoretic affirmation that all known finite existence belongs, either essentially or in a phenomenal sense, to the Divine nature. Both of these are positions which need to be established by a distinct philosophic process. Without this, Pantheism merely accepts the Theistic doctrine in the first stage of its development, in order to violate it in the second, thus becoming self-contradictory. To make good its claim to a place among philosophic theories, it must show first, how it reaches its theism, and next how it lifts up the 'all' into its theism, for legitimate construction of a Pantheism.

4. The first test of Pantheism is in the account it gives of its Theism. It does not profess to offer us any clearer or surer road from finite existence to a modified theism. Given the theistic point of vision, and it can descry the gleams of transcendent grandeur sweeping across all the varieties of finite form. But, how is the point of vision reached? Pantheism does not propose to resuscitate the argument from finite to infinite, from dependent to absolute. In every case, a theistic conception is regarded as natural to the mind, and the reality of the Divine existence is admitted as matter of natural belief. In so far, therefore, as the reality of theistic existence is concerned, Pantheism does not, by the structure of any new philosophic process, separate itself from the purely theistic doctrine.

5. The second test of the Pantheistic theory is concerned with the philosophic competency of its account of the relation of finite existence to the Divine nature. By what logical process can we identify the 'all,' with the Divine? The duality of existence being admitted as fact, to establish a real unity is the grand difficulty. If it be impossible in accordance with logical consistency to argue from a finite result to an infinite cause; the impossibility is still more manifest if we attempt to assign

finitude to the infinite, and thus seek to escape the necessity for a transition. The lower a Pantheistic theory descends, the greater the difficulty becomes. The higher the type of theory, the more it separates itself from the facts of the universe, and encounters difficulty of another sort. To say that the Divine nature embraces material existence, is theoretically to reduce absolute being to a level where its essential property is lost. The infinite becomes divisible. To say, finite existence is of the Divine nature, is to lift restricted existence to a level where its essential characteristics vanish. The dependent becomes absolute. The facts of a restricted, multiform universe are not solved; but simply overlooked, while men discourse in the language of transcendental faith. Man himself is the great obstacle to the acceptance of this philosophy; he is the living refutation of it. The Personality which makes independent action possible; the law which applies to such personality; the obligation which flows from that law; the action at one time in obedience to that law, at another in violation of it; all these are the indubitable facts of a present existence which make it impossible for us legitimately to embrace all being in unity. This is fatal to the philosophic claims of Comte's conception of a Great Being; the sum of all humanity. The Philosophy which declines the search for causes, is naturally at its weakest in seeking for a Deity, and arranging forms of worship.— Comte's *Politique Positive,* and *Catéchisme;* Lewes's *Hist. of Philos.* II. 635; M'Cosh's *Method of Div. Govt.* 7th ed. p. 240. From the Pantheistic position, personal freedom and responsibility are not facts but delusions, as Spinoza considers them. How, then, shall we discover the delusion? It is not discovered by constructing a dialectic and then pointing out the inconsistency of these alleged facts with the logical framework. This cannot satisfy the scientific demand. We must face the fact of absolute existence, since a theism of some sort is admitted. We must next take the finite universe as known to us, and propound its explanation. If no other course is satisfactory, an attempt must be made to prove that consciousness is illusory. The attempt is essential in order to claim philosophic rank for Pantheism. But such a line of proof has nowhere been offered.

6. The scientific insufficiency of the Pantheistic line of thought becomes apparent by examination of the philosophic

systems which may fairly be claimed as contributing in some degree towards a Pantheistic view of the universe. As Pantheism is not always openly avowed, it does not become any part of the duty of one recording historical facts to assign to every theory its exact place. No thinker is fairly chargeable with more than the results of his own reasoning; and if he do not carry out his theory to its full results, that must be because he has recognised reason sufficient to interpose some obstacle. On Pantheistic theories, see Cudworth's *Intellectual System: Modern Pantheism, Essays on Religious Philos.* by Emile Saisset, 2 vols., Edinburgh, 1863; Mansel's *Bampton Lect.* 5th ed. p. 38.

7. The whole philosophic system of Spinoza, as developed in the *Ethica,* is avowedly Pantheistic, and is properly taken as a test of the philosophic value of such a theory. Hume described it as Atheism, and spoke of its author as 'that famous atheist,'— *Treat. of Hum. Nat.* I. iv. 5,— and so the system has been described by others. Such representations are, however, altogether inconsistent with the structure of the theory. It may be logically competent to argue that Pantheism, consistently carried out, becomes Atheism, that the theistic element is lost in the All, and that materialism is the logical result. But it was not so in the hands of Spinoza. Neither in theory, nor in personal belief and practice, was Spinoza atheistic. His system has theism in its very centre, though it be a pantheism, and his whole frame of mind was alien to atheistic belief and feeling. See Spinoza's *Life, Correspondence, and Ethics,* by Willis, where the whole evidence on the subject is well presented to the English reader. With Spinoza, God is everything, and it is the overwhelming grandeur of the one conception which makes it impossible for him to admit a distinct existence for any other being. Take away all finite forms, and what remains for Spinoza is not Nothing, but God, the absolutely Infinite Being. Take the Deity out of his scheme of thought, and the theory becomes nothing. With him the existence of the Deity is a necessary and eternal truth. Account for other existence as you may, this is the fundamental certainty. The real strain upon Spinoza's theory is where it accounts for finite forms of existence, and attempts to gain Pantheism by maintaining that these are modes of the attributes of God. The point is reached at Prop. xv. Pars I., which, with its Demonstr. and Schol., must be mastered by the student in order

to reject or accept Spinoza. Any one may, indeed, legitimately refuse to pass the Definition of Substance. But, once entered on the argument, Prop. xv. is the testing point. His theory may be summarized thus,— Substance is self-existent; there is but one substance, God; one substance cannot produce another, I. Prop. vi.; a cause or reason must be assigned for everything, why it exists, as well as why it does not exist, Prop. XI. Demon. II.; 'whatever is, is in God,' Prop. xv.; 'all who have ever thought of the Divine nature in any proper way, deny that God is corporeal;' 'by body we understand a certain measure or quantity, having length, breadth, and thickness, and bounded by a definite outline;' but corporeal substance itself is not divisible, since divisibility applies only to the mode of an attribute, not to the attribute itself, much less to the substance; divisibility applies only to modality, not to reality — *modaliter, non autem realiter;* for example, 'water, as water, is produced and corruptible, but as substance it is neither produced nor corruptible;' God himself therefore is not corruptible, but only the modes of his attributes; God himself is *natura naturans,* 'nature acting;' all that follows from the necessity of his nature 'is *natura naturata,* nature acted upon,' prop. 29; therefore 'things could not have been produced by God otherwise than they have been,' prop. 33. The test of such a theory is twofold, from the theistic side, and from the finite side. *First,* it sacrifices the consistency of theism. The Absolute is represented as necessitated to act; God is a necessary cause, and is said to be free only in the sense of acting by the necessity of his own nature, a position which denies to Deity any choice in action. To aggravate the difficulty, God is necessitated to cause the changeable and corruptible; absolutely perfect attributes are necessitated to produce corruptible modes of existence, in other words, the modes of existence are not in harmony with their causes. *Second,* It fails to explain the facts of finite existence. Body is not mere measurement, but the thing measured; not mere modality, but reality, which every observer recognises as distinct from self. The theory of the 'All,' is not a theory of the universe as known to us. These are fatal objections to the logical coherence of the scheme, and they cannot be modified without destroying its essential features. The difficulties belong to the illogical attempt to reduce contradictory elements to unity of substance.

8. COUSIN says concerning his own treatment of this subject,— 'In the perplexing question of the relations of God to the world, we have constantly endeavoured to shun the double error of supposing a God of whom there may be no visible trace in the world, and a God so passed into the world that he may not be different from it; the dead God of the schools, and the grosser God of pantheism.'— *Hist. of Mod. Philos.* Note 3 to Lect. v.; so Pascal, in the preface to the *Pensées.* It is not clear that Cousin altogether succeeded in his intention, as, for example, in his views of creation and of universal reason. Speaking of the Deity as cause, he says, 'Being an absolute cause it cannot avoid passing into action; it cannot avoid developing itself.'— *Hist. of Mod. Philos.* I. 72. So also he has allowed himself to identify human reason with the Divine. 'Reason is not, then, individual, hence it is not ours; it does not belong to us, is not human . . . . Ideas are conceptions of this absolute and universal reason, which we do not constitute, but which appear in us.'— *Ib.* I. 76. It is on the ground of such passages as these that Cousin has been regarded as the exponent of a Pantheistic system. Much that might, at first sight, appear to warrant such a conclusion, admits of a different interpretation. If there are passages which seem more to favour the charge of Pantheism, Cousin himself did not regard them in that light.

9. The course which German thought took after the days of Kant, was decidedly in a Pantheistic direction, though it did not result in the construction of a pure Pantheism, such as that of Spinoza. The identification of the Ego (I) with absolute Reason by the elder Fichte; Schelling's absorption of the Ego (I) into the Absolute, and, the elaborate Dialectic of Hegel which makes the idea the essence and source of things, all point in the same direction. The system of Hegel is that which in form most approaches the appearance of Pantheism. Instead of the definitions of Spinoza, Hegel begins with pure Being and pure Nothing, that is, bare existence without any determinate quality, and its contradiction. With these there begin *moments,* or, more properly, movements. The combination of Being and Nothing, that is, the movement of the one into the other, leads to Becoming.— *Wissenschaft der Logik.*— Werke, III. 77, 78. In starting with Being, the possibility of a beginning of the world is denied.— *Ib.* p. 106. 'There can nothing begin, whether so far as

it is, or so far as it is not; for, in so far as it is, it does not first begin; but in so far as it is not, neither does it then begin.'— *Ib.* The movements of Becoming involve passing-into-being and passing-out-of-being — *Entstehen und Vergehen,* p. 108,— the disappearance of Being in Nothing and of Nothing in Being, and the result is determinate Being, or being existing in a definite place or state, p. 112. The determinate existence, or Being possessed of quality, is by its determinateness distinguished from some other. This is the interpretation of quality or determinateness,— 'It is something over against another, it is changeable and finite,'— *veränderlich und endlich.* The determinate Being is finite; it is a something contrasted with another something; each has another opposite to it, p. 122. This introduces the distinction of existence in itself, *Ansichseyn;* and existence-for-another, *Seyn-fur-Anderes,* p. 124. This existence-in-itself is the thing-in-itself, *Ding-an-sich;* but an answer to the question, what requires that determinations be assigned to being, is an impossibility, p. 127. 'The thing-in-itself is the same as that Absolute of which one knows nothing, but that in it all is one. We very well know what these things-in-themselves are; they are as such nothing else than truthless, empty abstractions,' p. 127. But the finite, with its relation of inner and outer, is the ending, perishing, or passing away; and if it merely pass away, it goes back to abstract nothing, and we make no progress, p. 139. But in passing away, it is. affirmative of the Infinite, a union with which is impossible. 'The Finite stands perpetually over against the Infinite,' p. 140. The limited is the bounded or bound. In this appears the ought-to, the necessity to pass over into something else. Something is raised above its limitation, and yet this ought-to has its limit, p. 142. The finite in passing away is not passed away, it has become another finite, and that becomes another, and so on to infinity, p. 147. This, as affirmative being, must have its other, or contrary, that is the Infinite, which in this aspect is only the negative of the finite, p. 148. But, as standing opposite each other, the Infinite is restricted by the finite, is in reality only another finite, p. 154. The finite passes over to the Infinite, and the Infinite passes over again into the finite for its realization. The finite and infinite thus relatively contain each other, and it is in the absorption of both that we attain the true Infinite,— the unity of finite and Infinite, p. 157.

For Hegel's Philosophy, see Schwegler's *Hist.;* Ueberweg's *Hist.;* Translation of first part of Hegel's Logic, in Dr. Hutchison Stirling's *Secret of Hegel,* beginning vol. I. 319, and *Lectures on Jurisprudence,* by same author.

This system may first be regarded as representative of a course of abstraction. In this light, every one will allow, that Being or Existence is the ultimate abstraction, and that from this ultimatum we may synthetically return to the complex order of things with which we are familiar. But that this can produce a theory of existence is not evident. It is a development of abstract thought, not a theory of existence; and to argue from thought to existence is incompetent.— V. p. 116 — 118.

Viewing the whole as a philosophic system, the following considerations are adverse to its logical competency. Its first requisite is moment or movement, which it assumes, but does not account for. And as movement cannot come from indeterminate being, nor from nothing, its presence is an inconsistency, unless it be merely mental movement which is intended, in which case the claim of the theory to be received as a theory of existence is abandoned. The line of progress from a negative to a positive is incompetent. At every stage in advance there is a violation of logical rule, by the assumption of more in the conclusion than is involved in the premises. It is admitted that the finite must have a beginning, and yet no explanation of such beginning is afforded, since the question of causality is ignored. Determinate being is placed before the Infinite, and leads to it. If this mean only that the mind seeks the explanation of the unite in the Infinite, Hegelianism has made a wide detour, with weary zigzag, to reach a position which may be taken at once. The whole question of the origin of existence lies outside the Hegelian Logic. Consciousness and thought are assumed and employed, yet not made account of: and all the while Hegel's offer is this,— Given the single contradictory Being and Nothing, and I shall create, not the universe merely, but even the Infinite.

CHAPTER IV
KNOWLEDGE OF THE DIVINE NATURE

1. Belief in the Divine existence implies knowledge of the Divine nature. This follows from the place which faith holds among our cognitive powers. TO classify belief otherwise would be an inconsistency. Sir W. Hamilton and Cousin agree in this, though differing so widely as to knowledge of the Infinite.— Hamilton's *Metaph.* 11. 15, and 350; Cousin's *Hist. of Mod. Philos.* i. 79. That a knowledge of the Deity belongs to man has been the general testimony of philosophic thought, from Socrates and Plato down through the Patristic period, even while it was held that none of the categories apply to God, as by Clement of Alexandria.— *Strom.* v., and Augustine, *De Vera Religione,* and *De Trin.* v. 2. And this knowledge of God has been maintained along with those acknowledgments of his incomprehensibility, of which Sir W. Hamilton has given examples in his philosophical testimonies to 'learned ignorance.'— *Discussions,* p. 634, and Mansel in his *Bampton Lect.,* Pref. to 5th ed. p. xx. The saying of Clemens Alexandrinus may be taken as axiomatic: ' Neither is there knowledge without faith, nor faith without knowledge.' So Cousin: ' To believe is to know and comprehend in some degree.'— *Hist.* i. 79. Hamilton, on the contrary, held that the Infinite is ' an object of belief, but not of knowledge.'— Letter to me in reply to first ed. of *Philos. of the Infinite,* given in the *third ed.* p. 497, and *Metaph.* II. 530. On this subject, see Prof. Fraser's *Essays in Philos.* p. 201, and *Rational Psychology;* Young's *Province of Reason;* and Prof. Noah Porter's *Human Intellect,* p. 645.

2. The knowledge of the Divine nature is not merely negative knowledge. As the reality of the Divine existence is not a conclusion reached by logical process, it is impossible to interpret the acknowledgment of a Supreme or Infinite Being, as if it were mere assent to an abstract proposition, or submission to the conditions of thought. Indeed, negation of one thing is possible only by affirmation of another, and consciousness bears witness to no such exercise as may with propriety be named 'negative thinking,' resulting in 'a negative notion.' Sir W. Hamilton's distinction between a positive and negative notion is given in the *Logic,* I. 102, and is defended in his Letter, *Philos.*

204

of Inf. p. 500, or *Metaph.* II. 534; and supported by Mansel, *Prolegomena Logica,* p. 48. This doctrine I have criticised at length, *Philos. of the Inf.* 3d ed., beginning at p. 272. See Cousin, *Hist. of Mod. Philos.* I. 86, and M'Cosh, *Intuitions,* 230.

3. Belief in an Infinite Being involves such knowledge of his nature as enables us to distinguish his existence from all existence besides. Belief is the assent of the mind to a truth, while the reality so acknowledged is not matter of observation. See Mansel's *Philos. of the Conditioned,* p. 129, and appendix to *Philos. of Infin.* 3d ed. p. 503. Thus, facts which we accept on the testimony of others, propositions to which we assent without being able to complete their verification, and such a transcendent fact as the Divine existence, are matters of faith. But faith is the exercise of an intelligent nature, apart from which it is impossible. Assent cannot be given except on condition of an apprehension of truth, sufficient to distinguish it from all other known truth. Since, then, a belief in the Divine existence belongs to us, this implies some knowledge of the Divine nature. That in this belief the mind meets the incomprehensible is beyond a doubt; but it meets a living being, an Intelligence, a Ruler, not an Abstraction. That this Being is possessed of intelligence and power is so far from being doubtful, that the admission is essential to the presence of the belief. And besides, all thought concerning this Being, in order to be logically competent in terms of the belief from which it springs, must reject every aspect of limitation which can apply either to this intelligence or power, acknowledging that any limits which we recognise are the measure of our thought, not of its object. Such denial of the objective application of the limits recognised in consciousness is not the result of any intellectual weakness, but of distinct intelligence resting on belief, as, in another sphere, the mind assents to the truth that the law of gravitation must apply in undiscovered regions of the world.

4. Knowledge of God is advanced by means of extending knowledge of nature, and especially of the conditions and possible attainments of personal existence. Widening knowledge of the facts to be explained gives increased knowledge of the nature and government of the Being whose action affords the explanation.

5. Knowledge of God on the ground of analogy between the Divine nature and human intelligence, presupposes a distinct knowledge of the attributes of Deity, fitting us to detect analogy,

and to determine where it fails. Neglect of this fundamental law of analogical reasoning is the glaring defect in Bishop Browne's works on this subject, otherwise so valuable.— *Proced. of the Hum. Understanding,* 2d ed., London, 1729; and *Things Divine and Supernatural,* London, 1733. The ability to recognise where analogy fails, saves us from resting content in anthropomorphic representations of Deity, which would vitiate the radical conception resting on the fundamental belief.— Buchanan's *Analogy as a Guide to Truth.*

6. Such knowledge as we have of the Divine nature, is knowledge of Infinite Being, not of Infinitude. Here the position of Sir W. Hamilton and Mansel is strong even to self-evidence. Human knowledge cannot compass the Infinite. But, on the other hand, it seems no less certain that Sir W. Hamilton was wrong, on psychological grounds, in maintaining that 'existence can only be an object, of thought, inasmuch as it is an object thought,'— Letter, *Philos. of the Infin.* p. 498,— and that partial knowledge of an object is knowledge of a part.— *Ib.* Mansel went still further wrong in making conception of an object equivalent to 'consciousness of Being,' or knowledge of 'a thing in consciousness.'— *Bampt. Lect.* 7th ed. p. 51. See Young's *Province of Reason,* London, 1860.

7. The Infinitude of the Divine Nature involves eternal incomprehensibility of the excellence of that nature, since no manifestation of the Divine power can discover the fulness of the Divine nature, and progress of human knowledge can be nothing more than relative approximation towards a fuller knowledge of the Divine.

8. Knowledge of the Divine nature being attainable only through knowledge of finite existence, we can formulate our knowledge only by regarding the Deity as possessed of such Attributes as are adequate for the accomplishment of recognised facts. While the facts of the universe guide us in postulating the Divine attributes, our belief in the infinitude of the Divine nature must regulate us in our affirmations and inferences. It is in this way that the original belief in the Divine existence delivers human thought from those contradictions set in array by Mansel as a barrier to systematic theology.— *Limits of Religious Thought, Bampt. Lect.*

CHAPTER V
RELATIONS OF THE ABSOLUTE BEING TO THE PROBLEMS OF MORAL LIFE

From the Psychology of Ethics there arise four metaphysical problems which have their solution essentially connected with the fact of Divine existence. These are, the foundation of Virtue; the relation of the human will to Divine sovereignty; the disorder of our moral nature; and the question as to a Future State of existence.

I. THE FOUNDATION OF VIRTUE

1. The first metaphysical question peculiar to Ethical science is this, What is the source of all morality, or, as it is often put, What is the foundation of Virtue? Granting that we, as moral beings, are capable of recognising moral law, and of putting it into application, so as to realize virtue in our life, what is the ultimate ground of that morality?

2. Here there are two alternatives: — Either a theory of the Impersonality of Reason, identifying it with Absolute Intelligence, so that it is God in us who unfolds his own excellence in moral life; or a theory that Human Reason, while distinct from Divine Intelligence, is a power for recognising absolute truth, implanted by the Author of our being, and for the explanation of which we are thrown back in thought upon that which belongs to the Divine nature itself.

3. There are no data on which to warrant a metaphysical conclusion to the impersonality of Reason. Cousin asks the question —'Is Reason, strictly speaking, purely human? or rather, is it only so far human as it makes its appearance in man?' To which he replies, 'Reason is not individual, hence it is not ours, it does not belong to us, is not human.'— *Hist. of Mod. Philos;* 1. p. 75; *Cours de Mod. Phil.* Leçon v. This statement rests on the basis, that we are not ourselves the source of the knowledge we have, which is at once granted by all who accept *a priori* truth. But is this basis sufficient to bear the theory built upon it? We are not ourselves the source of the knowledge we have of an outer world, but we do not think of attributing impersonality to the organ of knowledge. Though the conditions of knowledge are very different in the two cases, there is no warrant to regard Reason in any other or higher light than as an

organ of knowledge. All that Cousin pleads for in the exercise of the faculty is granted, without accepting his conclusion, and the reference to the Deity is not ignored, but merely presented in a different form.

4. Knowledge of moral law belongs to the exercise of our Reason, which discovers that law, without explaining how this discovery has been provided for, or on what ultimate basis the law rests.

5. Taking now the Divine Existence as the explanation of all finite being, it is in conformity with the solution of the earlier problem, that we regard the Divine nature itself as the foundation of Virtue. We cannot satisfy the intellectual demand in this case, by resting in the idea of mere Power, and affirming of it infinity of degree. There must be that in the Divine nature which explains the purpose and procedure realizing themselves in a moral race. We thus reach the metaphysical result, that the foundation of virtue is the moral purity or perfection of the Divine nature.

6. The relation of the Divine Will to the Divine nature must be such that the former is the sure exponent of the latter. Moral obligation and responsibility imply the exercise of Divine control subjecting us to moral law. We may, therefore, affirm that the source of all morality is in the Divine Will, but this can rank only as a provisional and partial statement, leaning upon the excellence of the Divine nature. Human morality cannot have its ultimate source in mere command, or exercise of authority over dependent being. Such a supposition would imply either that God might act capriciously, that is, without regard to his own perfection; or that he might act in violation of his own perfection. In appealing to the Divine nature, we do not affirm that God was necessitated to create, as if he were subjected to constraint from a superior power; or as if his power were not exercised in accordance with Will. It is simply affirmed that the action of the Deity must be in accordance with the perfection of his own nature,— never can fall beneath it.

In this appears the illogical character of Scholastic assertions, reproduced in a variety of forms in later times, such as that of William of Occam,— 'Nullum actum malum esse nisi quatenus a Deo prohibitum, et qui non possit fieri bonus si a Deo præcipiatur;'— there is no act which is wrong except as it is forbidden by God, and which cannot be made right, if commanded by God. Such a position can have no metaphysical sanction, and results from the attempt to interpret absolute nature by the negation of finite restrictions, in neglect at once of the testimony of our own moral nature, and of the application of our original belief in the Divine Being.

II. RELATION OF DIVINE SOVEREIGNTY TO FREE WILL

1. If the Divine existence is the explanation of all finite being, it follows that there is Divine sovereignty over all such being. This is a simple interpretation of the relation between the Absolute and the dependent. Dependence of origin, with independence of subsequent existence, were a contradiction. The dependent cannot restrict the Absolute. Sovereignty in originating dependent being, at the cost of surrender of sovereignty over the created existence, is impossible. The Absolute Being cannot restrict his own nature.

2. As Divine Sovereignty must apply to all forms of originated being, no creature can be so highly endowed as to be independent of Divine control. As independence could not be achieved by the dependent, it could not be conferred by the Absolute Being. Subjection to sovereign control must therefore hold true of the rational as well as of the irrational, and of activity as well as of sensitivity in creatures.

3. While Absolute Sovereignty of the Deity is a clear metaphysical deduction from the primary belief in His existence, it does not carry metaphysical warrant for a further inference as to the manner in which such absolute sovereignty is exercised. Inference on this subject must come from the facts of experience.

4. There are running all through the universe, lines of evidence which illustrate sovereign control. Whilst holding the highest place among the living agencies of the world, man is conscious of subjection to forces which he cannot control, and to which he must conform his efforts if these are to be attended with success. His experience is a lesson of continual subjection. The laws of existence he can discover; these laws he can in some degree employ for the attainment of his own ends; but he cannot alter their nature or change their applications. Physical laws, such as provide for supplies of light and heat, and for the currents of the air and ocean, are so beyond our power, that we are accustomed to describe them as laws of nature. The laws of

mind are equally definite and uniform in their action; they are laws of our nature, altogether superior to personal choice.

5. In observing and classifying the facts which indicate the action of a superior determining power in the universe, we discover evidence of diversity in the manner of control over the different forms of existence. These forms vary so greatly that they may be classified as animate and inanimate, rational and irrational, and the laws of their control may differ accordingly. Taking our own control over other beings as guide, we are able to reason by analogy towards sovereign control over dependent being. Our control over the productions of the soil, over animals, and over our fellow-men, varies so greatly, as to enable us to conclude that there may be diversity in the forms of sovereign control. We are not in possession of facts, however, by which to reach exact conclusions as to the manner in which Divine control is exercised over the actions of men. As we have no immediate consciousness of Divine control being exercised over us, the exact manner and measure of that control transcends the range of a legitimate philosophy. If this admission be made, it precludes an argument from Sovereignty to the denial of freedom of will, as we are precluded from reasoning from freedom of will to a denial of Divine Sovereignty. On exactly the same ground, our ignorance of the manner of exercise, we cannot reason from Divine foreknowledge to the denial of human freedom; any more than we are warranted to reason, as some have done, from freedom to the denial of foreknowledge.— See Ed. Williams, *Equity of Divine Govt.,* and *Defence of Mod. Calvinism;* and Mozley on the *Augustinian Doct. of Predestination.*

6. While granting that the facts of intelligent self-control are those which are most perplexing in view of our belief in the absolute sovereignty of the Deity, it is to be observed that Will itself bears witness to sovereignty. The analysis of consciousness has shown that our freedom is not an absolute, but a restricted freedom. A will capable of controlling our other powers, only by means of intelligent appreciation of the laws under which these powers operate, is not a faculty which can claim to possess freedom of such a nature as to be contradictory of our belief in Divine Sovereignty. On the other hand, a freedom which implies moral obligation and responsibility does, by its nature and exercise, carry a continual acknowledgment of the sovereignty of a Divine Ruler.

III. THE ORIGIN OF EVIL

1. If the Deity be the source of all dependent being, which exists only because he wills that it should, how does he permit the outbreak and continuance of moral evil? This is one of the darkest and most perplexing problems of moral philosophy.

2. The imperfection which belongs to a finite nature, occasions no perplexity, and affords no help towards a solution of our difficulty. To say that finite existence is imperfect, is only an identical proposition; it is to say, that finite existence is finite. The finitude of known existence raises the problem of existence, and originates inquiry without giving occasion for perplexity. Archbishop King puts it accurately when he says, 'Either nothing at all must be created, or something imperfect.'— *Origin of Evil,* chap. v. sec. v. subsec. i. 5th ed. p. 309. The question, then, is not, why does imperfect being exist, and why are all the natural evils belonging to restricted existence found in the universe, but why does moral evil exist, that is, why in the realm of creation is there any being out of harmony with the laws of its own nature, and out of harmony with the nature and will of the Deity?

3. The problem concerning the origin of moral evil has two aspects, the possibility of such evil, and its permission. (1.) How could moral evil be superinduced upon a nature morally pure? (2.) How could moral evil be permitted by the Supreme Being, who is at once absolutely pure and absolutely powerful? The first question is psychological, the second metaphysical. While, however, the first is psychological, being concerned with the laws of mind, the circumstance that we are conscious of the operations of our nature only in its disordered state, gives to the question in some degree a speculative character.

4. That the Deity himself is not the source of moral evil is involved in the acknowledgment of his existence as the Absolute Being. That which is inevitable on a Pantheistic scheme is impossible on a Theistic, which maintains essential duality of existence. Spinoza and Hegel did not hesitate to acknowledge that as all finite modes belong to the Infinite, all forms of evil must. The Theistic scheme, maintaining that no finite modes can belong to the Infinite, maintains that no evil can. The Pantheistic conclusion is merely an example of logical consistency, springing out of a scheme of thought, and nothing more; the Theistic conclusion is logical and metaphysical as well,

consistency of thought springing out of a scheme of being. This is the essential contrast between a philosophy based on a natural belief as to reality of existence, and a philosophy which rests only upon definitions or the forms of thought.

The impossibility of the Deity himself being the source of moral evil is apparent by reference to the moral perfection of his nature. This is only an amplification, by way of exposition of the nature of an Absolute Being. We find in the Divine nature the explanation of all that is noblest in us. Moral law, and obligation, and responsibility which apply to us, all rest upon absolute moral purity in him. In denial of this, the solution of the problem of existence is broken down. The fallacy, if there be any, must lie at an earlier stage; it cannot lie here. The present position can be turned only by an argument that the source of finite existence is not found in One Absolute Being. If the moral law in us is the expression of the Divine Will concerning us, he is a God of perfect moral purity.

5. In the laws of our moral nature as known in consciousness, we find some clue to the possibility of the outbreak of moral evil. Our nature, being complex, so that desires, affections, emotions, intelligence, and will, have their several parts to perform; and having its perfection secured only in the continued balance of all these; the possibility of its disorder is found in the peculiar nature of the Desires, or craving powers.— See before, *Psychol. of Ethics*, Pt. II. chap. i. sec. 7, p. 154. It is only the possibility of the outbreak of moral disorder which here concerns us, not the actual outbreak itself, which must be matter of history, not of philosophy.

The clue here obtained is nothing more, for there still remains the difficulty of deciding how a nature perfectly balanced could disturb its own harmony. So far as present experience can guide, the explanation lies in the freedom of the will, that is, the power to take or not to take the guidance of moral law. Why such a power should have been left to any being, is not a question at all, for without such power there could have been no morality. Why God should have created moral beings, is a question which is not concerned with the possibility of the disorder of their nature when created. But the possibility of disorder may be enough to account for the fact of disorder, in the event of its taking place.

6. The permission of the outbreak and continuance of moral disorder still remains the darkest mystery which the universe occasions. If there be absolute sovereignty, why is moral evil allowed? Archbishop King has well indicated the alternatives to which our thoughts may turn. 'There are three ways whereby God may be conceived able to have prevented bad elections: first, if he had created no free being at all; secondly, it his omnipotence interpose, and occasionally restrain the will, which is naturally free, from any wrong election; thirdly, if he should change the present state of things, and translate man into another, where the occasions to error and incitements to evil being cut off, he should meet with nothing that could tempt him to choose amiss.'— *Origin of Evil,* chap. v. sec. v. sub. 2, p. 312. More shortly,— No free beings;— free agents always restrained when tempted to transgress; or free agents whose freedom is never tried in such a way as to test voluntary submission to moral law. Of these, the first must be discarded as involving a claim for restriction upon the absolute; the second, as implying a breach on the nature of the creature; and the third, as inconsistent with the conditions of moral life.

7. It then we can see no way in which moral beings could certainly be guarded against an outbreak of moral evil, why did the Sovereign Being not visit with the punishment of destruction any moral agent who voluntarily destroyed the harmony of the moral world? This is the final form of a mystery, which is insoluble from the lower side of existence, and whose solution can lie only in the heights of Absolute Being.

IV. THE FUTURE STATE (IMMORTALITY OF THE SOUL)

1. With an Absolute Being as the Great First Cause, the final problem of the Metaphysic of Ethics concerns the question of future existence for ourselves as moral beings. Having moral life from him, what is our destiny? What are the rational expectations which may be formed as to a life beyond the present state? The immediate occasion for the question is the fact that there is a limit beyond which the present life cannot be continued. In seeking its answer, we must consider first the facts out of which the question arises, and afterwards the relation of the Absolute Being to the problem.

2. The facts which point towards the termination of our present state of existence are connected with our physical nature,

not with our mental. In physical life, there is a progression of bodily development until maturity is reached, after which there is gradual decay. But in mind, there is the law of progress, without evidence of the same law of decay. That our nature is one, and that weakness of body can entail restraint upon mental action, are admitted facts; but the latter places the source of restraint in the body, not in the mind. Besides, the body may be dismembered and the mind continue active as before. The phenomena of consciousness connected with amputation are of interest here. But chief importance attaches to the contrast between the facts of physical and mental life during the infirmities of age. At such a time, when the recollection of the occurrences of the day is difficult, recollections of events which happened threescore years before, are vivid and exact. Such facts point towards the possibility of continued existence of the spirit, apart from the body. See Taylor's *Physical Theory of Another Life.*

3. Besides these, the facts of our moral life seem to warrant a conclusion to the certainty of a future state. If there be moral obligation and responsibility, their full significance can be realized only in another state of being, where account of moral actions can be rendered. On this line of reflection, it is legitimate to conclude that the future state must be one of rewards and punishments. But the argument does not rest on what Comte has called 'the police consideration of a Future State,'— *Philos. Positive,* Martineau's Transl. II. 165; a consideration which is the legitimate logical accompaniment of the utilitarian and necessitarian view of responsibility, as expressed by Mr. Mill, 'Supposing a man to be of a vicious disposition, he cannot help doing the criminal act, if he is allowed to believe that he will be able to commit it unpunished,' *Exam.* 575; a consideration all trace of which is lost under a transcendental universalism, such as that of Spinoza or Hegel. I am not, however, looking along the line of a 'police consideration' of restraint, but along the line of higher intellectual and ethical possibilities, where, in full harmony with obligations held sacred here, the spiritual achievements of the present life will remain as a personal possession, whose real worth shall find acknowledgment from the Absolute Ruler. The argument, resting on our conception of perfection of character yet to be attained, our progress towards it, our aspiration after it, finds, in all these considerations, warrant

for anticipating that the Future which obligation implies, must afford scope for the realization of the possibilities after which we aspire.— See specially the very striking passages towards the close of the *Apologia* of Socrates, preserved by Plato.

4. While the most prominent facts of our life thus combine to support the belief that there is for man a great Future, there is nothing which logically warrants an inference to Immortality of existence. Such a conclusion can be sustained neither from the immateriality of the soul, the favourite logical basis — see Dr. S. Clarke's *Answer to Dodwell,* with Defences;— nor from the ceaseless motion of the soul, as with Plato in the *Phædrus;* — nor from the ideas of abstract beauty, goodness, and magnitude, as in the *Phædo;*— nor from the nature of the soul as a simple being, as argued by Moses Mendelssohn (1729 — 1786) in his *Phädon.* Mendelssohn's *Phädon* is a Dialogue after the Platonic model, preceded by a sketch of the character of Socrates, first published at Berlin, 1767, which reached a fifth edition in 1814, and is criticised by Kant, *Kritik der Rein. Vernf.,* Meiklejohn's Transl. p. 245. The finite, since it is not the self-sufficient, cannot afford an argument towards immortality. The nature which is dependent upon the Absolute Being for its origin, must be dependent on his will for its continuance. While, therefore, Futurity of Existence is clearly involved in the facts of the present life, Eternity of existence must depend upon the Divine Will, and can be known only as matter of distinct revelation, not as matter of metaphysical deduction. All that is greatest in us points towards an immeasurable future. Thither we must look for the solution of many of our dark problems, and for that purity and grandeur of personal life unknown in the present state. But Immortality, if it be ours, must be the gift of God. 'Over the best intellect, if it be restricted to pure speculation, must hang the great uncertainty which found utterance in the closing words of the *Apology* of Socrates,— 'The hour to depart has come,— for me to die, for you to live; but which of us is going to a better state is unknown to every one except to God,'— αδηλον παντι πλην η τω θεφ.

APPLIED ETHICS

The application of psychological and metaphysical conclusions to personal and social life is a task so much more simple than that of discovering the fundamental positions of the science, that the main points belonging to this division of the subject may be presented in brief outline.

The great leading questions here requiring attention are, the formation of moral character, the guidance of individual life, and the regulation of social life. To touch upon the more essential points involved in the disposal of these questions, is all that can be attempted in such a Handbook as the present. Connected especially with Sociology there is a vast range of intricate inquiry which cannot be embraced here.

I. Laws which regulate the Formation of Character

1. Character, as distinct from nature, is an established order of disposition which by development gradually acquires strength, in accordance with the rules of life most commonly acted upon. Its measure is found in the prevailing dispositions; the standard of measurement, in the moral law. Character is, therefore, good or bad, according as the reigning dispositions are in harmony with Conscience, or antagonistic to its authority. In accordance with the law of development, character may assume a selfish or benevolent, an upright or a dishonest type. The goodness temporarily manifested in a single action, may find an abiding representation in the disposition which prompts the moral agent readily to reproduce such forms of action when opportunity offers. The morally right disposition by development gains strength, and acquires an aptness to exert its influence which places it more at the command of the person.

2. Dispositions which incline the mind to duty are named Virtues. There are, then, as many virtues in the perfect human character as there are natural dispositions declared to be morally right, and fitted for influencing conduct in fulfilment of moral law.

3. The laws which regulate the formation of moral character are concerned with two distinct spheres — the one,

intellectual or guiding, the other, operative or executive; the one concerned with deciding what is right, the other with doing it. The law of Association rules in the one case, the law of Habit in the other.

4. The Law of Association, which provides generally for facility in retaining and recalling knowledge, enables us to classify actions and dispositions as right and wrong, that we may act upon the classification, without needing to test its accuracy on each occasion. In this we are naturally helped, as Herbert Spencer and others have maintained, by the moral convictions which have prevailed before our own time. The results of the observation and experience of previous generations are necessarily transmitted. But on no basis of ethical philosophy can it be warrantable that the moral judgments prevalent in society, whether in our own time or in earlier ages, should have unquestioning submission.

5. The Law of Habit, as concerned with our activity, is most important in the formation of character. It provides for greater facility in action by frequent repetition of the act. It must not be confounded with the law of Custom. Under the law of Habit, moral conflict in self-government is simplified; subjection of all the motive forces to rational control becomes more constant; and dispositions which incline to the performance of duty gain practical ascendency in co-operation with conscience. On this ground, Aristotle gave prominence to Habit.— *Ethics,* I. 8. Such Habit is not 'a mechanical necessity,' as Kant represents it — *Metaph. of Ethics,* 224,— but an aptness which is essentially dependent on personal direction, as it implies previous faithfulness in the application of Conscience.

II. The Number and Relations of the Virtues

1. In conformity with Conscience, a classification of the Virtues may be found in harmony of disposition with the known relations of personal existence to the Absolute Being, and to finite persons around. Three fundamental virtues are thus obtained, Reverence, Modesty, and Sympathy; Reverence for the Absolute Being, above all finite being; Modesty, which truthfully estimates personal dignity and efficiency; and

Sympathy, which respects and esteems others as persons to whom belong the dignity and responsibility of human nature.

2. From this wider and more general range of observation, embracing the foundations of character, we may pass to the virtues which belong essentially to the guidance of individual life. As concerning determinations to act, there is Faithfulness to known law, which, as a virtue of more general application, is often distinguished by the name of Conscientiousness; as concerning action itself, Courage in the execution of known law; as regards personal gratification, Temperance, in harmony with a rational nature; as concerning dealings with others, Love of Justice, founded on respect for the law of Justice.

3. The relations of the Virtues are such as to provide for special combinations among them, and perfect harmony of the whole in a single character. There are cardinal virtues, as ancient philosophy proclaimed, hinge or pivot virtues, on which dependent virtues turn. Thus, Reverence carries with it meekness and lowliness; Modesty, humility and penitence; Courage, endurance and perseverance. As all virtues are dispositions cultivated in subjection to moral law, the unity of that law provides for the harmony of the virtues.

III. Guidance of Social Life

1. The natural basis of society is biological. Society exists as a necessity of our life, in accordance with the constitution we have received, the laws of which are above our choice. Society is founded, not in Individualism nor in Associationalism, but in vital social organism. In this view, Comte's observation is strictly accurate and profoundly important, see p. 64, that the family is the primary unit in Society. Society is, therefore, strong only as family life is preserved in its integrity. It is this which is the natural condemnation of all speculative communism, such as that presented by Plato in the *Republic*.

2. The Ethical basis of Society is discovered in the identity of nature belonging to the race, placed as that is under common moral law, from which spring common obligations and common rights.

3. As Society is founded biologically, or as matter of life, on the union of the sexes; so is it founded ethically, or as matter

of rational combination, on the common application of the same moral law to both sexes. The obligation to physical, intellectual, and moral purity is exactly the same for both, and, being placed under common law, each of the sexes is constituted the guardian of purity in the other.

4. Diversity of nature given to the sexes, implies diverse application of a common moral law for the attainment of a moral unity in social life. To man is given robustness, to control and provide for the other; to woman, such fineness of nature as requires support, yet elevates by refining the stronger nature with which it is associated. In these facts, biological and ethical law are seen to combine in the regulation of both sexes, for the consolidation and progress of Society. On the other hand, the harmony of personal and social life is disturbed, if in the one case robustness degenerate to coarseness, or in the other fineness degenerate to weakness. The man who uses his strength to defend the purity of woman, performs the moral part assigned to him in life, and he only is manly in the true ethical sense. The man who uses his power to corrupt woman, is self-degraded, cruel, and cowardly. The woman who, in receiving the protection which is her birthright, uses her influence to refine and elevate, performs her moral part in life. She who uses her influence to corrupt others, debases herself, and makes her life a moral anomaly, specially glaring and offensive because of the refining influence intrusted to her keeping.

5. The marriage bond is the only adequate acknowledgment of the biological and ethical laws appointed to regulate human society. In this alone is there realization of the truth, that the family is the primary form of society. In accordance with the common obligations imposed by moral law, interpreted and applied to the special relations of husband and wife, marriage implies a mutual pledge to life-long, consistent endeavour to reach in family history a high standard of attainment in physical, intellectual, moral, and religious life. A lower ideal is unworthy of rational government of the social life.

6. In the family circle, with the relations of husband and wife, parents and children, brothers and sisters, moral law provides for the series of relative duties incidental to the natural relations of life.— Maurice's *Social Morality.*

7. On a wider and less close relationship of individuals, where the relation rests upon the general rights of contract, such as the union of employers and employed, it is still universal moral law,— the undeviating principle of Justice,— which determines relative obligations. In this way, Political Economy rests ultimately on an ethical basis.

IV. Moral Conditions or Political Government

1. The basis of Political Organization must be found in the biological and moral structure of Society. Men in arranging, or organizing themselves for the guidance of the more general relationships of the race, can find rational warrant for procedure only in acknowledgment of the laws of human life, physical and moral.

2. As the basis of Society is the unity of the race, and the moral equality of all, Political Government can be legitimately constructed only on condition of the acknowledgment of natural obligations and rights as inviolable. Political or Positive Law comes into existence only with the acknowledgment that there is natural law superior to itself, for moral law has universal and uniform sway.

3. As moral action is possible only by personal direction of motive, the attainment of moral ends is beyond the reach of Political Government. Political law may, nevertheless, greatly favour or retard a pure moral life among the people living under it. But the healthy relations of Political Government to a sound morality can be secured only by providing that Positive Laws, which transcend the moral sphere in their applications, are in nature harmonious with moral law. Such security is attained only where legislators and people have reverence for moral law. All legal reform, other than that which is merely formal, is an attempt to bring positive law more completely into harmony with the principle of equity, as advancing experience may guide.

4. As the ultimate end of Political Organization is community of interest, it is implied in its existence, that the real, abiding interests of all men are the same, and that when present, temporary interests come into competition, these are to be regulated on the principle of Justice, that is, the equality of all,— for in the eyes of the Law, all men are equal.

5. As Political Government involves a modified limitation of personal liberties for the purpose of securing the common good, it is essential to its constitution and procedure, that it be acknowledged that there are liberties which men cannot, consistently with moral law, surrender, and with which political government cannot interfere without stepping beyond its natural boundaries. If only there be protection for the rights of all, and provision for the common good, there must be unfettered liberty of thought, utterance, and action. Political Government becomes the bulwark of civil and religious liberty only by rigid acknowledgment of the limits of its own sphere.

6. Political Government, in seeking the common good, must restrict by punishment wilful injury as infraction of natural or acquired rights. In this, however, by its constitution and aim, it acts only as the guardian of common interests, not as the judge of personal motives, that is, political cannot pass over into moral government.

V. Morality in its Relations to Religion

1. As there is a Natural Theology springing out of morality, so is there a Natural Religion. It has been already indicated, p. 231, on what ground it seems legitimate to conclude that religious sentiment is a natural instinct, acting as an impulse, and checking the low materialism to which the mind is in some ways prone. But on the ground of the metaphysical conclusions as to the Divine existence and nature, it becomes here matter of legitimate deduction, that religious thought and feeling rest on a rational basis, and are capable of being elevated and purified by application of our original belief to the guidance of our life, in harmony with personal obligation and responsibility.

2. Philosophy thus becomes the vindicator and upholder of reverential and submissive acknowledgment of the Absolute Being, affording in itself a rational basis of religious homage. Such was recognised as the result of philosophic thought by the best spirits which preceded the Christian era, as in the case of Socrates, *Apologia,* and of Plato, *Republic,* Book vi. And since the dawn of that era, the Christian system has shed its grand light over the darkest mysteries of philosophic thought, and opened for Philosophy itself new courses of inquiry, culminating in a fuller devotion. So Hume, whose thought at many points seems antagonistic to this admission, says, 'There is only one occasion

when philosophy will think it necessary and even honourable to justify herself, and that is, when religion may seem to be in the least offended; whose rights are as dear to her as her own, and are indeed the same.'— *Treat. on Hum. Nat.* Book I. sec. 5, vol. i. p. 435,

3. As the existence of the Deity is the transcendent fact of philosophy, the rational homage offered to Him is the highest exercise of mind. In such exercise, intellect is occupied with the highest conceptions which it can reach, and our sensibility proves competent for companionship with thought, as it goes forth on its most exalted range. The unity of both sides of our nature in this exercise is the loftiest and surest indication of the possibility of attainment far beyond everything that has yet come within the limits of consciousness.

4. In accordance with the conclusion thus reached, religion becomes the loftiest element of individual, family, and social culture, as it is the obvious duty of every intelligence contemplating God as the source of finite existence and of all forms of good with which restricted being is blessed.— See Chapters on *Worship,* in Maurice's *Social Morality.*

5. In the application of Moral Law, there is provision for the development of a life of purity; of consistent activity, seeking the attainment of those ends which our powers are fitted to secure; and of generous regard for others, making us their helpers in well-doing. But our highest greatness appears in the appreciation of Absolute Greatness, and dedication of all our energies to the fulfilment of the will of Him who has bestowed upon us a moral nature. The religious life and the moral are thus essentially related. For, we yield a true and full homage to the Author of our being, not when we observe forms of worship merely, but when we use our whole nature aright, realizing Moral Law in action, because it has been vitalized in personal character.

Printed in the United States
24219LVS00004B/229